Groups of Companies

AUSTRALIA
The Law Book Company Ltd.
Sydney: Brisbane: Melbourne: Perth

CANADA
The Carswell Company Ltd.
Agincourt, Ontario

INDIA
N.M. Tripathi Private Ltd.
Bombay
and
Eastern Law House Private Ltd.
Calcutta and Delhi

M.P.P. House
Bangalore
and
Universal Book Traders
New Delhi

ISRAEL
Steimatzky's Agency Ltd.
Jerusalem: Tel Aviv: Haifa

PAKISTAN
Pakistan Law House
Karachi

Groups of Companies

edited by

Clive M. Schmitthoff
LL.M., LL.D. (London), Dr. jur. (Berlin), Dres. h.c., F.J.Ex.

and

Frank Wooldridge
LL.M., Ph.D.

London
Sweet & Maxwell
Centre for Commercial Law Studies
1991

Published in 1991 by
Sweet & Maxwell
South Quay Plaza
183 Marsh Wall, London
Computerset by
Mendip Communications Ltd.
Frome
Printed and bound in Great Britain by
BPCC Hazell Books
Aylesbury, Bucks, England
Member of BPCC Ltd.

**A catalogue record for this book is available from the British
Library**

ISBN 0–421–432403

Publisher's Announcement

Professor Schmitthoff died on September 30, 1990, although much of the editorial work had been completed at the time of his death. The publishers are grateful to Dr. Wooldridge for his work in preparing the final texts for publication.

Preface

All except one of the articles in the present volume was originally presented at the conference on groups of companies chaired by Professor Clive Schmitthoff and Roy Goode, and held at the Waldorf Hotel on May 18, 1988. The chapter by Professor Alan Page was not presented at the conference, but it forms an additional contribution to the present book. Professor Schmitthoff was, one of course of the greatest scholars in international and domestic company and commercial law of his time, and he retained his intellectual powers and prodigious energy into extreme old age. However, it is very unfortunate that owing to his illness and subsequent death in September 1990, he was unable to complete his work of editing the contributions to the book.

The task of completing the editing of these contributions was consequently very gratefully assumed by me. I have the advantage of having been a former friend, colleague and PhD. student of Professor Schmitthoff, and also of having worked in the area of groups of companies. It is thus to be hoped that my small contribution to the final format of the book will be deemed satisfactory. Despite the prolonged failure of the Commission of the EC to agree upon a harmonising text in this area, the importance of the law governing groups of companies to businessmen, practitioners and scholars in the field of national and comparative company law requires no exaggeration. It is to be hoped that the present book will contribute to a more general understanding of this difficult area of the law, and that it may perhaps have some influence on national legislation concerning groups, and on the possible future harmonisation of the law concerning them.

F. Wooldridge

November 7, 1990

Introduction

The legal problems raised by the activities of Groups of Companies
provide continuing fascination for the commercial lawyer. This
fascination is due to the fact that here there exists an obvious gap
between commercial reality and legal regulation and that this gap
discloses a serious shortcoming of the law. English law, like most legal
systems including that of the United States but excluding perhaps
that of Germany, approach the group problem from the point of view
of company law which is primarily designed to regulate the single
company and regards the group merely as an appendage to that law.
But in modern business life, particularly on the transnational level,
the single public limited company has virtually ceased to exist and
one encounters only groups of companies. The law takes as its starting point the concept of the company as a separate legal entity, a
doctrine briefly called the entity doctrine, but makes concessions to
reality by admitting a long (and growing) list of exceptions in which
the corporate veil is "pierced" or "lifted". The economist rejects the
legal approach as dealing merely with matters of form. In his view the
essential point is that the various companies combined in a group act
in the market place as one economic unit. The lawyer has to concede
that there is strength in the economist's argument. But how can this
situation be remedied? This is the problem which Professors Klaus
Hopt and André Tunc and Mr. Tom Cashel consider in their contributions to this volume. The next contribution consists of an
account by Mr. James Keir, Q.C., the former Secretary of Unilever,
of the practical operation of group management in a large transnational group. These chapters are followed by Dr. Dan Prentice's
examination of the key problem in the law of groups, that of group
indebtedness. The volume is concluded by an account by Professor
Alan Page of the relationship between the state and corporate groups
in the United Kingdom.

1. The dominant shareholder's fiduciary duty

Professor Tunc in his chapter entitled "The Fiduciary Duties of a
Dominant Shareholder" examines the question whether English law
might develop a system of law of groups by attributing a fiduciary
duty to the dominant shareholder. Such a duty would be owed in the
first place to the subsidiary and other subordinated companies, but
Professor Tunc does not rule out the possibility that it may also be
owed to outside minority shareholders of controlled companies.
Professor Tunc admits that he cannot support his thesis by reference
to an English precedent but he refers to several modern English cases
in which the court has held that in a single company the majority

shareholder is under an equitable obligation not to treat the minority shareholder unfairly, even if the provisions of section 459 of the Companies Act 1985 (or one of its predecessors) cannot be invoked.

In the second part of his chapter, Professor Tunc refers to American law in support of his proposition. In American law the fiduciary duty is much further developed than in English law. Fiduciary duties are imposed in American law (as in English law) on the directors but, unlike English law, there are also a few cases in which the American courts held that a dominant shareholder was under such a duty to the subsidiary or its minority shareholders. Professor Tunc makes extensive references to the *Principles of Corporate Governance* published by the American Law Institute, beginning in 1980. This project contains partly a restatement of the law and partly a set of recommendations.

Professor Tunc concludes that in the present state of English authorities "the door seems open to the recognition of the fiduciary duty of a dominant shareholder towards the company and perhaps the minority shareholders". He suggests that in England the continuing duties of the dominant shareholder should be defined, similar to the American Principles of Corporate Governance, either in the Companies Act or in a document of voluntary self-regulation, *e.g.* a Code of Transactions within a Group of Companies.

Professor Tunc's suggestions open a new vista on the law of groups. The regulation which he suggests would be supplemental to, or even in place of, the application of the traditional rule *viz.* the identity doctrine, subject to frequent exceptions admitting the piercing of the corporate veil, if justice so demands.

2. The richness of the American scene

Mr. Tom Cashel has written on "Groups of Companies—Some US Aspects". His contribution surveys the amazing plethora of case law produced by the American courts on group problems and the wealth of academic writing on the subject. But the result at which Mr. Cashel arrives can be stated in fairly simple terms. The American courts, like the English courts, apply the traditional identity doctrine, *i.e.* treat, in principle, each company of the group as a separate legal entity, a rule which the English lawyer is wont to express as the principle in *Salomon* v. *Salomon & Co. Ltd.* [1897] A.C. 22. But American courts, like the English courts again are prepared to admit exceptions, where equity so demands. Mr. Cashel refers to these exceptions as the "instrumentality rule", an expression apparently coined by the New York courts. The instrumentality rule comprises such metaphors as piercing the veil, instrument of the controlling company, alter ego, dummy or agent and as is shown by Mr. Cashel a number of others.

Mr. Cashel sums up the American position thus: "In reviewing the authorities mentioned above, the reluctance of the courts to ignore the separate identity of corporations is apparent. Yet piercing the corporate veil concepts, while perhaps imperfect, are available where equity requires."

3. Practical problems of group management

Mr. James Keir Q.C.'s chapter deals with "Legal Problems in the Management of a Group of Companies". Mr. Keir was the Secretary of the Unilever Group for nearly 30 years. In this capacity he had an opportunity of observing the management conduct of the group and his paper deals with this experience. The Unilever group is a transnational group of great strength. It is an unusual group in that it has two parent companies, one Dutch and the other English.

The surprising fact is that the management of this large conglomerate of companies in many parts of the world works so smoothly in practice. The secret of this success is that the constitution of the Unilever group is, in Mr. Keir's words, "tailor-made". The directors of both parents, the Dutch NV and the English PLC, are identical. The Dutch NV does not have a supervisory board, as required by Dutch law; a special Dutch enactment had to be passed to dispense with this requirement. This solution neatly disposed of the requirement of representation of independent persons on the supervisory board, which is the Dutch substitute for employee representation.

The Unilever group is founded on several Agreements, the principal being the Equalisation Agreement, the terms and operation of which are explained by Mr. Keir. The Equalisation Agreement lays down the principle that the dividends of the NV and PLC shall be equal and contains detailed rules on the calculation of the dividends; it also admits some exceptions from the principle of equivalence.

Mr. Keir gives several examples of the way in which legal problems arising in the group are resolved. One of them was caused by the statutory dividend control which existed in the United Kingdom for a long time and ended only in 1979. A similar measure did not exist in the Netherlands. This differential treatment made the application of dividend equalisation unworkable. The solution of this problem was found by obtaining Bank of England permission that the limited company (the predecessor of the plc) should declare a dividend in excess of the statutory limit but not pay it until either the regulation on statutory dividend control was revoked or the Bank of England granted permission for payment. The limited company's shareholders thus received a bonanza in 1979.

The Unilever group includes many interests in the countries of Africa and the Far East, which became independent after the end of the British Empire. Here the question of indigenisation raised legal problems. Mr. Keir emphasises the importance of these matters. The group must pursue a policy of making a visible contribution to the social fabric of the host country and of treating outside shareholders of its local companies with absolute fairness. Mr. Keir says: "If we continued to be seen as a valued adviser and provider of useful services and a fair dealer, it enabled us to preserve the value of our existing interest while increasing the worth of the enterprise as a whole."

4. Group indebtedness

"Group indebtedness" is the subject of Dr. Prentice's contribution. His article contains a comprehensive exposition of the present English position. It indicates how deeply modern English law is already involved in the group problem.

Dr. Prentice divides his chapter into two parts. In the first part he deals with situations in which one company in the group assumes liability for another, *e.g.* by guaranteeing the other's debt or by providing security for it. The second part deals with situations in which the law imposes a liability for the debts of some members of the group on other members. In the first part Dr. Prentice takes *Salomon* as the starting point; he indicates that the assumption of liability by a group company for the debts of another member of the group may be challenged on the ground of lack of capacity of the company assuming liability, breach of duty by its directors, or the existence of similar circumstances; these problems arise, in particular, if the company which assumes liability does so gratuitously.

In the second part of his chapter Dr. Prentice explains that the law may impose liability on a group member for the debts of another group member in three cases, *viz.* in piercing the veil situations, if the group members or its directors were engaged in wrongful trading, and under the rule in *West Mercia Safety Ltd.* v. *Dodd* [1988] BCLC 250, where the Court of Appeal held that in certain circumstances the directors owed a duty to the creditors of an insolvent company; a case which raises the hope that one day the English courts may be prepared to go through Professor Tunc's "open door".

As regards piercing the veil situations, Dr. Prentice, like Mr. Cashel in his contribution, recognises the piecemeal character of this solution, but he makes a few generalisations. He thinks that piercing is likely to be admitted where the subsidiary is grossly under-capitalised; where the affairs of the parent and subsidiary are commingled, or where the subsidiary is set up to enable the parent to perpetuate a fraud.

Of particular interest is Dr. Prentice's view that in certain circumstances group liability may arise under the provisions on wrongful trading. These provisions are contained in section 214 of the Insolvency Act 1986. They provide, in essence, that if in the insolvency of a company, *e.g.* a subsidiary, the court holds that a director knew or ought to have known that the company would have to go into insolvent liquidation, the court may order that the director shall be personally liable. The term "director" in this section includes a shadow director, and that may well be the parent company or its controlling director.

At the end, Dr. Prentice comes to the conclusion that although the principle in *Salomon* is still the main starting point in determining the liability of members of a group for each other's debts "the reality is that in many situations the principle will either be contracted out of by the parties or circumvented by rules of law".

5. In search of a law of groups

Professor Hopt entitles his contribution "Legal Elements and Policy Decisions in Regulating Groups of Companies". He examines whether the German law on the subject provides a satisfactory system of regulation. The significance of his critical evaluation lies in the fact that until recently, when legislation governing groups was introduced in Brazil (1976), Portugal (1986) and Hungary (1988), Germany was the only country which had placed the law of groups on a comprehensive statutory basis. Germany has done so in its Companies Act 1965; Book III of it deals in a number of articles with the *Konzernrecht*, as the German regulation of groups of companies is called.

The statutory regulation of the *Konzernrecht* has significance beyond the borders of Germany. It has been used by the European Community as a model for the contemplated regulation of the law of groups of companies in the Community. It was contemplated that this regulation would be proposed in the Ninth Directive on Company Law Harmonisation. This Directive is still at a preparatory stage; it has not even been formally submitted by the Commission to the Council of Ministers. But its intended contents are known as a preliminary draft was published in 1985.

Professor Hopt examines the German regulation from every angle, including that of comparative law. He extends his examination to the leading decisions of the *Bundesgerichtshof* on group issues. But his main quest is whether the statutory regulation of the *Konzernrecht* has closed the gap between reality and the law, in other words, whether it has been accepted by the practice. He is evidently doubtful about the success of the statutory regulation. He concludes his chapter with these significant words: ". . . there is no doubt that the reality of the business enterprise today is not the independent corporation but the group of companies. The question remains to be discussed whether the lacunae achieved this reality and the national and European laws should remain unfilled for a significant period of time." So the search for a system of the law of groups has to go on.

6. The state's involvement with groups in the United Kingdom

Professor Alan Page has written an interesting and original contribution entitled "The State and Corporate Groups in the United Kingdom". The author demonstrates that from the perspective of the state it is clear that the problems posed by the development of corporate groups have been recognised and tackled in the United Kingdom. The state's involvement with the corporate group phenomenon is dealt with under three headings by Professor Page, these consist of state assistance, state participation and state regulation or supervision.

The state has attempted to control the behaviour of parents of companies to which it has extended assistance. Furthermore, it has been forced to address the question of its liability for the debts of such companies and of companies in which it has a substantial participation. The state regulation or supervision of corporate groups is of considerable contemporary importance; such regulation has been particularly apparent in the financial services sector. As is shown by Professor Page, there would seem to have been five responses to the emergence of financial service groups in the United Kingdom. These are the adjustment of supervisory regimes; consolidated supervision; coordination between supervisors; the regulation of group organisation, and the use of letters of comfort. Letters of comfort are now sought from all shareholder controllers, *i.e.* institutions and other persons controlling 15 per cent of more of the voting power, of a bank. This policy has been extended to gilt-edged market makers and participants in the wholesale money markets. Although letters of comfort are not usually legally binding, as Professor Page points out, they may well be administratively enforceable. Thus the Banking Supervision Division has begun to monitor the ability of givers of letters of comfort to honour their responsibilities should the need arise. It remains to be seen how far this *de facto* removal of limited liability will be extended, and how successful it will be. Similar questions may also be asked about the other techniques mentioned in the present paragraph.

Summing up

The research of the eminent experts presented in this volume shows that there are four approaches possible to the creation of a system of law of groups of companies: the statutory approach (Germany, Hopt); the development of a fiduciary duty of the dominant shareholder (Tunc); the separate entity doctrine, with exceptions where the veil of corporateness is pierced (Cashel);) and the approach from the insolvency law angle (Prentice). It is not suggested that any one of these approaches deserves to be preferred at the expense of the others.

The most radical solution is, of course, the statutory solution but, to say the least, in the form in which it is operative at present in Germany, it is capable of improvement. Eventually the European Community will have to work out a system of group law which is generally acceptable. The other three solutions are important tools for the judge to apply according to the circumstances of the case before him.

At the end, the urgency of establishing a system of the law of groups should be emphasised. The present position is highly unsatisfactory. Dr. Prentice rightly observes that the case law does not permit any confident prediction whether the courts will rely on *Salomon* or pierce the veil and there are conflicting decisions on very similar facts. It is not important whether the principles of group law are laid down in an EC Directive, a national statute, a self-regulatory Guide, as Professor Tunc suggests, or by the judicial process. But some degree of certainty should be provided. The American experience described by Mr. Cashel shows that, if nothing is done, the situation may get out of hand and end in near-chaos. Although at present it seems that, as Professor Page says the chance of the United Kingdom adopting a fully developed law of corporate groups is remote, some intermediate solutions would nevertheless seem both desirable and necessary in this and in certain other countries.

Clive Schmitthoff

March 6, 1989

Contents

Table of Cases

Table of Secondary Legislation of the European Communities

Table of National Legislation

I

The Fiduciary Duties of a Dominant Shareholder

Professor André Tunc*

It is a well known, but not yet remedied, paradox that company law seems principally devised for independent bodies, while most important companies are integrated in a group. As regards Great Britain, among the 50 biggest companies, the typical one seems to have 230 subsidiaries operating on five levels; one of them has more than 800 subsidiaries working on 11 levels.[1] The take-over bid of *Cerus* for the *Société Générale de Belgique* has shown that the network of holdings, cross-holdings and circular holdings is currently such that, in some circumstances, a large company[2] is bound to take a decision which, while profitable overall, will conflict with its interests in a part of itself. The simple reason why the paradox has not been remedied is that no satisfactory remedy has been found. Witness the disappointing German experience with the *Konzernrecht*[3] or the long and presently sterile efforts of the Commission of the European Communities to devise a directive on the subject.[4]

This is not to say, of course, that the group phenomenon is completely ignored by English law.[5] In extreme cases, the courts, in

---

* Professor Tunc of Centre d'Etudes Juridiques Comparatives, Université de Paris, Panthéon-Sorbonne.

[1] R. I. Tricker, *Corporate Governance* (1984) pp. 54–69.

[2] *E.g. Suez*, which sided with SGB while holding 10 per cent. of *Cerus* (which itself held 1·5 per cent. of *Suez*).

[3] *cf.* Frank Wooldridge, *Groups of Companies. The Law and Practice in Britain, France and Germany* (1981); Herbert Wiedemann, "The German Experience with the Law of Affiliated Enterprises," in Klaus J. Hopt (ed.), *Groups of Companies in European Laws, Les groupes de sociétés en droit européen*, (1982) 21–43; Ulrich Immenga, *Company Systems and Affiliation* (1985), Chap. 7 of vol. XIII, *Business and Private Organizations* (Alfred Conard, ed.) of the *International Encyclopedia of Comparative Law*; Klaus J. Hopt, "Le droit de sociétés. Expériences allemandes, perspectives européennes, in *Revue des sociétés* (1987), p. 371 *et seq.*

[4] *cf.* Wooldridge, *supra*, n. 3; Yves Guyon, "Examen critique des projets européens en matière de groupes de sociétés (le point de vue français)," and Welf Muller, "Group Accounts under the Proposed Seventh EEC Directive: A Practitioner's View" in Hopt (ed.) *supra*, n. 3, respectively at 155–174 and 175–193; Richard M. Buxbaum and Klaus J. Hopt, *Legal Harmonization and the Business Enterprise* (1988) p. 250.

[5] See in particular Wooldridge, *supra*, n. 3; D. D. Prentice, "Groups of Companies: The English Experience," in Hopt (ed.), *supra*, n. 3, 99 ss; Tom Hadden, *The Control of Corporate Groups* (1983); Clive M. Schmitthoff, "The wholly owned and the controlled subsidiary" [1978] J.B.L. 218. See also Clive M. Schmitthoff *et al* (ed.), *Palmer's*

"lifting the veil" of a company, will consider a parent company and a subsidiary as a single corporate entity.[6] If the power of a dominant shareholder is such that the directors are accustomed to act in accordance with his directions or instructions, he becomes a "shadow director" and as such is subject to some of the duties of a director, even though a parent company escapes a part of the duties.[7] Legislation on the holding-subsidiary relationship, which is decades old, has recently been broadened and in part extended to relations between fellow subsidiaries of the same holding company. The legislation provides against the purchase by a subsidiary of shares in the parent company[8]; for the issue of information for the shareholders and the public, especially through group accounts[9]; against directors' unfair dealing with subsidiaries.[10] Increasingly, company legislation acknowledges the existence of relations between companies and takes them into account in the regulation of financial assistance by a company for the acquisition of its own shares,[11] of substantial property transactions,[12] of the powers of inspectors during an investigation,[13] in the definition of "connected persons",[14] or companies "associate" of others,[15] and in the definition of "investment business."[16] But this legislation, important as it is, only deals with specific points. English law has not developed a coherent body of rules governing the relationships of companies forming part of a group.[17] In particular, in its judicial as well as in its legislative form, it remains silent on the duties of a parent company towards the share-

---

Company Law, vol. 1, (24th ed., 1987), paras. 18–22, 18–32, 38–24, 50–09, 73–08, Chap. 74; Robert R. Pennington, *Pennington's Company Law*, (6th ed., 1990) Chap. 20; J. H. Farrar, *Company Law*, (1985) Chap. 32; A. J. Boyle, John Birds, Graham Penn, *Boyle and Birds' Company Law*, (2nd ed., 1987) para 1.14; J. H. Farrar, "Ownership and Control of Listed Public Companies. Revising or Rejecting the Concept of Control," in B. G. Pettet (ed.), *Company Law in Change. Current Legal Problems* (1987) 39.

[6] *cf.* Schmitthoff *et al*, *supra*, n. 5, paras. 18–22, 18–23; Pennington, *supra*, n. 5, pp. 58–63; Farrar, *supra*, n. 5 pp. 58–60; L. J. Leigh, V. H. Joffe, D. Goldberg, *Northey and Leigh's Introduction to Company Law* (4th ed., 1987) pp. 20–26; Andrew Beck, "The two sides of the corporate veil, in John H. Farrar" (ed.), *Contemporary Issues in Company Law* (1987) 71.

[7] C.A. 1985, (as amended) s.741.

[8] C.A. 1985, (as amended) s.23.

[9] C.A. 1985 (as amended), ss.227–232 and Schedules 4–6. *cf.* Schmitthoff *et al*, *supra*, n. 5, Chap. 74; Leigh, Joffe, Goldberg, *supra*, n. 6 pp. 165–166; Geoffrey Morse, *Charlesworth's Company Law* (13th ed., 1987) pp. 532–544; Pennington, *supra*, n. 5.

[10] C.A. 1985 (as amended), ss.318(1)(c), 319(1), 320(1), 323(3), 324, 330.

[11] C.A. 1985 (as amended), ss.151, 153.

[12] C.A. 1985 (as amended), s.321.

[13] C.A. 1985 (as amended), s.433.

[14] C.A. 1985 (as amended), s.346.

[15] I.A. 1986, s.485(6).

[16] F.S.A. 1986, Schedule 1, para. 18.

[17] See Wooldridge, *supra*, n. 3; Prentice, *supra*, n. 5; Schmitthoff, *supra*, n. 5 para. 74–02; Pennington, *supra*, n. 5 pp. 792–807; Farrar, *supra*, n. 5 pp. 460–467; Boyle, Birds, Penn, *supra*, n. 5 para. 1.14; L. S. Sealy, *Cases and Materials in Company Law* (3rd ed., 1985) pp. 57–59.

holders and the employees and the creditors of a subsidiary.[18] Does the valuable position of a dominant shareholder[19] create duties which do not fall on an ordinary shareholder?[20] This is the problem which the German *Konzernrecht* has tried to solve, apparently with little success. This is the problem which, notwithstanding its difficulty, I would like to consider as a conceptual framework to our research and without forgetting other aspects of the problem.[21] My thesis is the following: English law is very close to recognising the fiduciary duties of a dominant shareholder; it should go one step further and actually recognise them. What then would be the consequences? To try to answer the question, I shall turn to American law in the second part of this chapter. This choice of American law on the part of a French lawyer may be surprising. The truth is that French law and more broadly, and as far as I know, continental laws, ignore the doctrine of fiduciary duties of directors and replace them by a mere regulation of the director's dealings with the company. This is strange. We pride ourselves on relying on principles and leaving it to English purists to look for regulations. The reverse is true in this field. Certainly, Great Britain now has detailed legislation on the enforcement of fair dealing. But at least it has kept the basic principle, and this principle has gained increased importance in the United States, while the French never expressed it. This is the reason why I shall cover successively English and American law.[22]

---

[18] For the sake of simplicity, the employees' interests shall be considered equivalent to the shareholders' interests: *vis-à-vis* a dominant shareholder, both ordinary shareholders and employees have the same interest in the prosperity of the company.

[19] On the value of the controlling share interest in a private company, see *Lloyd's Bank plc* v. *Duker* [1987] 1 W.L.R. 1324 and Clive M. Schmitthoff in [1987] J.B.L. 421. When the City Code applies, the principle that all shareholders of the same class of an offeree company must be treated similarly by an offeror prevents a sale of the value of the control. On the duties of a controlling shareholder in the City Code, note the 8th Principle: "Rights of control must be exercised in good faith and the oppression of a minority is wholly unacceptable" and the first note on Rule 3.1: "The requirement for competent independent advice is of particular importance in cases where the controlling shareholder is making an offer." Also notice, in the Yellow Book, the requirement of the disclosure of the interest of a "substantial shareholder" (as defined in s.6, Chap. 1, 1.2) in a "Class 4 transaction": s.6, Chap. 1, 6.3.

[20] *cf.* John H. Farrar, "The duties of controlling shareholders," in Farrar (ed.), *Contemporary Issues in Company Law* (1987) p. 187; Philip Anisman, "Majority-minority relations in Canadian corporation law: an overview," (1986–1987) 12 Can. Bus. L.J. 473. An excellent thesis has recently been written on the subject: Sylvie Maze, *Les devoirs des actionnaires prépondérants en droit comparé (français, anglais et nord-américain)* (Paris I, 1987, mimeo; arrangements are being sought for its publication). The tension between the "right" aspect and the "function" aspect of the voting right in French and German laws is the subject of another excellent thesis of Jean-Marc Hauptmann, *Le droit de vote de l'actionnaire en droit français et en droit allemand* (Nancy, 1986, mimeo).

[21] See the authors referred to *supra*, nn. 3, 4 and 5, and *e.g.* Diane M. Hare and Anna T. Archimandritou, "Intra-group transactions. The importance of disclosure" [1986] J.B.L. 249.

[22] On the French law of groups, see among many other studies: René Roblot, *Traité élémentaire de droit commercial de Georges Ripert*, Vol. I, Nos. 711–715 (12th ed., 1986); Yves Guyon, *Droit des affaires*, nos. 580–623 (4th ed., 1986); Pierre Bézard, *La société*

English law

In 1980, Dr. Prentice could sum up English law on the matter by the following statement:

> "It is a direct consequence of the entity doctrine that directors of a company owe their fiduciary duties to their company and not to other members of the group; thus, the directors of a parent or a subsidiary will owe their duties to their respective companies and they will be entitled to take into consideration the interests of other constituent members of the group only to the extent that this furthers the interests of their own companies."[23]

While the statement is basically correct, it illustrates a fundamental and dangerous paradox: while the group only exists to further the interests of the group as a whole or even, more precisely, to further the interests of its dominant corporate body, this basic reality is completely ignored by law. When a company, for its own benefit, has created a subsidiary and controls the composition of the latter's board of directors, the subsidiary's directors are supposed to disregard entirely the parent company's interests and manage the affairs of the company with an entirely independent mind.[24] This is truly unrealistic, but then the subsidiary's directors are in an untenable position. And yet, the law does not provide them with any guidance. Certainly, the question must be explored whether Dr. Prentice's statement represents the whole of the matter at the present time or whether it needs a number of qualifications.

Dr. Prentice himself, in a further development, remarks that "[t]he allocation of corporate opportunities between the various companies of a group gives rise to vexing (and as yet relatively unexplored) problems."[25] Dr. Prentice is shocked by the logical conclusion that the parent company would have full power to take a corporate opportunity for itself, or to allocate it to a subsidiary if this is in its own interest, in full disregard of another subsidiary's interests. This is probably what happens in practice. It was tolerable when the directors had no duty towards the employees and to the extent to which the interested subsidiaries were 100 per cent. owned by the parent company. But it is no longer acceptable as soon as the sacrificed sub-

---

anonyme, nos. 1662–1732 (1986); Maurice Cozian et Alain Viandier, *Droit des sociétés*, nos. 1630–1815 (1987); Philippe Merle, *Droit commercial, Sociétés commerciales*, nos. 641–671 (1988).

[23] Prentice, *supra*, n. 5 p. 112.

[24] *cf.* Lord Denning M.R. in *Boulting* v. *ACTT* [1963] 2 Q.B. 606, 626, speaking of the appointment of nominee directors: "There is nothing wrong in it. It is done every day. Nothing wrong, that is, so long as the director is left free to exercise his best judgment in the interests of the company which he serves. But if he is put upon terms that he is bound to act in the affairs of the company in accordance with the directions of his patron, it is beyond doubt unlawful."

[25] Prentice, *supra*, n. 5 p. 125. *cf.* Klaus J. Hopt, "Self-Dealing and the Use of Corporate Opportunity and Information: Regulating Directors' Conflicts of Interest," in Klaus J. Hopt and Gunther Teubner, *Corporate Governance and Directors' Liability* (1985) p. 285, pp. 310–312.

sidiary has outside shareholders and, in any case, now that the directors "must have regard to the interest of the company's employees in general."[26] Dr. Prentice turns to American authors and American judicial decisions to conclude that:

> "At the minimum in this situation a parent should be treated as owing a fiduciary duty to its subsidiary and as under an obligation to treat its subsidiary with fairness."[27]

The traditional view of the matter creates difficulties which extend beyond the allocation of corporate opportunities. Companies of a group are often linked by frequent contracts either long-term or short-term.[28] Under the traditional view, it is not only the right, but the duty of the parent's directors to consider only the parent's interests; they may impose on the subsidiary unfair contracts, the only limit to unfairness being an economic one, *i.e.* the need to let the subsidiary survive. Again, the conclusion is not acceptable. Unfortunately, the case is not purely hypothetical. The danger of unfair dealings is particularly serious in situations of vertical integration. Some years ago, two companies created a common subsidiary to be their supplier; each of them provided 40 per cent. of the capital, and 20 per cent. was obtained from the public; but it had been rumoured that, by secret agreement between the parents, the prices of the supplies would be such that the subsidiary would never prosper.

It may be that no remedy to such a situation can be found in a purely conceptual framework of parents, subsidiaries and sister companies, as separate entities. The idea of the interest of the group is no longer of use: as the interest of a political society might be to sacrifice some of its members (a solution which can be accepted only by authoritarian States), the interest of the group could be to sacrifice one of the subsidiaries, a solution which can no longer be acceptable.[29] What is needed is a harmonisation of the group's interests and of its members' interests, a harmonisation somewhat comparable to the one which John Rawls, in his *Theory of Justice*, has tried to establish for the political society. I submit that the only hope of approaching such harmonisation exists in regarding the parent, not as an entity distinct from the subsidiary, but as its dominant shareholder.

It has been said, it is true, that "the shareholder's vote is a right of

---

[26] C.A. 1985, s.309. *cf.* Peter G. Xuereb, "The jurisdiction of industrial relations through company law reform" (1988) 51 M.L.R. 156.

[27] Prentice, *supra*, n. 5 p. 126.

[28] On the practical importance of intra-group borrowing, see Hadden, *supra*, n. 5 p. 15.

[29] See Pennycuick J. in *Charterbridge Corporation Ltd.* v. *Lloyd's Bank Ltd.* [1970] Ch. 62; [1969] 2 All E.R. 1185: "Mr. Bagnall for the bank contended that it is sufficient that the directors of Castelford looked to the benefit of the group as a whole. Equally, I reject that contention. Each company in the group is a separate legal entity and the directors of a particular company are not entitled to sacrifice the interest of that company."

property, and prima facie may be exercised by a shareholder as he thinks fit in his own interest."[30] However, the dictum of Lindley M.R. in *Allen* v. *Gold Reefs of West Africa Ltd.*[31] that shareholders in exercising their vote must exercise it bona fide for the benefit of the company as a whole, if of dubious impact, greatly moderates the previous dictum; it brings the right to vote closer to a function or, at least, implies a duty of the shareholder towards his fellow members. A number of contradictory dicta can be collected on the subject.[32] But this mere fact shows that the road is opened to the idea that, while an ordinary shareholder may vote as he thinks fit in his own interest, a dominant one should consider himself as a member of an association, with a power which commands duties towards his fellow members.[33]

This injection of equitable considerations into the voting right has received considerable support in recent years. It is hardly necessary to recall Lord Wilberforce, in *Ebrahimi* v. *Westbourne Galleries Ltd.*,[34] underlining

> "the fact that a limited company is more than a mere legal entity, with a personality in law of its own; that there is room in company law for recognition of the fact that behind it, or amongst it, there are individuals, with rights, expectations and obligations *inter se* which are not necessarily submerged in the company structure"

and the same Lord Wilberforce stating that

> "... equity always does enable the court to subject the exercise of legal rights to equitable considerations" and that "considerations ... of a personal character arising between one individual and another, ... may make it unjust, or inequitable, to insist on legal rights, or to exercise them in a particular way."

---

[30] Lord Maugham in *Carruth* v. *Imperial Chemical Industries Ltd.* [1937] A.C. 707. See also Jessel M.R. in *Pender* v. *Lushington* (1877) 6 Ch.D. 70; 46 L.J. Ch. 317; Nolton J. in *Northern Counties Securities Ltd.* v. *Jackson and Steeple Ltd.* [1974] 1 W.L.R. 1133; [1974] 2 All E.R. 625. *cf.* Lord Cozens-Hardy M.R. in *Phillips* v. *Manufacturers Securities Ltd.* (1917) 116 L.T. 290, 296: "members of a company voting at a general meeting properly convened have no fiduciary obligation either to the company or to the other shareholders." *cf.* also the robust support for this view by Lord Wedderburn (1981) 44 M.L.R. 202, 208–210, or L. S. Sealy, "Equitable and other fetters on the shareholder's freedom to vote," in Nancy E. Eastham and Boris Krivy (eds.) *The Cambridge Lectures 1981* (1982) p. 80.

[31] [1900] 1 Ch. 656, 671.

[32] See the contradictory dicta collected by L. C. B. Gower *et al, Gower's Principles of Modern Company Law* (4th ed., 1979, with a *Second Cumulative Supplement*, 1988, by B. G. Pettet) pp. 614–630; D. D. Prentice (1976) 92 L.Q.R. 502, 505–506; Lawrie (1982) 3 *Co. Law* 160, 163; Maze, *supra*, n. 20, Title I. See also Peter G. Xuereb, "The limitation on the exercise of majority power" (1985) 6 *Co. Law* 199; R. G. Rixon, "Competing interests and conflicting principles: an examination of the power of alteration of articles of association" (1986) 49 M.L.R. 446, especially at 464–471; Peter G. Xuereb, "Voting rights: a comparative review" (1987) 8 *Co. Law* 16.

[33] *cf.* Gower, *supra*, n. 32 pp. 623–630.

[34] [1973] A.C. 360, 379.

What is said by Lord Wilberforce of the relationship between individual persons in a quasi-partnership company seems equally realistic when applied, in a quite different situation, to relationships between companies of a group. More recently, in *Eastman Co. (Kilner House) Ltd.* v. *Greater London Council*,[35] Megarry V.-C. stated:

> "Plainly there must be some limit to the power of the majority to pass resolutions which they believe to be in the best interests of the company and yet remain immune from interference by the courts. It may be in the best interests of the company to deprive the minority of some of their rights or some of their property, yet I do not think that this gives the majority an unrestricted right to do this, however unjust it may be, and however much it may harm shareholders whose rights as a class differ from those of the majority."

One should admit that these statements were uttered in cases which did not involve the problem concerned here: the fiduciary duties of a dominant shareholder. However, they are sweeping statements, which have their roots in the originally broad powers of a judge of equity, and which are capable of bringing consequences to bear on many problems of company law. It was on the basis of Lord Wilberforce's statement that, in *Clemens* v. *Clemens Bros. Ltd.*,[36] a resolution of the general meeting legally carried by the votes of the majority was set aside as depriving the minority of its negative control.

Other authorities reinforce the feeling that English law is coming closer to the recognition of the fiduciary duties of a dominant shareholder.[37] In *Daniels* v. *Daniels*,[38] Templeman J. on three occasions in his judgment equated directors and majority shareholders as regards the "duty" (or the breach of duty) "which they owe to the company." When Templeman J. in *Re Hellenic and General Trust Ltd.*,[39] denied the right to vote on a scheme of arrangement to the wholly owned subsidiary of the company proposing the scheme,[40] is not his

---

[35] [1982] 1 W.L.R. 2, 11; [1982] 1 All E.R. 437, 444.

[36] [1976] 2 All E.R. 268.

[37] It does not seem possible to consider here the cases which allowed an exception to the rule in *Foss* v. *Harbottle* on the ground of "fraud on the minority," in order to see whether or not they imply a duty of a dominant shareholder toward the company or the minority shareholders. A valuable research on the matter has been made by Maze, *supra*, n. 20 Title II, Ch. II, s.I, ss.I. On the "fraud on the minority" concept, see Schmitthoff, *supra*, n. 5, paras. 65–09, 65–10; Gower, *supra*, n. 32 pp. 616–630; Pennington, *supra*, n. 5 pp. 734–736 (warning in conclusion against the idea of a fiduciary duty); Farrar, *supra*, n. 5 pp. 364–367; Sealy, *supra*, n. 15 pp. 455–573; W (1981) 44 M.L.R. 202, 205–211; H. R. Hahlo and J. H. Farrar, *Hahlo's Cases and Materials on Company Law* (3rd ed., 1987) pp. 490–519.

[38] [1978] Ch. 406.

[39] [1976] 1 W.L.R. 123; [1975] 3 All E.R. 382.

[40] *cf. Re Holders Investment Trust Ltd.* [1971] 1 W.L.R. 583; [1971] 2 All E.R. 289; *Pennell Securities Ltd.* v. *Venida Investments Ltd.*, unreported but commented upon by Susan J. Burridge (1981) 44 M.L.R. 40 and Cosmo Graham (1985) 6 *Co. Law* 183.

decision a recognition of the fact that a controlling shareholder in fact imposes his will? Is not his decision capable of far-reaching consequences on the regime of the contracts between a parent and a subsidiary, of consequences comparable to the ones derived from the fiduciary duties of a director as regards contracts in which he is interested? Legislation goes in the same direction. When, under section 210 of the Companies Act 1948, a remedy was provided against the "oppression" of a minority shareholder, was not this remedy the recognition of the principle that a dominant shareholder should not always be allowed to exercise fully his legal rights? As said by Lord Simonds, quoting Lord Cooper[41]:

> "Whenever a subsidiary is formed ... with an independent minority of shareholders, the parent company must, if it is engaged in the same class of business, accept as a result of having formed such a subsidiary an obligation so to conduct what are in a sense its own affairs as to deal fairly with its subsidiary."

It may be that this passage does not impose a fiduciary duty on majority shareholders towards the minority,[42] but the same result would be reached if a fiduciary duty was recognised, which would impose a fair allocation of business opportunities. Finally, under the new legislation, if a dominant shareholder was to make an unfair use of his legal power to the prejudice of ordinary shareholders, any shareholder of that category could either present the court with a winding up petition[43] or apply for a remedy under section 459. Section 459, much resorted to,[44] may be considered as a statement in the negative of the duty of directors and dominant shareholders alike to conduct the company's affairs with fairness which is another way of expressing their fiduciary duties.

Thus, while it does not seem possible to claim that English law at present recognises the fiduciary duties of a dominant shareholder toward the company and a fortiori towards his fellow shareholders,[45] it seems possible to consider that the highest judicial authorities and the legislator have opened a door which would permit recognition of such duties.[46] The question may be asked: which consequences would flow from this recognition? For reasons already explained, we shall turn to American law in quest of an answer, rather than to speculate on the

---

[41] *Scottish Co-operative Wholesale Society Ltd.* v. *Meyer* [1959] A.C. 324, 343; [1958] All E.R. 66, 72.

[42] Pennington, *supra*, n. 5 p. 749.

[43] I.A. 1986 s.122(g).

[44] *cf.* A. J. Boyle, "The judicial interpretation of Part XVII of the Companies Act 1985," in B. G. Pettet, *Company Law in Change. Current Legal Problems* (1987) p. 23; Peter G. Xuereb, "Remedies for abuse of majority power" (1986) 7 *Co. Law* 53; Ralph Instone, "Unfair prejudice: an interim report" [1988] J.B.L. 20; Pettet, *Supplement* to *Gower*, pp. 669–670, *supra*, n. 32; D. D. Prentice, "The theory of the firm: Minority shareholder oppression; sections 459–461 of the Companies Act 1985" (1988) 8 Ox. J. Leg. St. 55.

[45] See also the *caveat* of Gower, *supra*, n. 32 p. 630.

[46] *cf.* Farrar, *supra*, n. 5 pp. 392–395, Morse, *supra*, n. 9 pp. 422–426.

matter. However, since the group phenomenon also creates a well known danger for the creditors of a subsidiary,[47] another problem should briefly be considered: would it be possible to admit a duty of a dominant shareholder toward the company's creditors?

A negative answer seems self-evident. No English decision has ever been based on a duty of the directors towards the company's creditors.[48] *A fortiori* it would seem impossible to admit any duty of a mere dominant shareholder. The question, however, should not be dismissed too lightly. The existence of a fiduciary duty seems eliminated, as one does not see the relation of trust which would link directors and creditors of a company. But a duty of care from the former toward the latter should not be ruled out. It has been recognised by a number of Commonwealth and American decisions.[49] In English law, it seems more and more implicitly recognised by the legislator. Since 1976, an auditor's notice of resignation should state whether there are circumstances connected with his resignation which in his opinion should be brought to the notice of the members or creditors of the company.[50] The Secretary of State may order an investigation into the affairs of a company if it appears to him that there are circumstances suggesting that the company's affairs are being or have been conducted with intent to defraud its creditors or the creditors of any other person.[51] Indeed nearly the whole of Parts V and VIII of the Companies Act 1985, on the share capital, its increase, maintenance and reduction, and the distribution of profits and assets, seem intended for the protection of creditors as well as that of the shareholders.[52] More to the point, a director or former director who has led his company to insolvency may be the subject of a disqualification order by the court.[53] The Insolvency Act 1986, sections 213 and 214, provides sanctions for fraudulent trading and wrongful trading. Finally, the *City Code* also expresses the duties of the directors toward the creditors.[54] To the extent to which the com-

---

[47] *cf. Multinational Gas and Petrochemical Co.* v. *Multinational Gas and Petrochemical Services Ltd.* [1983] 3 W.L.R. 492 and Wedderburn in (1984) 47 M.L.R. 87. See also Schmitthoff, *supra*, n. 5; Prentice, *supra*, n. 5 at pp. 104–112.

[48] See however Nourse L.J. in *Brady* v. *Brady* (1987) 3 B.C.C. 535, commented upon by A. G. J. Berg [1988] J.B.L. 65, John Kiggundu (1987) 8 *Co. Law* 270, Kenneth Polack [1988] C.L.J. 24; Dillon L.J. in *West Mercia Safetywear* v. *Dodd*, noted [1988] J.B.L. 68 n. 11 and commented upon by D. D. Prentice in Chapter 3 below.

[49] *cf.* Reginald Barrett, "Directors' duties to creditors" (1977) 40 M.L.R. 226; J. H. Farrar, "The obligation of a company's directors to its creditors before liquidation" [1985] J.B.L. 413; Sealy, *supra*, n. 17 pp. 248–249; Boyle, Birds and Penn, *supra*, n. 5 para. 20.5; Beck, *supra*, n. 6.

[50] C.A. 1985 (as amended) ss.392, 392A and 394.

[51] C.A. 1985 (as amended) s.432(2)(a).

[52] See, however, Buckley L.J. in *Re Horsley and Weight Ltd.* [1982] Ch. 442; [1982] 3 All E.R. 1045: "It is a misapprehension to suppose that the directors of a company owe a duty to the company's creditors to keep the contributed capital of the company intact."

[53] Company Directors Disqualification Act 1986 ss.6–8.

[54] The City Code on Take-overs and Mergers, General Principles, 9: "... It is the

pany's creditors would be recognised as beneficiaries of a duty of care on the part of the directors, the recognition could be extended to a similar duty on the part of a dominant shareholder.

American law

In the United States, it is no longer disputed that dominant shareholders have fiduciary duties towards the corporation and the other shareholders.

As in England, shares are considered the private property of the shareholders, who in principle are allowed to vote with their shares as they desire.[55] The situation is different, however, for controlling or dominating shareholders. Fiduciary duties are imposed on them, either because they have the power to govern the corporation through directors and officers or, more directly, because it is considered that their power should in equity carry with it its counterpart, fiduciary duties.[56] And, as the principle of *Percival* v. *Wright* is set aside in most jurisdictions, those fiduciary duties exist both towards the corporation and towards the other shareholders. As early as 1919, the Supreme Court of the United States could state:

"The rule of corporation law and of equity invoked is well settled and has been often applied. The majority has the right to control; but when it does so, it occupies a fiduciary relation toward the minority, as much so as the corporation itself or its officers or directors."[57]

Again, in 1939:

"A director is a fiduciary ... So is a dominant or controlling stockholder or group of stockholders... Their powers are powers in trust."[58]

The doctrine seems unanimously accepted by the various states.

---

shareholders' interests taken as a whole, together with those of employees and creditors, which should be considered when the directors are giving advice to the shareholders" (on a take-over bid).

[55] Harry G. Henn and John R. Alexander, *Laws of Corporations and Other Business Enterprises* (3rd ed., 1983) para. 240.

[56] Henn and Alexander, *ibid.*; William L. Cary and Melvin Aron Eisenberg, *Cases and Materials on Corporations* (5th ed., 1980) pp. 613–637; Richard W. Jennings and Richard M. Buxbaum, *Corporations. Cases and Materials* (5th ed., 1979) pp. 466–480; Lewis D. Solomon, Russell B. Stevenson, Jr., Donald E. Schwartz, *Corporations. Law and Policies. Materials and Problems* (1982) pp. 608–613, 986–1021; Alexander H. Frey, Jesse H. Choper, Noyes E. Leech, C. Robert Morris, Jr., *Cases and Materials on Corporations* (2nd ed., 1966) pp. 180–188 (3rd ed. in preparation); Maze, *supra*, n. 20 Title I. Ch. II, s.II, Title II Ch. III; Farrar, *supra*, n. 20.

[57] *Southern Pacific Co.* v. *Bogert*, 250 U.S. 483, 39 S.Ct. 533, 63 L. ed. 1099 (1919).

[58] *Pepper* v. *Litton*, 808 U.S. 295, 60 S.Ct. 238, 84 L. ed. 281 (1939). Among many similar decisions, see *Perlman* v. *Feldmann*, 219 F. 2d 173 (2nd Cir. 1955), and *Singer* v. *Magnavox*, 380 A.2d 969 (Del.S.Ct. 1977). Compare André Tunc, "The Not So Common Law of England and the United States, or, Precedent in England and in the United States, A Field Study by an Outsider" (1984) 47 M.L.R. 150, at 166–167.

Unanimity, it is true, does not extend to the implications of the doctrine. While many states have passed legislation governing transactions between directors and their corporations, only two states have enacted a general principle which authorises contracts between a parent corporation and its subsidiary subject to certain conditions of fairness, approbation or ratification. In the other states, while the fiduciary duty of the dominating shareholder, including the parent corporation, is recognised, there is much hesitation and much variation notwithstanding an important volume of case law and doctrinal writings, as to the consequences it carries in specific circumstances.[59] The situation, however, is in the process of evolution and clarification. The American Law Institute launched, in 1980, a project which, after a difficult start, has received the name of *Principles of Corporate Governance: Analysis and Recommendations*. It is partly a restatement of the law and partly, as its name indicates, a set of recommendations addressed, as the case may be, to the courts or to the legislatures. Its Chief Reporter is now Professor Melvin A. Eisenberg. Seven Parts are in preparation, covering the objects and conduct of the business corporation, the structure of the corporation, the duty of care and the business judgment rule, the duty of loyalty, transactions in control, and shareholders' remedies. It is in Part V, on the duty of loyalty, that a full chapter, Chapter 3, covering 40 pages, has been devoted to the duties of dominating shareholders.[60] While the text is not final and the whole project faces some opposition, it can hardly be disputed that the draft is the result of a thoughtful and balanced deliberation by competent and independent experts on the basis of the case law and the doctrinal writings on the subject, and that it deserves great consideration. In particular, no comparable effort had previously been undertaken to embrace in its generality the subject of the duties of a dominating shareholder. Chapter 3 is composed of three sections, governing transactions with the corporation, use of dominating position, or of information or property, and corporate opportunities. A preliminary problem is the definition of a dominating shareholder. In the last version of the *Principles*[61] "a dominating shareholder" means a shareholder who, either alone or pursuant to an arrangement or understanding with one or more other persons:

(a) owns, and has the unrestricted power to vote, more than 50 per cent. of the outstanding voting securities of a corporation; or

(b) otherwise in fact exercises control[62] over the management of the business of the corporation or the transaction in question.

---

[59] See the authors referred to *supra*, n. 56, in particular Maze.

[60] Tentative Draft No. 3 (1984), pp. 231–271, revised in Tentative Draft No. 5 (1986), pp. 155–195.

[61] Tentative Draft No. 5 (1986) s.1.12.

[62] The word "control" is defined in s.1.05 (Tentative Draft No. 5) as "the power, directly or indirectly, either alone or pursuant to an arrangement or understanding with one or more other persons, to exercise a controlling influence over the management or policies of a business organization through the ownership of equity interests, through one or more intermediary persons, by contract, or otherwise ... A person

11

A shareholder who either alone or pursuant to an arrangement or understanding with one or more other persons owns, or has the unrestricted power to vote, 25 per cent. or more of the outstanding voting securities of a corporation is presumed to exercise control over the management of the business of the corporation. This is a definition which is comparable to the definition of a holding company under the Companies Act 1985, section 736. Transactions between a dominating shareholder and the corporation are governed in section 5.10 by a general rule which reads as follows:

> "A dominating shareholder who enters into a transaction with the corporation, fulfils his duty of loyalty to the corporation concerning the transaction if:
> (1) the transaction is fair to the corporation when entered into; or
> (2) the transaction is authorized or ratified by disinterested shareholders, following disclosure concerning the conflict of interest and the transaction, and does not constitute a waste of corporate assets at the time of the shareholder action."[63]

Another part of the section specifies who carries the burden of proof. If the transaction was duly authorised or ratified, the burden of proof is on the challenging party. Otherwise, the dominating shareholder has the burden of proving that the transaction was fair to the corporation.

The commentary in the *Principles* considers that "Section 5.10 reflects the view generally taken by the courts that a dominating shareholder will have the burden of proving that transactions with a dominated corporation are fair. Section 5.10 also adopts the view taken in some decisions that where a transaction is approved by disinterested shareholders, the burden will shift to the party attacking the transaction to prove waste of corporate assets."[64] The commentary also specifies that a dominating shareholder is not expected in the normal course of dealing to obtain the informed authorisation of disinterested shareholders: it is only a course of dealing which is open to him if he does not want to carry the burden of proving fairness if the transaction happens to be challenged.[65] The commentary also provides useful guidance as to the appreciation of fairness. A transaction is fair if "it falls within a range of reasonableness." "Where the dominating shareholder is selling goods or services to the corporation

---

who, either alone or pursuant to an arrangement or understanding with one or more other persons, owns or has the power to vote more than 25 per cent. of the equity interest in any business organization is presumed to be in control of the organization..." *cf.* Farrar, "Ownership," *supra*, n. 5.

[63] The words and expressions "disinterested shareholders," "disclosure concerning a conflict of interest," "disclosure concerning a transaction," "waste of corporate assets," are defined in other parts of the *Principles* (Tentative Draft No. 5).

[64] pp. 155–156.

[65] p. 157.

that are of comparable quality and are sold at the same price and upon the same terms as those in transactions with third parties in contemporaneous transactions at arm's length, the dominating party will have satisfied the burden of proving fairness."[66] Where transactions with third parties are not available as a guide to fairness, it might be wise for the corporation to entrust the contemplated transaction to an independent negotiating committee of its non-executive directors.[67]

The commentary finally deals with the conflicting duties of loyalty owed by directors who sit on the boards of a parent corporation and a subsidiary. They are subject to the duty of fairness. "In the absence of total abstention of an independent negotiating structure, common directors must determine what is best for both the parent and the subsidiary."[68]

The following section, Section 5.11, deals with the use of dominating position, information, or property. According to the commentary, it is "generally consistent with existing law."[69] The general rule is the following:

"A dominating shareholder may not advance his pecuniary interest by using his dominating position, material non-public information concerning the corporation, or corporate property, in a manner that:

(1) causes reasonably foreseeable harm to the corporation or to its other shareholders in their capacity as shareholders; or

(2) allows him to secure a pecuniary benefit, including a pecuniary benefit received as a shareholder that is not made proportionately available to other shareholders similarly situated, except as permitted by Part VI (transactions in control), unless his conduct is authorised or ratified in accordance with the standards of para. 5.10(a)(2) (transactions with the corporation), or, in case of use of corporate property or services, he gives fair value for any benefit received. The allocation of the burden of proof is comparable to what it is in the preceding section.

---

[66] p. 159.
[67] cf. p. 158.
[68] p. 160. The comment refers to *Weinberger* v. *UOP, Inc.*, 457 A.2d 701, 710–711 (S.Ct. Delaware, 1983): "The requirement of fairness is unflinching in its demand that where one stands on both sides of a transaction, he has the burden of establishing its entire fairness, sufficient to pass the test of careful scrutiny by the courts ... There is no dilution of this obligation where one holds dual or multiple directorships, as in a parent-subsidiary context ... Thus, individuals who act in a dual capacity as directors of two corporations, one of whom is parent and the other subsidiary, owe the same duty of good management to both corporations, and in the absence of an independent negotiating structure, or the directors' total abstention from any participation in the matter, this duty is to be exercised in light of what is best for both companies." cf. Leigh Thomson, "Nominee and multiple directors and confidential information," in John H. Farrar, *Contemporary Issues in Company Law* (1987) p. 161.
[69] p. 165.

13

If the dominating shareholder's conduct was duly authorised or ratified, the challenging party has the burden of proof. Otherwise, it falls on the dominating shareholder to prove that his conduct was fair to the corporation and its shareholders."

One should perhaps underline that the commentary confirms that abuse of its power by a parent corporation is a current practice, sanctioned by the courts when submitted to them. It may be worth reproducing part of the commentary:

"Although some of [the cases of abuse] deal with individuals who are dominating shareholders, many deal with relationships between parent and partly owned subsidiary corporations. The cases involve such matters as misuse of position to obtain a tax benefit at the expense of a subsidiary, to influence dividend policy, to preclude a subsidiary from engaging in certain business activity, to obtain a profit from the sale of the dominated corporation's property to the exclusion of other shareholders similarly situated, and to preclude competition with the dominating shareholder. Section 5.11 synthesizes the results reached in these cases by setting forth the principle that a dominating shareholder may not, without proper disclosure and approval by disinterested minority shareholders, utilise corporate property, material non-public information, or his position to obtain a pecuniary benefit not shared with other shareholders similarly situated, unless such use would be fair to the corporation and the other shareholders."[70]

Otherwise, the commentary illustrates all the implications of the general rule set forth in the section. The Reporter's Note refers to a case to show to what length an American court may be willing to go in order to oblige a dominating shareholder to deal fairly with minority shareholders: the well-known case of *Jones* v. *H. F. Ahmanson and Co.*[71] Briefly stated, the case involved a saving and loan association (the stock of which had a very narrow market, chiefly because the stock had a high book value and was closely held), and the decision of a majority of its members to enhance the value of their investments in bringing them to a holding company; the shares of which would be much lighter (250 shares of the holding for each share of the association) and which could make public offerings of stocks and debentures, thus creating a substantial trading market. The operation had been a very successful one. It had nothing illegal in it. But it had been realised by some shareholders only, forming a majority, and was not open to the others. In an opinion written by Chief Justice Roger Traynor, the Supreme Court of California decided that the majority's conduct had been unfair: "The Courts of Appeal have often recog-

[70] pp. 165–166.
[71] 1 Cal. 3d 93, 460 P.2d 464.

14

nised that majority shareholders, either singly or acting in concert to accomplish a joint purpose, have a fiduciary responsibility to the minority and to the corporation to use their ability to control the corporation in a fair, just, and equitable manner. Majority shareholders may not use their power to control corporate activities to benefit themselves alone or in a manner detrimental to the minority. Any use to which they put the corporation must benefit all shareholders proportionately...". The decision is remarkable, not only for the strength and breadth with which the fiduciary duty of a majority is asserted, but mainly for the fact that it is asserted in a case relating not to an operation of the corporation, but to an operation purely bearing on individual properties of the majority, their shares, and by the additional fact that minority shareholders had not suffered any loss, but had simply not been offered an opportunity.

This decision thus constitutes a transition to the consideration of the last section of the chapter, which deals with the allocation of corporate opportunities.[72]

The drafters of Section 5.12 had to define what is, for the purpose of the rule, a corporate opportunity. They did it in the following terms:

"For the purposes of this section, a corporate opportunity means any opportunity to engage in a business activity that is held out to shareholders of the corporation as being within the scope of the business in which the corporation is presently engaged or may be reasonably expected to engage, and that is neither developed nor received by the dominating shareholder within the scope and regular course of his own business activities. 'A business activity' includes the acquisition or use of any contract right or other tangible or intangible property".

Corporate opportunities thus defined are governed by the following general rule: "A dominating shareholder may not take advantage of a corporate opportunity unless:

(1) The taking of the opportunity is fair to the corporation; or
(2) The taking of the opportunity is authorised or ratified by disinterested shareholders following disclosure concerning the conflict of interest and the facts concerning the corporate opportunity, and the shareholders' action is not equivalent to a waste of corporate assets."

---

[72] The allocation of corporate opportunities may be one of the most important and difficult problems in the parent-subsidiary relations. Recent research on the subject has led the authors to suggest the following rule: "all business opportunities that may be taken by either a parent company or its partially owned subsidiary are deemed to belong to the subsidiary, and their taking by the parent is therefore a wrongful usurpation, unless the parent shows by clear and convincing evidence that the opportunity would have a substantially higher value if taken and developed by the parent than if taken and developed by the subsidiary." Victor Brudney and Robert Charles Clark, "A New Look at Corporate Opportunities," (1981) 94 Harv.L.Rev. 997, 1045–1060, at 1055; see also Robert Charles Clark, *Corporate Law* (1986) para. 7.8. The rule does not give a solution to the problem of allocation of corporate opportunities between the various sister subsidiaries of a common parent company.

The Provision of Section 5.12 dealing with the burden of proof offers no surprise, but attention should be paid to the commentary on this section.

First, while there is a large number of American judicial decisions involving the duty of directors and senior executives to offer corporate opportunities to the corporation, there are relatively few decisions dealing with the similar duty of a dominating shareholder.[73] Still, it is common experience that a parent corporation has currently to decide allocations of corporate opportunities between itself and its various subsidiaries. Thus, we face a field of relations where unfair practices are certainly current and which, nevertheless, has largely been ignored by law, even in the United States. It seems of special importance to work out a proper rule.

Second, the definition of a corporate opportunity in this context is more narrow than in general, "in order to balance the right of the dominating shareholder to engage in business in competition with the corporation against the need to assure that the dominating shareholder does not seize for itself opportunities which could fairly be said to belong to the corporation."[74] The commentary explains that, for the purposes of para. 5.12, several factors must be considered in determining whether a corporate opportunity exists which must be offered to the corporation:

> "(1) Has an expectation been created in the corporation's shareholders that its existing or anticipated scope of operations will include the business activity or geographical area of operation under consideration? ... (2) Even if the first question is answered in the affirmative, ... two further questions must be asked: (a) Was it contemplated that the corporation exclusively engage in the particular business activity or geographical area, or that the dominating shareholder would also engage in such activity or area? (b) How did the dominating shareholder gain access to the opportunity? Specifically was the opportunity developed by the dominating shareholder or received by it within the scope and regular course of his own business activities? If it was, then the dominating shareholder has no duty to offer the opportunity to the corporation unless it is an activity that was held out generally to shareholders of the corporation as within its area of activity. If the dominating shareholder is not engaged in the particular activity and the corporation is actively engaged in the activity, then the fact that the dominating shareholder received the opportunity will not be determinative, since it may be fairly inferred in the absence of other facts that under the circumstances he would not have received the opportunity but for the existing business of the corporation."[75]

[73] p. 185.
[74] p. 186.
[75] pp. 186–187.

16

The definition of a corporate opportunity may be the most delicate problem of a codification of the dominating shareholder's duty in this field. On the other hand, the duty itself can be stated with clarity. As stated in the commentary:

"Section 5.12(a) sets forth the general rule that a dominating shareholder may not take a corporate opportunity unless the taking is fair to the corporation or the taking has been approved or ratified by disinterested minority shareholders, in which event a party attacking the transaction must prove that the shareholder's action is equivalent to a waste of corporate assets. As in the case of para. 5.10, the dominating shareholder is not obliged to disclose material facts concerning the opportunity unless he seeks the approval of disinterested shareholders. If he does seek such approval, then para. 5.12(a)(2) obliges him to disclose material facts known to him concerning the corporate opportunity. Unlike directors and senior executives, the dominating shareholder is not subject to a duty of loyalty not to compete with the corporation, and therefore ... para. 5.12 does not require that the taking of a corporate opportunity must place the dominating shareholder in competition with the corporation. However, if the dominating shareholder uses his position to take a corporate opportunity and thereby precludes the corporation from competing with him, he will have breached his duty of loyalty under para. 5.11 as well as para. 5.12."[76]

A last quotation from the *Principles* should be made. The introductory note to Part V gives an important clue to the philosophy in which the whole part has been conceived:

"Great emphasis is placed in Part V on the desirability of providing the corporation with disinterested representation as a technique for dealing with conflicts of interest. The board and committee structure in Part III and Part IIIA for large publicly held corporations is designed to provide a general board environment conducive to objective decision-making in recurring conflict-of-interest situations. It is to be expected that courts will take into consideration the presence of such an environment in determining how capable the board of directors or a board committee are of performing their function of approving conflict-of-interest transactions objectively. In approaching a breach of duty of loyalty case, a court will be expected to give close scrutiny to the objectivity of those who are acting on behalf of the corporation in the transaction. This scrutiny should involve consideration of such factors as whether receipt of fees from the corporation that are material to the director impair his objectivity, whether the directors have sought the assistance of independent advice to the extent appropriate to their decision, and

[76] pp. 185–186.

17

whether the directors have otherwise followed procedures designed to enhance the objectivity of their deliberations."[77]

If we now turn briefly to the duty of a dominant shareholder towards the corporation's creditors, we find at least some recognition of this duty.[78] The Supreme Court of the United States has often decided that the claims of a controlling shareholder should be subordinated to those of ordinary creditors.[79] It has sometimes justified the solution by "simply the violation of rules of fair play and good conscience by the claimant, a breach of the fiduciary standards of conduct which he owes the corporation, its stockholders and creditors."[80]

Conclusion

Thus, the contrast is striking between the English and the American scenes. In England, one may argue that the door seems open to the recognition of the fiduciary duty of a dominant shareholder towards the company and perhaps the minority shareholders. In the States, the matter is no longer the object of dispute: the existence of the duty has been recognised for decades and, if it has given rise and still gives rise to innumerable decisions, the problem is only, in these decisions, whether, in the circumstances of the case, the duty has been fulfilled or broken. From this contrast, can we derive some conclusions?[81]

(1) Merely the number of American cases on the matter probably reveals or rather confirms that unfairness is common in the relationships of a dominant shareholder and the company, in particular in the relationships of a parent company with its subsidiaries.

(2) It would simply be an acknowledgment of the facts to recognise that, while an ordinary shareholder is free to vote as he thinks proper, a dominant shareholder should behave as a *member* of a company and is subject to a duty of loyalty and fairness toward the company and toward his fellow shareholders.

(3) It would then be desirable that the relationships of a dominant shareholder with the company, in particular the relationships of a parent company with its subsidiaries, be governed by a set of rules based on the duty of loyalty and fairness.

(4) In the interest of all parties involved, these rules should be as clear as possible. However, they should above all other con-

---

[77] p. 17.

[78] Henn and Alexander, *supra*, n. 55, s.231. See also Philip I. Blumberg, *The Law of Corporate Groups. Bankruptcy Law* (1985) and *The Law of Corporate Groups. Substantive Law* (1987); "Liability of Parent Corporation for Hazardous Waste Cleanup and Damages" (1986) 99 Harv.L.Rev. 986, note.

[79] Cary and Eisenberg, *supra*, n. 56 pp. 108–111.

[80] *Pepper* v. *Litton*, 308 U.S. 295, 60 S.Ct. 238, 84 L, ed. 281 (1939).

[81] *cf.* Prentice, *supra*, n. 5 p. 128, and the authors referred to *infra*, n. 82.

sideration be flexible enough.[82] The interests of a subsidiary should not be sacrificed to the interests of the group, neither can they be divorced from the interests of the group. Furthermore, the normal working of the group and the normal process of decision should be hampered as little as possible.

(5) It is submitted that the duties of a dominating shareholder, as articulated in the *Principles of Corporate Governance*, constitute a most interesting model based on a long American experience and devised after due consideration of all relevant factors.

(6) The American situation, where directors and executives make decisions under the permanent threat of a law suit, should be avoided.[83] However, the recognition of rules governing what directors and executives should do in difficult situations, should not have this effect. On the contrary, in case of doubt, the directors and executives could seek competent independent advice, comparable to the advice required in the case of a take-over bid from the board of the offeree company.[84]

(7) If a set of rules, comparable to those of the *Principles of Corporate Governance*, had to be introduced in England, it might take place either in the *Companies Act*, or, more probably among the continuing obligations of listed companies,[85] perhaps as a *Code of Transactions Within a Group of Companies*.

---

[82] *cf.* Clive M. Schmitthoff, *supra*, n. 5 p. 229; Wedderburn in (1984) 47 M.L.R. 87, at 91; Hopt, *supra*, n. 25 p. 312; Farrar, "Ownership," *supra*, n. 5; Maze, *supra*, n. 20, Conclusion; *Even* v. *Peoria and E. Ry. Co.*, 78 F.Suppl. 312 (DCSDNY 1948); Trib. Gr. Inst. Mulhouse 25 mars. 1983, *Dalloz* 1984. 285 note Claude Ducouloux-Favard.

[83] *cf.* Sealy, *supra*, n. 30, 85: "An indulgent legislature has, in most of our jurisdictions, given the minority a new remedy in cases of 'oppression' or now, in England, 'unfairly prejudicial' acts. The proper role of the courts is surely to develop this into a workable remedy, and content themselves with a less interventionist function in the corporate decision-making process."

[84] See *The City Code on Take-overs and Mergers*, Rule 3.1.

[85] *Admission of Securities to Listing*, s.5, Chap. 2.

II

Groups of Companies—Some US Aspects

T. W. Cashel*

1. INTRODUCTION

A number of highly publicised shipping and industrial disasters and
resulting litigation in part prompted the conference for which this
chapter was originally prepared.[1]

After experiencing the feeling of deep concern such events inspire,
the practitioner in commercial law is likely to ask a question. What
particular company was involved? There would then follow a mental
review of traditional concepts of corporate law: the separate legal
personality of a corporation, the limited liability of its shareholders
and whether or not the veil of incorporation would be "pierced" or
"lifted."

While it may be that scholars and courts have begun to examine the
interactions of various bodies of law across corporate groups, it is
submitted that analysis of legal issues relating to corporations most
often centres on a single acting entity. Analysis of fact patterns in
cases involving corporations is usually focused by reliance on traditional corporate law concepts of separate legal personality or corporate entity.[2] Where an attempt is made to question the separateness of
the corporation from its shareholders, analysis focuses upon a search
for some abuse of corporate personality, such as dominating control
by a majority shareholder, inadequate capital, or a failure to observe
corporate formalities, in order to test *alter ego* or instrumentality
theories.[3] The aim of such analysis is, largely, to determine whether

---

* Senior Visiting Fellow, Queen Mary & Westfield College, University of London;
  Member, New York Bar.

[1] See, for example, *In re Oil Spill by the "Amoco Cadiz" off the Coast of France on March 16,
  1978*, Docket No. 376 (ND Ill Apr 18, 1984) printed in 20 *Environmental Reg. Cases*
  2041 (BNA); *In re Union Carbide Corp. Gas Plant Disaster at Bhopal, India in Dec 1984*, 634
  F Supp. 842 (SDNY 1986), *aff'd* in part 809 F 2d 195 (2d Cir. 1987). The conference
  was held on May 18 1988.

[2] See Fletcher, *Cyclopedia of the Law of Private Corporation*, 25, 41, 6213 (Perm. Ed.). (This
  Cyclopedia is hereinafter referred to as "*Fletcher.*")

[3] Fletcher, ss.43.10 and 41.10, 6213, 6222; *Brunswick Corp.* v. *Waxman*, 459 F Supp. 1222,
  1229 (EDNY 1978); *Lowendahl* v. *Baltimore & O R Co.*, 247 A.D. 144, 287 N.Y.S. 62
  (1st Dept.), *aff'd* 272 N.Y. 360, 6 N.E. 2d 56 (1936). Lowendahl is a leading case
  decided by New York's highest state court. It sets out a tripartite "instrumentality"
  rule.

the attributes of corporateness of a particular entity can be avoided in a particular case.[4]

These concepts of corporate entity and limited liability are venerable, however. They were developed largely before the emergence of modern corporate structures involving affiliated companies under common control of a holding or parent company through intercorporate group shareholders. The hypothetical, but I believe instinctive, analysis just outlined highlights the absence of a developed law of corporate groups as such. However, there is a developing jurisprudence in the United States on the relationships and rights and duties of companies doing business in groups. The proliferation of subsidiaries, conglomerate companies and multi-national companies and their interaction with other traders and consumers in domestic and transnational business and financial markets inevitably leads to disputes which will have to be resolved. While we will see that focus on the individual entity acting remains the predominant approach, the presence of the larger group to which the entity belongs is a reality whose relevance to the particular case has to be considered.

The conduct of business through groups of affiliated companies, has developed swiftly since the Second World War. The grouping of companies, subsidiary and affiliate, often on a multi-national scale, is now commonplace. Their organisational structures, like models of chemical molecules, are complicated.[5] Their economic and social importance is obvious. It is against this background of far reaching economic activity and corporate structure, that legal notions of corporateness play.

The notion that each corporation is a separate legal entity with rights and duties separate from its shareholders is the generally accepted principle of corporate law both in the United States and in England.[6] Analysis of issues relating to such an entity in terms of the entity itself forms what Professor Philip I. Blumberg terms entity law.[7]

A succinct history of the development of corporate concepts

---

[4] See Henn and Alexander, *Laws of Corporations and Other Business Enterprises*, Ch. 7, s.146 (3rd ed., 1983) (hereinafter referred to as "*Henn and Alexander*").

[5] See, for example, Industrial Groupings in Japan, Dodwell Marketing Consultants, Tokyo (7th ed. 1986/87). See also Hadden, "Inside Corporate Groups," 12 Int'l. J. Soc. L. 271, 274 (1984).

[6] *United States* v. *Milwaukee Refrigerator Transit Co.*, 142 Fed. 247, 253 (CCED Wis. 1905). See *Fletcher*, ss.20, 25, 41, 6213; *Henn and Alexander* at Ch. 3, 145; *Gore Browne on Companies* 1–2 (1984); Gower, *The Principles of Modern Company Law*, Chap. 5 (4th ed., 1979) (hereinafter referred to as "*Gower*").

[7] Blumberg, *The Law of Corporate Groups: Tort, Contract and Other Common Law Problems in the Substantive Law of Parent and Subsidiary Corporations*, Introduction xxxi (1987) (hereinafter referred to as "*Blumberg, Substantive Law*"). Various other theories are discussed in *Henn and Alexander* at Ch. 3, *Fletcher*, ss. 24–28. Fletcher also discusses the nature of corporations as fact or fiction and the artificial personality and entity doctrine. For our purposes, whether or not a corporation is a fiction "... it is a fiction created by law with intent that it be acted upon as true." *Klein* v. *Board of Tax Supervisors of Jefferson County, Kentucky* 282 U.S. 19 (1930). See also n. 16 below.

(including English trading companies and joint stock companies)[8] from early times through modern American corporate law, has been developed in the United States by Professor Henn.[9] In summarising the entity theory of corporations, he notes that in early writings the emphasis of corporateness was on an artifical person having perpetual succession, but little was apparently made of the concept of limited liability.[10]

The notion of the limited liability of corporate shareholders is today an essential part of entity law. It is generally accepted that a stockholder is not personally liable for corporate obligations.

> "Limited liability is the rule, not the exception: and on that assumption large undertakings are rested, vast enterprises are launched, and large sums of capital attracted."[11]

This can be argued to flow from the notion of separate legal personality, but the concept of limited liability apparently was developed relatively late in the history of corporations.[12]

In a brilliant series of books Professor Blumberg has brought together through exhaustive research a remarkably comprehensive analysis of the law dealing with groups of companies. His series, "The Law of Corporate Groups"[13] contrasts traditional corporate law and economic fact.[14] The economic effect of a group enterprise is slowly giving rise in some areas of law to concepts of what he calls enterprise law.[15]

The development of a concept of enterprise law would challenge many traditional aspects of entity law, particularly if it led to the

---

[8] *Henn and Alexander* at 19. *Fletcher,* s.2.

[9] *Henn and Alexander* at 14–36.

[10] *Ibid.* at 18, 19.

[11] *Anderson v. Abott,* 321 U.S. 349, 362 (1944). See *Henn and Alexander* at 19; *Fletcher,* s.6212, p. 16. This rule may be varied by constitutions or statutes in various states. See, *e.g.* New York Business Corporation Law, para. 630 (McKinney 1986) (liability of largest stockholders for wages); Delaware Corporation Law s.102(b)(6); New York Banking Law ss.114, 609 (McKinney 1971). Blumberg also discusses in depth the development of limited liability, highlighting issues and examples of unlimited liability, pro rata liability and double liability for certain types of companies and corporations, and distinguishes the liability of a shareholder for an uncalled assessement of his original subscription for shares. *Blumberg, Substantive Law,* at 27, n. 16.

[12] *Henn and Alexander* at 19. *Fletcher* at ss.6212, p. 17; *Blumberg, Substantive Law* s.1.03; *Gower,* at 25, 26.

[13] Blumberg, *The Law of Corporate Groups: Procedural Problems in the Law of Parent and Subsidiary Corporations* (1983); Blumberg, *The Law of Corporate Groups: Bankruptcy Problems in the Law of Parent and Subsidiary Corporations* (1985); Blumberg, *The Law of Corporate Groups: Tort, Contract, and Other Common Law Problems in the Substantive Law of Parent and Subsidiary Corporations* (1987); Blumberg, *The Law of Corporate Groups: Problems of Parent and Subsidiary Corporations Under Statutory Law of General Application* (1989).

[14] *Blumberg, Substantive Law,* at xxxi.

[15] *Ibid.* See *Gower,* at 131. See Priest, *The Invention of Enterprise Liability: A Critical History of The Intellectual Foundations of Modern Tort Law,* 14 J.Leg.Stud. 461 (December 1985). This article deals with product liability and is one of a series of papers on tort law presented at a conference at Yale Law School.

imposition of duties on controlling group members arising out of action by one of the group entities.[16]

In the presence of such exhaustive scholarship by Professor Blumberg one hesitates to attempt here more than a review of some issues of interest to business lawyers, including those dealing with "piercing the corporate veil" jurisprudence, and a review of the approach taken by some distinguished commentators thereon.

2. US STRUCTURE

Before discussing specific issues, one should recognize that the body of law of business enterprises in the United States is largely comprised of statutes adopted in the various states, with interpretations thereof by state and federal courts, as well as common law decisions in various state courts. There is no extensive federal law of corporations as such, although the federal government has enacted some statutes that grant chartering authority (notably for national banks) and has superimposed a level of federal regulation of busness through anti-trust laws, federal tax laws and various federal statutes governing the issue of, and dealing and trading in, securities.[17] An extensive body of federal court case law can also be found in these areas. Federal bankruptcy laws relating to business enterprises in general override state law in the case of insolvency proceedings relating to corporations.

3. CORPORATE GROUPS—SOME ISSUES

Development of limited liability

In the modern corporation the concepts of separate entity and limited liability form the basis of business structures and expectations.[18]

---

[16] *Blumberg, Substantive Law,* at 685. An early insight into a broader view of the corporation appears in *Farmers' Loans & Trust Co* v. *Pierson,* 130 Misc. 110, 119, 222, N.Y.S. 532, 543–544 (Sup. Ct. 1927) as follows:

> "The concrete import of these views is that a corporation is more a method than a thing, and that the law in dealing with a corporation has no need of defining it as a person or an entity, or even as an embodiment of functions, rights and duties, but may treat it as a name for a useful and usual collection of jural relations, each one of which must in every instance be ascertained, analyzed and assigned to its appropriate place according to the circumstances of the particular case, having due regard to the purposes to be achieved. . ."

It does not appear, however, that in tort and contract cases where liability of shareholders is at issue this approach has been followed by courts. *Fletcher,* s.24 at n. 12 cites this case for the total fiction theory, but points out that New York's highest court decisions treated corporations as entities. For an analysis of various theories of corporate personality, see Blumberg, "The Corporate Entity in an Era of Multinational Corporations." 15 Delaware J. of Corp. L. 283 (1990).

[17] See *Henn and Alexander* at 7, 29–47. See *Fletcher,* ss.2,10; 2.55

[18] See *Lowendahl, supra* n 3. *Gore-Browne on Companies,* 1–3 (1984); *Fletcher,* s.25. *Salomon* v. *Salomon & Co. Ltd.* [1897] A.C. 22. The *Salomon* case adopted the corporate entity

Blumberg clearly analyses the significance of limited liability to the concept of separate entity in English, American and civil law.[19]

Modern corporate structures rely on the expectation of predictable results arising from the observance of corporate norms. Investors and businessmen in domestic and international transactions must be able to evaluate risks and limit liabilities. Accordingly, the statutory and common law of corporations recognising limited liability as legitimate will not lightly be disregarded.

A discussion of corporate groups will inevitably have to deal with an evaluation of the concept of separate entity and, more importantly, with the concept of the limited liability of corporate shareholders. It goes without saying that the limited liability concept is ingrained in Western corporate theory. Yet, as has been pointed out by others, the doctrine did not develop contemporaneously with the concept of a corporation as a separate entity.[20]

The limited liability of shareholders initially extended to the individual investors in a corporate entity. It is apparently the case that the concept became settled in England by 1855 and slightly earlier in the United States.[21] At the time it became the rule in the United States there was apparently little or no authority for corporations to own shares in other corporations.[22]

When general corporation laws permitted investment by a corporation in other companies, the concept of limited liability was extended to the parent corporate shareholder. On its face, this extension appears to be simply a logical parallel to the treatment of individual shareholders investing in a company. As Professor Blumberg makes clear, however, a fundamental change was effected, perhaps without much analysis of its effects. Starting from a policy (largely to promote investment in business) of protecting an individual person as a shareholder from the liabilities of the corporation by limiting his liability to the capital he invested, he shows that the law moved to permit in effect the conduct of an overall business enterprise under which parent and affiliated corporations were protected from the liabilities of one another.[23] The development of a theory of the group as a single enterprise, as studied by Blumberg, would significantly affect this result.

principle in England. *Gower*, at 97–100. It is apparently fairly rigidly applied. Gower, "Corporation Law in England and America," 11 *The Bus Lawyer* 38, 46 (1955); *Gower*, at 118–120, 123.

[19] *Blumberg, Substantive Law*, ss.1.02–1.05.

[20] *Blumberg, Substantive Law* at 7–8. See *Henn and Alexander* at 19, 130, 147–148; *Gower* at 25, 35. Blumberg, "Limited Liability and Corporate Groups." 11 J. Corp. L. 573 (1986) (indicating that the concepts of separate entity and limited liability are not essentially interrelated).

[21] *Gore-Browne on Companies*, Chap. 1 (1984). See Gower, Ch. 2 and 3; *Henn and Alexander*, 130 n. 1; *Blumberg, Substantive law*, s.1.03.3.; *Fletcher*, s.20.

[22] Blumberg, *Substantive Law*, Chap. 3, s.3.02.

[23] *Blumberg, Substantive Law*, at 4, 56; *Gower* at 118. *Henn and Alexander*, at 19. See *Gower*, at 124, 128.

A brief history

The terminology used today by English solicitors and American lawyers in describing their areas of practice as "company" law and "corporation" law, respectively, has its origins in an interesting history.[24]

In the United States, corporation law developed from the "embryonic" legal framework[25] in place at the time of the Revolution. Apparently, before the mid-eighteenth century in England corporations were used primarily for non-commercial purposes. Corporate charters for commercial and industrial corporations had to be obtained from Parliament. The states of the United States succeeded Parliament as the source of corporate charters there and apparently granted them more readily (albeit in small numbers).[26]

The English experience is a fascinating history, both legal and political.[27] Limited liability was controversial and most of the development of the concept of limited liability there derived not from the law dealing with corporations but from the law of joint stock companies with an evolving case law and statutes.[28]

The processes in England and America over the years ultimately led to formation of corporations through general incorporation statutes, rather than by special legislative charters. In the United States, limited liability of stockholders was upheld in early common law cases, and in many states the concept of limited liability was treated in various ways in state legislation.[29]

This oversimplified detour through history has been taken in order to make the point that the current general acceptance of limited liability in England and America, while not necessarily a requirement of the concept of separate entity, represents a definite political and economic choice, in some cases codified by statute, and constitutes a clear statement of policy.[30]

Blumberg's thinking about the liability of parent companies in a corporate group enterprise for obligations of affiliates is in contrast to the neglect of the issue at the time that corporation laws were changed to allow corporations to hold shares in other corporations. His approach recognises that in some cases the conceptual rigidity of entity law may require what he terms a "safety valve" which the

---

[24] *Gower*, "Corporation Law in England and America," 11 The Bus Lawyer 39, 40 (1955). *Gower*, Chap. 2 and 3; *Fletcher*, ss.1, 2.

[25] For a very succinct historical account contrasting the American and English development of corporation law, see Gower; n. 24 above.

[26] See *Fletcher*, s.2; Brandeis, J, dissenting in *Louis K Liggett Co.* v. *Lee*, 288 U.S. 517 (1933); Gower, "Some Contrasts Between British and American Corporation Law," 69 Harv.L.Rev. 1369, 1370 (1956).

[27] *Blumberg, Substantive Law*, at 17; *Gower*, Chap. 2.

[28] See *Blumberg, Substantive Law*, Ch. 1; *Henn and Alexander* at 19–23.

[29] See *e.g.* Delaware Corporation Law, s.102(b)(6) and n. 11 above. Compare old Delaware Corporation Law s.102(a)(7), discussed in Folk, *The Delaware Corporation Law, A Commentary and Analysis*, 20 (2d ed., 1988).

[30] For discussion on statutory enactments of limited liability in continental civil law, see *Blumberg, Substantive Law*, at 38 and authorities cited.

principles developed by the courts in "piercing the corporate veil" cases has provided in exceptional cases where equitable and societal pressures were so strong as to require its use.[31]

Piercing the corporate veil jurisprudence[32]

Piercing, or lifting, the corporate veil is a colourful figure of speech. It seems descriptive of both a process and a result. It is more, however, if we accept that it is the basis on which courts can evaluate the impact of group structures in a particular case and thereby construct by precedent a law of corporate groups over many cases over time. However, commentators and judges have pointed out that such figures of speech and attendant metaphors more often than not cripple analysis in many cases.[33]

> "The whole problem of the relation between parent and subsidiary corporations is one that is still enveloped in the mists of metaphor. Metaphors in law are to be narrowly watched, for starting as devices to liberate thought, they end often by enslaving it. We say at times that the corporate entity will be ignored when the parent corporation operates a business through a subsidiary which is characterised as an 'alias' or a 'dummy.' All this is well enough if the picturesqueness of the epithets does not lead us to forget that the essential term to be defined is the act of operation."[34]

Henn's treatment of this area is in terms of disregard of corporate entity where otherwise technically correct incorporation has been achieved.[35]

> "If any general rule can be laid down ... it is that a corporation will be looked upon as a legal entity as a general rule and until sufficient reason to the contrary appears; but when the notion of legal entity is used to defeat public convenience, justify wrong, protect fraud, or defend crime, the law will regard the corporation as an association of persons ..."[36]

Beginning with an entity theory and the attributes of corporateness, Henn discusses situations in which courts have disregarded

---

[31] Blumberg, "The Corporate Entity in an Era of Multinational Corporations," 15 Delaware J. of Corp. L. 283, 321 (1990); *Blumberg, Substantive Law*, at 56. See Brandeis, J. *supra*, n. 26 at 556.

[32] See in general *Fletcher*, ss.41–48; *Gower*, Chap. 6; *Henn and Alexander* s.146; *Blumberg, Substantive Law*, Ch. 6; *Fletcher*, s.41.30 at p. 431; *Gower*, Ch. 6; I. Wormser, *Disregard of the Corporate Fiction and Allied Corporation Problems* 42–85 (1972); "Annotation, Disregarding Corporate Existence," 1 A.L.R. 610, 34 A.L.R. 597; *Gore-Browne on Companies*, 1–4 (1984).

[33] *Blumberg, Substantive Law*, at 107.

[34] *Berkey v. Third Avenue Railway*, 244 N.Y. 84, 94–95, 155 N.E. 58, 61 (1926).

[35] *Henn and Alexander* at 344–375.

[36] *United States v. Milwaukee Refrigerator Transit Co.*, 142 Fed. 247, 255 (CCED Wis. 1905), cited by *Henn and Alexander* at 346. See also *Bangor Punta Operations, Inc. v. Bangor & Arrowstoock R Co.*, 417 U.S. 703, 713 (1974); *Fletcher*, ss.25, 41–41.30, 6213.

corporateness. In essence, the analysis centres on determining whether the corporate fiction has been abused.[37]

At the outset, Henn quite properly points out that securing limited liability is one of the primary purposes of incorporation, and that seeking incorporation in order to avoid unlimited liability is not improper.[38] It follows therefore that controlling shareholders as well as other shareholders generally are entitled to limited liability.[39]

Further, it is clear that the mere fact of ownership of all or a controlling block of stock in a corporation and common management is not itself grounds for disregarding a corporate entity.[40]

In contract cases, shareholders are generally not liable for contract obligations of a corporation.[41] Similarly, parent companies are not generally responsible for debts of their subsidiaries. Further, if a contracting party has selected a particular corporate obligor, freedom of contract and principles of entity law carry out the intention of the parties to the transaction, in the absence of other circumstances.[42]

Likewise, in tort cases shareholders are not generally liable for torts of their corporation.[43]

However, shareholders could become liable for corporate contracts or torts if fact patterns could be shown leading to successful invocation of piercing the corporate veil principles.

Henn and Blumberg have pointed out that in attempting to deter-

---

[37] See *Henn and Alexander* at 345, n. 3 (citing *Mayo* v. *Pioneer Bank & Trust Co.* 270 F. 2d 823, 830 (5th Cir. 1959); *reh. denied*, 274 F. 2d 320 (5th Cir. 1960), *cert. denied*, 362 U.S. 962 (1960)) and at 354. *State Dept. of Environ. Protection* v. *Ventron Corp.*, 94 N.J. 473, 500, 468 A. 2d 150, 164 (1983). A court will not usually disregard the corporate entity for the benefit of a shareholder. See *Henn and Alexander* at 357; See *Blumberg, Substantive Law*, s.15.03, dealing with attempts to assert *alter ego* theories by a parent to avoid general tort law liability granted by workmen's compensation laws in cases involving injured employees of subsidiaries. *cf.* *U.S.* v. *Cohn*, 682 F. Supp. 209 (SDNY 1988).

[38] *Henn and Alexander* at 347. *Fletcher* s.41.20. See *CM Corp. Oberer* v. *Development Co.*, 631 F. 2d 536 (7th Cir. 1980); *Brunswick Corp.* v. *Waxman* 459 F. Supp. 1222 (EDNY 1978), *affirmed* 599 F. 2d 34 (2d Cir. 1979); *Bartle* v. *Home Owners Co-operative, Inc*, 309 N.Y. 103, 127 N.E. 2d 832 (1955); *American Protein Corp.* v. *AB Volvo*, 844 F. 2d 56, 60 (2d Cir. 1988); *Crown Cent Petroleum* v. *Cosmopolitan Shipping Co.*, 602 F. 2d 474, 476 (2d Cir. 1979); *Zubik* v. *Zubik*, 384 F. 2d 267, 273 (3d Cir. 1967).

[39] *Fletcher*, ss.6216, 6222.

[40] See *Ventron, supra*, n. 37; *Steven* v. *Roscoe Turner Aeronautical Corp.*, 324 F. 2d 157, 161 (7th Cir 1963); *American Bell Inc.* v. *Federation of Telephone Workers* 736 F. 2d 879, 886–7 (3rd Cir. 1984); *Fletcher*, s.6222; Annotation, "Liability of Corporation for Contracts of Subsidiary," 38 A.L.R. 3d 1102, 1111; Annotation, "Liability of Corporation for Torts of Subsidiary," 7 A.L.R. 3d 1343, 1350.

[41] *Henn and Alexander* at 348. *Fletcher*, ss.29, 6213, 6222. *Kingston Dry Dock Co.* v. *Lake Champlain Transp Co.*, 31 F. 2d 265 (2d Cir. 1929), Annotation; "Liability of Corporation for Contracts of Subsidiary," 38 A.L.R. 3d 1102. See Miller, *The Great Salad Oil Swindle*, 222 (1965), reviewed in 24 Wash. Lee.L.Rev. 394 (1967) and 11 N.Y.L. Forum 593 (1965).

[42] *Henn and Alexander* at 348 and n. 20; *Fletcher* s.41.85. See *Kingston, supra*, n. 41.

[43] *Henn and Alexander* at 349, *Fletcher*, ss.33, 6214, 6222; Annotation, *supra*, n. 40. "Counsel have been unable to cite a case where the corporate entity was disregarded to make an individual liable for tort." *Zubik* v. *Zubik*, 384 F. 2d 267, 273 n. 14 (3rd Cir. 1967), *cert. denied*, 390 U.S. 988 (1968). See *Craig* v. *Lake Asbestos of Quebec Ltd.*, 843 F. 2d 145 (3rd Cir. 1988), using the *Lowendahl* test of dominance.

mine in a specific situation whether limited liability can be avoided, courts have often indiscriminately[44] mixed precedents from contract, tort, fraudulent conveyance and other cases involving disparate areas of law.[45]

The traditional approach regards entity law as the general rule. Under this approach, Blumberg points out that disregarding the entity would only take place reluctantly and in the exceptional case. Such cases exist only where dominance and control by a parent coupled with strong equities can be shown.[46]

The method of application of the piercing approach by many courts concerns Blumberg, in that he stresses that the policies of the particular area of the law involved in a particular case should be controlling of the outcome and that it is not appropriate to use a precedent in one area of law (say, procedure, or tort, or bankruptcy) to decide a case in another area (say, contract).[47]

In very general terms, the metaphors used in piercing the veil cases, such as instrumentality, *alter-ego*, dummy, or agent (and myriad others),[48] will be subsumed for convenience in this chapter under the term "instrumentality."[49]

The traditional New York instrumentality rule used in determining when a parent can be liable for debts of its subsidiary was set forth in *Lowendahl* v. *Baltimore & Ohio Railroad Co.* as follows:

> "Restating the instrumentality rule, we may say that in any case, except express agency, estoppel, or direct tort, three elements must be proved:
>
> '(1) Control, not mere majority or complete stock control, but complete domination, not only of finances but of policy and business practice in respect of the transaction attacked so that the corporate entity as to this transaction had at the time no separate mind, will or existence of its own; and
>
> '(2) Such control must have been used by the defendant to commit fraud or wrong, to perpetrate the violation of a statutory or other positive legal duty, or a dishonest and unjust act in contravention of plaintiff's legal rights; and
>
> '(3) The aforesaid control and breach of duty must proximately cause the injury or unjust loss complained of.' See Powell,

---

[44] *Henn and Alexander* at 348. Blumberg, *Substantive Law*, at 107–108

[45] *Ibid.* See *Gower*, at 138.

[46] Blumberg, *Substantive Law*, at 106–107. See *Gorrill* v. *Icelandair/Flugleider*, 76 1 F. 2d 847, 853 (2d Cir. 1985); *Fletcher*, s. 41.10 and text at n. 3.50 (1987 Cum. Supp.) and s.41.30 at 429; *Zubik* v. *Zubik, supra*, n. 43 at 273. Although equitable in nature, the issue of disregard of the entity is a question for the jury according to *American Protein Corp.* v. *AB Volvo* 844 F. 2d 56, 59 (2d Cir. 1988). See *e.g. Walter E. Heller & Co.* v. *Video Innovations Inc.*, 730 F. 2d 50, 53 (2d Cir. 1984). Disregard of the entity rates only for the issue in the particular case and not for other purposes. Blumberg, *supra*, n. 31 at 362.

[47] Blumberg, *Substantive Law*, at 108.

[48] See *Henn and Alexander* at 146, n. 2.

[49] This, despite distinctions that instrumentality implies separateness whereas *alter ego* implies unity. See n. 57, below.

'Parent and Subsidiary Corporations,' chapters I to VI, passim, and numerous cases cited."[50]

In *Worldwide Carriers, Ltd* v. *Aris Steamship Co.*,[51] a case applying New York law, the court articulated various factors relevant to determining whether a provisional attachment of assets belonging to a debtor's subsidiary would be valid. The case arose out of an order to show cause challenging an order of attachment brought on by several defendants who were joined in the principal action solely for purposes of attaching their assets. The defendants argued that the plaintiff's affidavit in support of its motion for attachment did not constitute a prima facie showing that the defendant subsidiaries acted as the instrumentality of the defendant parent.

In denying the defendant's motion, the court held:

"In order to establish that a subsidiary is the mere instrumentality of its parent, three elements must be proved: control by the parent to such a degree that the *subsidiary has become its mere instrumentality*; fraud or wrong by the parent through its subsidiary, *e.g.* torts, violation of a statute or *stripping the subsidiary of its assets*; and unjust loss or injury to the claimant such as *insolvency of the subsidiary*."[52]

The court then set out factors that had historically been used by courts to determine whether a parent's control over a subsidiary would support liability. These factors include controlling stock ownership, common management, undercapitalisation, financing of subsidiary expenses by the parent, lack of separation of property or business, direction of the subsidiary's affairs by the parent and non-observance of formal corporate norms.[53]

The court found that the parent had substantial stock interests in each of its subsidiaries and that "there was practical identity of officers and directors among the parent and its subsidiaries."[54] It also

[50] Lowendahl, n. 3 above, 287 N.Y.S. at 76.

[51] 301 F. Supp. 64 (SDNY 1968). See *Fidenas AG* v. *Honeywell Inc.*, 501 F. Supp. 1029 (1980); *Brunswick Corp.* v. *Waxman*, n. 38 above.

[52] *Ibid.* at 67 (emphasis in original), quoting from *Steven* v. *Roscoe Turner Aeronautical Corp.*, 324 F. 2d 157, 160–61 (7th Cir. 1963) and citing *Fisser* v. *International Bank*, 282 F. 2d 231, 238 (1960) and *Lowendahl*, n. 3 above 287 N.Y.S. at 76. See discussion and history of this tripartite test in *Blumberg, Substantive Law*, 112–114, and *Lowendahl*, n. 3 above. The instrumentality test comprising these three factors is the predominant New York rule. See discussion in Brunswick, n. 3 above. *Lowendahl* is the classic formulation. The *Lowendahl* case was quoted with approval in *Gorrill*, and cited in 1988 in *American Protein*, n. 46 above.

[53] *Ibid.* at 67–68 (citations omitted). The eleven factors listed by the court are set out in *Roscoe Turner*, n. 52 above quoting from *Taylor* v. *Standard Gas & Electric Company*, n. 77 below, which in turn quotes from an earlier book, Powell, *Parent and Subsidiary Corporations* (1931). See *Fletcher*, s.41.30; *Henn and Alexander*, s.148. See *American Bell Inc.* v. *Federation of Telephone Workers*, 736 F. 2d 879, 886–7 (3rd Cir. 1984). Again, exhaustive listing and discussion of these and many other issues determinative of whether to pierce the corporate veil in contract cases is contained in *Blumberg, Substantive Law*, Chaps. 19 and 20. See also *Gower*, at 130.

[54] *Ibid.* at 68.

found that assets for the parent were traditionally purchased through its subsidiaries, that the parent's credit facilitated these purchases and that the parent and its subsidiaries cross-guaranteed loans, resulting in payment by one subsidiary to third-party creditors of the parent. The court upheld the attachment.[55] The case is not necessarily typical as to its result however, particularly in New York where the more conservative approach of an established commercial jurisdiction is likely and, since it was a decision on a pre-trial motion, is not a decision on the merits. The case is interesting in reiterating that the factors to be applied derive from the earlier cases cited.

It is clear that no one factor should be determinative. The varied fact situations one would meet in contract and tort cases and the combination of various elements like those mentioned above will have to be analysed on a case by case basis.[56]

Another commentator sorting through the inconsistencies of piercing the veil jurisprudence attempts to synthesize a rule for decision which he submits is more objective.[57] Dobbyn's article is a concise and effective summary and analysis of the law. He points out that in cases where a plaintiff has dealt with a corporation and seeks to pierce the corporate veil, the plaintiff's case could be that the controlling shareholder should be personally liable because he has abused the corporate privilege to the plaintiff's detriment. Courts could also consider the shareholder/plaintiff nexus and look for some action by the shareholder or parent which directly caused loss to the plaintiff. Dobbyn shows that this presents many problems since in most cases it is likely that there has been no specific action directed at the plaintiff by the shareholder.[58]

An examination of the shareholder/corporation nexus is the alternative approach. Here Dobbyn finds that the effort to unite[59] the shareholder and his corporation is usually conducted with more concern for corporate form than regard to the direct effect of the shareholder's dealings with his corporation upon the plaintiff's claim.[60] This is the same basic point made by Blumberg.

Dobbyn refers to the difficulties presented to courts by settled business expectations and acceptance of limited liability principles, and points out that in the absence of generally accepted rules, a court could not simply analyse alleged inequities in a particular case and

---

[55] The court did not discuss the elements of wrong or damages as set out in its basic standards. See *Blumberg, Substantive Law*, at 117. See also *Galgay* v. *Gangloff et al.*, 677 F. Supp. 295, 299 (1987).

[56] *Fletcher*, s.41.30, p. 431; *Berkey*, n. 34 above; *American Bell*, n. 53 above at 887.

[57] Dobbyn, "A Practical Approach to Consistency in Veil-Piercing Cases," 19 Kansas L.Rev. 185 (1971), reprinted in *American Bar Association, Selected Articles on Corporate Law*, 1151 (Osborn and Schmutz ed. 1977), (herein referred to as "ABA").

[58] *Ibid. Hazeltine* v. *General Electric Co.*, 19 F. Supp. 898, 902 (D. Md. 1937) (no "... clear cut rule ..."). See Gower, at 138.

[59] A.B.A. at 1152. See Blumberg's discussion of instrumentality and *alter ego*/identity theories in *Blumberg, Substantive Law*, Chap. 6, s.602, 603 and in his article, n. 16 above. Fletcher discusses *alter ego* theories at s.41.10.

[60] A.B.A. at 1153.

ignore settled corporation law.[61] Thus, in his view, the more a court looked at the relation between a corporation and its shareholder and could perceive some unity, a decision to pierce the corporate veil did not appear to be an extreme departure,[62] but that the problem with such an approach is the search for technical points, and uncertainty as to which combination of the many factors enumerated in the cases[63] is fatal.

Dobbyn believed that by the 1970s enough cases had been decided to enable him to distill a proposed rule to the effect that shareholder liability in contract or tort should rest upon an exercise of control to hinder unjustly a plaintiff's ability to collect a claim.[64] It cannot be said that this theory has been adopted explicitly by courts.

Recognising that if a corporation has funds to pay claims against it, there is no need for a plaintiff to assert the personal liability of the shareholder,[65] Dobbyn's rule focuses on the responsibility of shareholders to set up their company with adequate capitalisation to meet reasonably perceived risks of the business.[66] Undercapitalisation, not in the sense of the impairment of assets during good faith attempts to operate a business, but in that of the use of control initially or by subsequent diversion of assets to allow the corporation to function so that only unreasonably inadequate assets are available to meet claims, would be his test.

To sum up, piercing the veil jurisprudence can be seen as a narrow exception to an accepted principle and policy in favour of limited liability. The economic realities may be argued to be overlooked in such cases, but absent domination and control by a parent to an

---

[61] "Throughout all the discussions there runs, of course, as the dominant theme, the eternal quest for justice, checked, to a lesser extent than usual it seems to me, by the countervailing considerations that courts exist for the purpose of administering, not the judge's personal idea of justice, but justice under law, and that a rule which leaves everyting to "justice in the particular instance' really is not a rule, not law, at all." *P.S. & A. Realities Inc.* v. *Lodge Gate Forest Inc.*, 205 Misc. 245, 254, 127 N.Y.S. 2d 315, 323–24 (1954). See *Gower*, at 138.

[62] A.B.A. at 1154.

[63] See for example text at n. 53.

[64] A.B.A. at 1156.

[65] See *Blumberg, Substantive Law*, at s.11.11.

[66] See *Fletcher*, s.41.30 at p. 430 and n. 49 (and in 1987 Cum. Supp. n. 49, citing *Walter E. Heller & Co.* v. *Video Innovations Inc.*, 730 F. 2d 50 (2nd Cir. 1984) (applying New York law)). Blumberg feels that the cases in which undercapitalisation is referred to are equivocal. *Blumberg, Substantive Law*, s.11.12. See Annotation, "Inadequate Capitalization as a Factor in Disregard of Corporate Entity," 163 A.R.L. 2d 1051. One New York case rejects this consideration where corporate formalities are observed. See *Fisser* v. *International Bank*, 282 F. 2d 231, 240 (2d Cir. 1960), reflecting a conservative New York position, at least in contract cases. *Fisser* relies substantially on *Lowendahl*, n. 3 above and *Powell*, n. 53 above. *Mull* v. *Colt*, n. 21 below, discusses inadequate capitalisation as a factor, and would seem to be in accord with Dobbyn. See also *Weisser* v. *Mursam Shoe Corporation*, 127 F. 2d 344 (2d Cir. 1942). *Blumberg, Substantive Law*, s.11.12. See *Refco Inc.*, v. *Farm Production Asociation Inc.*, 844 F. 2d 525 (8th Cir. 1988) an alternative holding piercing the corporate veil to find a sole stockholder liable personally on a commodity trading agreement where undercapitalisation is cited as a factor among others.

extent which causes the separation between corporations and shareholders to be ignored and a wrong causing unjust loss to the plaintiff, courts should uphold the broader policy underlying the entity theory.

Duty of loyalty

The duty of dominating shareholders (including parent corporations) in dealings with the corporation and issues of loyalty in connection with the use of status to obtain position, information, property and corporate opportunity have been set out in a study by the American Law Institute.[67] Little is specifically said about parent-subsidiary relationships, although conflicts would arise in cases where a controlling parent and common directors and officers of the parent and subsidiary enter into transactions with one another. The best interests of both corporations must be determined by essentially the same persons.[68]

Actions against Foreign states and "instrumentalities" of a foreign state

The United States Foreign Sovereign Immunities Act of 1976 defines a foreign state entitled to sovereign immunity for purposes of the Act to include an "agency or instrumentality" of the foreign state.[69] This in turn is defined to include any entity which is a separate legal person, corporate or otherwise, and which is an organ of, or a majority of whose shares or other ownership interest is owned by, a foreign state.[70] The term "organ" is not defined.

Under Section 1606 of the Act, as to any claim for relief with respect to which the state is not immune, the state ". . . shall be liable in the same manner and to the same extent as a private individual under like circumstances . . ."[71]

This language may suggest that entity law and piercing theories are applicable to government owned corporations in US courts. Different policy considerations however are likely to make successful use of piercing of the corporate veil theories more difficult.[72] There have however been attempts to treat an entity as an instrumentality

---

[67] American Law Institute, "Principles of Corporate Governance: Analysis and Recommendations" Part V (Tent Draft No. 3, 1984, and Tent Draft No. 5, 1986). Ruder, "Duty of Loyalty—A Law Professor's Status Report," 40 *The Bus Lawyer* 1383, 1389 (1985), citing *Sinclair Oil Corp.* v. *Levien*, 280 A. 2d 717 (Del. 1971).

[68] See *Ibid.* at s.5.14, Comment (f) to 1984 Draft, and Reporters' Notes.

[69] 28 U.S.C. s.1603(a).

[70] ; 28 U.S.C. s.1603(b).

[71] 28 U.S.C. s.1606. This language indicates that the Act is not intended to affect the substantive law of liability and does not affect attribution of responsibility among foreign state entities. See *Bancec* n. 74 below. However, under s.1610(b) of the Act, execution against the property of one agency or instrumentality in order to satisfy a judgment against another was not contemplated according to the legislative history, although a court might find that property of one agency is really that of another. See *Bancec*, 462 U.S. at 621 n. 8. See also *Hercaire*, n. 75 below.

[72] See *Fletcher* s.41.30 at 429 and discussion at n. 75 below.

(not in the statutorily defined sense, but in a piercing sense) of a government for purposes of set-off and attachment and execution of judgment.[73]

In *First National City Bank* v. *Banco Para el Comercio Exterior de Cuba*[74] (*"Bancec"*), Citibank was sued by a Cuban bank as beneficiary of a letter of credit. The letter of credit had been issued by Citibank in support of a contract for delivery of sugar to a customer in the United States. The sugar was delivered and Bancec requested collection under the letter of credit. Within a few days, Citibank's assets were nationalised by Cuba. Citibank credited the amount of the draft to Bancec and then set off Bancec's account balance for the value of the expropriated assets. Bancec sued to recover on the letter of credit and Citibank counterclaimed, asserting a set-off for its seized assets. The Supreme Court upheld Citibank's right to set off amounts due to Bancec under the letter of credit against the debt owed to Citibank by Cuba.

The Court acknowledged that the creation of government instrumentalities as entities separate from the government itself aided economic development. It warned that "[f]reely ignoring the separate status of government instrumentalities could frustrate the purpose of their creation by raising uncertainty as to whether their assets would be diverted to satisfy a claim against the sovereign . . . ." and concluded that ". . . government instrumentalities established as juridical entities distinct and independent from their sovereign should normally be treated as such."[75]

However, the Court concluded that this presumption that instrumentalities are separate from their sovereign may be overcome in certain circumstances. The court mentions piercing the veil theories

---

[73] See Ryan, "Defaults and Remedies Under International Bank Loan Agreements with Foreign Sovereign Borrowers—a New York Lawyer's Perspective," 1982 U. of Ill. L.Rev. 89, 106–109 (1982); "American Hostages in Iran," 239 (Council on Foreign Relations 1985); *Banco Nacional de Cuba* v. *Chemical Bank New York Trust Company, et al.*, 822 F. 2d 230. (2d Cir. 1987). See also *DeLetelier* v. *Republic of Cuba*, 748 F. 2d 790 (2d Cir. 1984), *cert. denied*, 471 U.S. 1125 (1985).

[74] 462 U.S. 611, 626 (1983).

[75] *Ibid.* at 626, also citing English cases, *I Congreso del Partido*, [1983] (1) A.C. 244; *Trendtex Trading Corp.* v. *Central Bank of Nigeria*, [1977] Q.B. 529; and *C. Czarnikow Ltd.* v. *Centrala Hardlu Zagramicznego Rolimpex*, [1979] A.C. 351. In *Hercaire International Inc.* v. *Argentina*, 821 F. 2d 559 (11th Cir. 1987), the plaintiff obtained a directed verdict against Argentina for breach of Centrala Hardlu Zagramnnicznego contract and obtained an order permitting attachment of any property used in the United States for commercial activity belonging to either Argentina or one of its agencies or instrumentalities. The plaintiff levied upon an Aerolineas Argentinas ("Aerolineas") aircraft at Miami International Airport. The district court upheld the levy, stating "where, as here, the sovereign owns 100 per cent. of the assets of the agency at issue, the presumption that [Aerolineas] is an entity separate from Argentina is overcome." 642 F. Supp. at 130. On appeal, the Eleventh Circuit reversed the district court and vacated the order of attachment. Relying on the Supreme Court's analysis in *Bancec*, the court concluded that the presumption of Aerolineas' separate juridical existence could not be overcome by a simple showing that the government of Argentina owned 100 per cent. of its stock.

developed in domestic corporate law,[76] but in the circumstances of this case did not use them and relied instead on "the broader equitable principle that the doctrine of corporate entity, recognised generally and for most purposes, will not be regarded when to do so would work fraud or injustice ..."[77]

Cases applying an equitable doctrine of *alter ego* do not set out clear rules and depend upon their facts.[78] Indeed, the Supreme Court stated in *Bancec* that its decision under the facts and circumstances of the case,

"... announces no mechanical formula for determining the circumstances under which the normally separate juridical status of a government instrumentality is to be disregarded. Instead it is the product of the application of internationally recognised equitable principles to avoid the injustice that would result from permitting a foreign state to reap the benefits of our courts while avoiding the obligations of international law."[79]

---

[76] *Ibid.* at 628–630 (although it disparages the metaphors at 611). "[W]here a corporate entity is so extensively controlled by its owner that a relationship of principal and agent is created, we have held that one may be held liable for the actions of the other." *Ibid.* at 629. A distinction should be made here. Piercing the veil cases and *alter ego* theories sometimes use the term "agent" or "agency," but the facts in such cases usually do not support the consensual contractual basis necessary for an agency contract. Liability of a parent as principal could be found however where either a true agency relationship can be shown or an apparent agency relationship or an estoppel exists. See *Fletcher*, s.43; Blumberg, *Substantive Law*, ss.6.06, 8.02, 14.01; Annotation, n. 40 above, 38 ALR 3d at s.4 and s.6. See *Lowendahl*, n. 3 above at 287 N.Y.S. 76. See discussion of estoppel in New York in *Weisser* v. *Mursam Shoe Corporation*, n. 66 above. See also *Gower*, at 123.

[77] *Ibid.* at 629 quoting *Taylor* v. *Standard Gas & Electric Company*, 306 U.S. 307, 322 (1939). *Taylor* is a case dealing with subordination of a parent company's claim against its subsidiary in bankruptcy. See n. 85 below. The court noted that because of Bancec's dissolution subsequent to commencement of its action and succession to its claim by Cuba's Ministry of Foreign Trade, any recovery under the letter of credit would inure directly to the benefit of the Cuban government.

> "Giving effect to Bancec's separate juridical status in these circumstances, even though it has long been dissolved, would permit the real beneficiary of such an action, the Government of the Republic of Cuba, to obtain relief in our courts that it could not obtain in its own right without waiving its sovereign immunity and answering for the seizure of Citibank's assets—a seizure previously held by the Court of Appeals to have violated international law. We decline to adhere blindly to the corporate form where doing so would cause such an injustice."

Ibid. at 632 (citations omitted).
For discussion of the case and of a somewhat similar approach in Germany see Schodermeir, "Piercing the Corporate Veil of State Enterprises," 4 J.I.B.L. 36 (1989).

[78] See A.B.A. at 1154. See *American Bell Inc.* v. *Federation of Telepone Workers*, 736 F. 2d 879, 886–7 (3rd Cir. 1984).

[79] 462 U.S. at 633–34 (footnotes omitted).

Bankruptcy

(i) *Equitable subordination*

In bankruptcy cases, the issue has frequently arisen as to the extent to which a claim by a parent against a bankrupt subsidiary company should be disallowed or subordinated to claims of unrelated creditors.[80]

The writing and case law in this area of the law of corporate groups is extensive. Again, the authorities have been collected and comprehensively analysed by Blumberg.[81]

Contract or tort cases involve determining liability, and limited liability concepts evolved to meet these concerns. It is difficult to ignore the limited liability doctrine in cases where the liability of shareholders is being pressed.

In bankruptcy, however, equity and fairness among creditors is the principal consideration. Bankruptcy courts analysing transactions involving a group of related companies could look through the corporate form if it would accomplish equity and fairness among creditor groups.[82] Blumberg argues therefore that issues of substantive liability of shareholders relevant to tort and contract cases have little applicability in this area because the underlying policies differ.[83]

In analysing decisions involving the treatment of a claim of a parent company or controlling shareholder in relation to creditors of an insolvent company in bankruptcy, Blumberg asserts that there has been a shift away from entity law.[84] Again, however, we must keep in mind that bankruptcy courts act within policies of equity. While piercing the veil concepts, with their arguments that the bankrupt entity was an instrumentality or *alter ego* of its parent have of course been made, the bases for decision in bankruptcy cases have rapidly shifted to fairness issues.

In the leading *Deep Rock* case, *Taylor* v. *Standard Gas & Electric Company*,[85] equitable subordination of a parent's claim to holders of preferred stock was ordered because of unfair behaviour by the parent vis à vis the preferred shareholders. The *Deep Rock* doctrine considers issues of inadequate capital and patterns of control designed to prefer the parent over public investors.

Again, in *Pepper* v. *Litton*,[86] where fiduciary standards of conduct applicable to the controlling shareholder were breached, the claim of

---

[80] See 3 *Collier, Bankruptcy*, para. 510.05 (15th ed., 1984); 11 U.S.C. s.510(c); *Henn and Alexander*, s.152.

[81] Blumberg, *The Law of Corporate Groups: Bankruptcy Law* (1985) (hereafter referred to as "*Blumberg, Bankruptcy*").

[82] *Blumberg, Bankruptcy*, at 6–8; s.1.03. See *Zubik* v. *Zubik*, n. 43 above, at 273.

[83] *Ibid.* at 9.

[84] *Ibid.*, citing *In re Vecco Const. Indus. Inc.*, 4 Bankr. 407, 409 (Bankr. ED Va 1970).

[85] 306 U.S. 307 (1939); discussed in *Henn and Alexander*, 369–372; *Blumberg, Bankruptcy*, at 63–68.

[86] 308 U.S. 295 (1939).

a parent was subordinated in the distribution of the bankrupt's assets.

These cases do not disregard the shareholder's claims or disregard corporateness. Instead, they subordinate the shareholder's interests to achieve fairness.[87]

(ii) *Successor liability*

A recent and novel case[88] presented the question in bankruptcy whether a corporation's liability for damages consisting of back pay for unfair labour practices assessed by the National Labor Relations Board under the National Labor Relations Act survives a Chapter 7 bankruptcy proceeding and attaches to an *alter ego* formed after the bankruptcy by the same shareholders. Under Chapter 7, only individual and not corporate debts may be discharged.

The shareholders of a roofing company were found to have conducted business for a period of years through several different companies. When one company was assessed for damages for unfair labour practices, the shareholders ceased to do business through that company and formed another. The court, found the companies to be *alter egos* because of the extent of common control, management and financing. Subsequently, additional companies were formed to conduct roofing business and finally the individual shareholders and their then corporations filed for bankruptcy under Chapter 7.

After the proceedings were concluded, the shareholders formed a new company. This company was ordered to pay the NLRB damages.

The court found that a corporation that succeeds another which has a liability for damages under the Act would also be liable for the damages if it were an *alter ego* of the first corporation. The shareholders did not challenge this nor the conclusion that their companies were *alter egos*. They argued that the back pay judgment was discharged and that therefore there was no debt due. However, since corporate debts cannot be discharged in a Chapter 7 proceeding, they also argued that the finding that the companies were *alter egos* of one another because of the personal involvement of the shareholders should mean that the debts were not corporate debts, but personal debts, and as personal debts they were discharged in the Chapter 7 proceeding.

The court rejected this argument. Applying control, common management and financial control tests to determine that the companies were *alter egos* was not deemed to be relevant to determining whether the court should impose corporate liability on the shareholders in their individual capacities. Under Washington law, a shareholder would only be liable for a corporate liability when

---

[87] *Blumberg, Bankruptcy*, at 18 and see Chapter 3. See also Bankruptcy Code provisions requiring a reorganisation plan to be fair and equitable in 11 U.S.C. s.1129 (b).

[88] *National Labor Relations Board* v. *Better Building Supply Corp. et al.*, 837 F. 2d 377 (9th Cir. 1988).

"... the liability-causing activity did not occur only for the benefit of the corporaton ... or [when] the liable corporation had been 'gutted' and left without funds by those controlling it in order to avoid actual or potential liability."[89] The court held that the involvement of the shareholders was not sufficient to result in personal liability. Hence, the debt was a corporate debt and not discharged.

This is an interesting use of entity law to avoid liability of share-holders to achieve a result in bankruptcy that the court perhaps perceived as equitable.

(iii) *Substantive consolidation*

Another equitable doctrine arising out of the bankruptcy court's power to adjudicate equities among creditors is substantive con-solidation of parent and subsidiary companies or consolidation among subsidiaries.[90] Substantive consolidation technically may be ordered in a liquidation or in a reorganisation proceeding where one of the companies in a group has filed for relief. If substantive con-solidation is ordered, inter-company claims would be eliminated, assets would be pooled, and the creditors of the various group com-panies would be treated as creditors of the common fund.

Substantive consolidation is an extraordinary remedy.[91] It has been permitted where there has been a fraudulent transfer of signifi-cant assets to a controlled corporation.[92] It has also been used where the subsidiary "has in reality no separate existence, is not adequately capitalised and constitutes a mere instrumentality of the parent corporation or a mere 'corporate pocket' or department of its business."[93] In one case it was allowed where auditing "would entail great expenditure of time and expense without assurance that a fair reflection of the conditions of the debtor corporations would in the end be possible."[94]

The power to consolidate should be used sparingly because of the possibility that some creditors may have dealt with one company without knowledge that it was part of a group. In *Anaconda Bldg. Materials Co.* v. *Newland*,[95] the parent organised finance subsidiaries to acquire mortgages taken by the parent when it sold prefabricated homes manufactured by it. These subsidiaries obtained funds by selling debentures to the public. Although all four subsidiaries and the parent had filed bankruptcy proceedings, the subsidiaries were in better financial condition than the parent. The creditors of the parent

---

[89] *Ibid.* at 379. Courts also do not usually disregard corporate personality to benefit shareholders. See n. 37, above.

[90] See *Sampsell* v. *Imperial Paper Corp.*, 313 U.S. 215, 219 (1941), consolidation of corporation and bankrupt individual controlling shareholder.

[91] See, *e.g. In re Auto-Train Corp.*, 810 F. 2d 270, 275–276 (D.C. Cir. 1986).

[92] *Sampsell*, 313 U.S. 215, 220–21.

[93] *Stone* v. *Eacho*, 127 F. 2d 284, 288 (4th Cir. 1942), *reh. denied*, 128 F. 2d 16, *cert. denied*, 317 U.S. 365 (1942).

[94] *Chemical Bank New York Trust Co.* v. *Kheel*, 369 F. 2d 845, 846 (2d Cir. 1966).

[95] 336 F. 2d 265 (9th Cir. 1964).

sought substantive consolidation in order to reach the assets of the subsidiaries. Debenture holders and the Securities and Exchange Commission objected. The court refused substantive consolidation because the finance subsidiaries were operated as separate entities, the parent was the beneficiary of the inter-corporate relationships, and the creditors of the parent did not rely upon the credit of the subsidiaries and were not prejudiced by their operations.

Since substantive consolidation can prejudice substantive rights of creditors of the individual entities, bankruptcy courts will have to determine if there are equitable circumstances in a particular case which would warrant consolidation and to balance carefully whether the prejudice from consolidation is outweighed by the prejudice that would result from a failure to consolidate the various estates of the companies in the corporate group.[96]

Corporate guarantees

It is common for parent companies to guarantee debts of subsidiary companies. Such guarantees may be subject to corporation laws or corporate charters restricting the power or the right of a company to issue a guarantee. The formalities of authorisation, whether guarantees must be authorised by the Board of Directors or whether they must be approved by shareholders, are also the subject of statutes, charters or by law provisions.[97]

The doctrine of *ultra vires* reflected the need to comply with corporate law in the creation of corporate obligations,[98] but in a sense it also highlights the usual rule that a company is not generally responsible for the debts of its subsidiaries or its parent or affiliates, in the absence of a successful invocation of veil-piercing circumstances.

Short of guarantees, we have also seen the development of so-called "comfort letters." These are often obtained when a guarantee of a parent company cannot be obtained. Whether or not such letters give rise to legal rights and, if so, what rights, have presented interesting questions.[99] The legal effect of "keep-well" or "comfort" letters is beyond the scope of this Chapter, but again their use highlights that separate corporate entities are not generally responsible for debts of affiliates.

In the case of guarantees or pledges by a subsidiary either to a creditor of the parent (so-called "upstream" guarantees) or to a creditor of a sister company (so-called "cross-stream" guarantees),

---

[96] *In re DRW Property Company* 82, 54 B.R. 489 (Bankr ND Texas 1985). The factors determining whether substantive consolidation is warranted are set out in this decision. Several are reminiscent of factors discussed above in piercing the veil cases.
[97] See *Henn and Alexander*, 970–971.
[98] See *e.g. Commercial Trading Co.* v. *120 Jane Corp.*, 27 A.D. 2d 533, 275 N.Y.S. 2d 621 (1966). See *Telefest* v. *VU–TV Inc.*, 591 F. Supp. 1368, 1379 (D.N.J. 1984).
[99] See, for example, *Kleinwort Benson Ltd.* v. *Malaysian Mining Corp. Berhad*, FT Law Report, January 12, 1988, commented on in Business Law Briefing, 4 (February 1988) reversed by Court of Appeal, see *The Times*, February 5, 1989.

issues are raised as to the corporate benefit to and business purpose of a guaranteeing subsidiary in connection with the guarantee.[1]

In order to avoid application of the assets of a subsidiary for the benefit of another company's creditors and to the detriment of the subsidiary's creditors, as a matter of corporate law an upstream or cross-stream guarantee by a subsidiary should be in furtherance of its own corporate purposes and be issued in consideration of some corporate benefit derived by the subsidiary.[2] Similarly, such guarantees would have to pass the tests of fraudulent conveyance statutes in various states and the fraudulent conveyance sections of federal bankruptcy law.[3]

In *Rubin* v. *Manufacturers Hanover Trust Company*,[4] debtors issued upstream and cross-stream guarantees for affiliates to a bank and subsequently went into bankruptcy. The trustee in bankruptcy argued that these secured guarantees were fraudulent conveyances because the bank's loan's were not made to the debtors but to the guaranteed affiliates. The lower court found for the bank. The bank had argued that there was an indirect benefit to the guarantors. The Court of Appeals rejected these arguments. The Court of Appeals held that it was an error to have found that fair consideration had been given for the guarantees without a finding of economic benefit to each guarantor company and a further error to have determined the financial health of the debtor company by reference to related entities and the solvency of the "enterprise as a whole."[5] The case was remanded for a factual determination of the economic benefit to each guarantor.

The recent *Gleaneagles* case involved the effect of the Pennsylvania Fraudulent Conveyance Act on, among other things, upstream guarantees within a corporate group in connection with a leveraged buyout transaction. The court held, first, that the Act applied to

---

[1] See New York Business Corporation Law, ss.202(a) and 908 (McKinney 1986); *Henn and Alexander*, 970–971. See *In re Security Products Co.*, 310 F. Supp. 110 (E.D. Mo. 1969), distinguished in *Geremia* v. *First National Bank of Boston*, 653 F. 2d 1, 7 (1st Cir. 1981). See *In the Matter of Xonics Photochemical Inc.*, 841 F. 2d 198 (7th Cir. 1988).

[2] See *Collier* on *Bankruptcy*, para. 548.09 at p. 548–113 to 115 (15th ed., 1987); *Rubin* v. *Manufacturers Hanover Trust Company*, 661 F. 2d 979, 991–992 (1981). But see *Telefest Inc.* v. *VU–TV Inc.*, 591 F. Supp. 1368 (D.N.J. 1984), distinguished in the *Gleneagles* case since fair consideration was not disputed (*Tabor Court*, 803 F. 2d at 1305). See *Xonics*, n. 1 above. Cherin, Ash & Burlingame, "Enforceability of Guarantees and Credit Support Provided Among Members of a Corporate Group: A Bibliography," 34 The Bus Lawyer 2029 (1979).

[3] See Uniform Fraudulent Conveyance Act and Uniform Fraudulent Transfer Act, 7A Uniform Laws Annotated (West 1985) and cases cited thereunder; *NY Debtor and Creditor Law*, ss.270–281 (McKinney 1945 and 1987 Supp.); U.S. Bankruptcy Code, 11 U.S.C. s.548, and cases cited thereunder; *United States of America* v. *Gleneagles Investment Co. Inc.*, 565 F. Supp. 556 (1983), aff'd. sub nom *United States of America* v. *Tabor Court Realty Corp.*, 803 F. 2d 1288 (3rd Cir. 1986), cert. den. *McClellan Realty Co.* v. *United States*, 107 S. Ct. 3229 (1987); Rubin, supra, n. 2. See also *Kupetz* v. *Wolf*, 845 F. 2d 842 (9th Cir. 1988); *Xonics*, n. 1 above.

[4] n. 2 above.

[5] *Rubin*, 661 F.2d 979 at 995.

leveraged buyout situations, and, second, that the guarantees should be set aside on the facts as fraudulent conveyances.[6]

In another recent leveraged buyout case,[7] a creditors' committee in a Chapter 11 reorganisation sought to set aside upstream guarantees and other security documents under Section 548 of the Bankruptcy Code, the fraudulent conveyance section. The court held, as a matter of law, that Section 548 (as well as the Ohio fraudulent conveyance law) may be applied to leveraged buyouts.[8] The court then adopted the *Rubin* test that it is necessary to demonstrate an economic benefit to the entity which incurs an obligation or makes a transfer.[9] The court recognised that the benefit to a debtor guarantor or pledgor may be indirect, through benefits to a third party where the consideration is ultimately given to the debtor or otherwise confers an economic benefit on the debtor.

What is of significance to our analysis of corporate groups, however, was the argument of the defendants that the transactions met the tests of the fraudulent conveyance statutes because reasonably equivalent value was given.

"...and that as long as some entity received a reasonably equivalent value for the incurring of the loan obligation or the transferring of a security interest, Plaintiff's case must fail regardless of whether *Ohio Corrugating* benefitted from the transaction."[10]

The court rejected this attempt to apply an enterprise theory of a benefit received by a corporate group, instead holding that it is necessary to show specific economic benefit to the entity within the group which incurs an obligation or makes a transfer.

Thus, despite the general application of equitable principles in bankruptcy cases, as discussed above in connection with equitable subordination, in the area of corporate guarantees, entity law still appears with considerable vitality.

Tort law

It is not possible to address here the sweeping changes in tort law in the United States, particularly in product liability cases.

What is emerging in the product liability area of modern tort law generally are the attempts to apply tort principles based on policies to spread economic risks of loss. Such policies are not based on breach of warranty with its related concepts of contract privity, or on traditional negligence law.[11]

---

[6] *Gleneagles*, n. 3 above, 565 F. Supp. 556 at 576.
[7] *In the Matter of The Ohio Corrugating Company*, 70 B.R. 920 (B. Ct. ND Ohio 1987).
[8] *Ibid.*, at 927.
[9] *Ibid.*
[10] *Ibid.* See also *Telefest*, n. 98 above.
[11] For a general discussion see *Prosser and Keeton on Torts*, Ch. 13 (discussing strict liability and which also discusses the reaction of U.S. courts to *Fletcher* v. *Rylands*, (1865), 3H. & C. 774, 159 Eng. Rep. 737, *rev'd. Fletcher* v. *Rylands*, (1866), L.R.1 Ex.

Priest summarises some of the salient changes and the positions of various prominent scholars in tracing the intellectual history, and then presents his advocacy of strict liability in product liability cases.[12]

Blumberg also finely analyses modern developments in tort law, not only in product liability cases but in various other tort areas, with his special emphasis on the effects of various tort law theories on corporate groups.[13]

Clearly, social policies, economic considerations, and remoteness of manufacturers from consumer all affect attitutes toward tort liability. Also, as far as corporate groups are concerned, entity law and veil-piercing techniques may be argued to be inadequate approaches given the non-consensual nature of relationship between an injured party and a corporation in tort cases.[14] In any event, it should be remembered that strict liability is not the norm for tort law generally.

The concept embodied in Section 402A of the Restatement of Torts[15] dealing with product liability has been referred to as "enterprise" liability; that is, a form of strict liability without fault, which would make an enterprise liable for all costs associated with the enterprise. In other words, in product cases it looks to providing an effective remedy and spreading costs through the price of products.[16]

However interesting developments in product liability to consumers may be, they cannot be said now to have supplanted tradi-

---

265, aff'd. Rylands v. Fletcher, (1868), L.R. 3 H.L. 330), and Ch. 17 (which discusses strict liability in the context of products liability), (5th ed., 1984).

[12] Priest, n. 15 above at 464. See as to product liability generally, Prosser and Keeton, n. 11, above, Chap. 17. Although Priest refers to strict liability as "enterprise" liability, the term is not used in the sense of Blumberg's usage to connote the interrelationship of a corporate group. See also, Prosser, "The Assault upon the Citadel (Strict Liability to the Consumer)," 69 Yale L.J. 1099 (1960); criticised to some extent by Priest, n. 15 above at 516–518. See Restatement of Torts (2nd ed., American Law Institute 1965) s.402A. The materials in this footnote deal primarily with strict liability in product liability cases. See, also, a critique of Priest's article and views in Owen, "The Intellectual Development of Modern Products Liability Law; A Comment on Priest's View of the Cathedral's Foundations," J. of Leg. Stud. 592 (Dec. 1985). See Schmalz, "Superfunds and Tort Law Reforms—Are They Insurable?," 38 The Bus Lawyer 175 (1982).

[13] Blumberg, Substantive Law, Chaps. 8–16.

[14] See Blumberg, Substantive Law, at s.10.01 n. 1 and s.11.01. Fletcher, s.41.85. Fletcher also notes that, unlike contract cases, no proof of fraud is necessary.Ibid. at n. 2.20.

[15] Under s.402 A, there is special liability of a seller of a product for physical harm to a user or consumer if the product is in a defective, unreasonably dangerous condition, if the seller is engaged in the business of selling such product, and regardless of the seller's care and whether or not the consumer was in privity with the seller. Restatement of Torts, n. 12, above. See Prosser and Keeton, n. 11, above, at 693. The scope of s.402A covers both manufacturers and distributors, and federal legislation attempting to limit strict liability for non-manufacturers has been proposed in the past. See Cohen, "Analysis of the Products Liability Act (S. 44, 98th Congress) as Reported," J Prod. Liab. L. 1, 32, 35–54 (1984).

[16] As to the concept of strict liability generally, see Prosser and Keeton, n. 11 above, at Ch. 13. See also Blumberg, Substantive Law, Chap. 13.

41

tional negligence law outside this special area and outside more traditional strict liability situations, and it would appear that traditional tort and corporate law will continue to be operative in cases dealing with corporate groups.[17]

Cases involving railway companies provided interesting facts upon which to develop group tort liability. As Blumberg points out, the great railway systems developed by combining individual companies incorporated in various states into interconnected systems of nationwide scope.[18] Early railway tort cases found liability on the basis of the continuous system. Regardless of the ownership of the line on which the incident occurred, the overall system and not the part operated by a subsidiary could be liable.[19] However, Blumberg concludes that piercing the corporate veil analysis seems to have replaced the approach of these early cases and the *Berkey* case is most often cited.[20]

Numerous cases arose in New York City involving taxicab accidents. In many cases[21] large taxi fleets were set up and centrally operated. Injured passengers and others who may have thought they were dealing with a single business enterprise in fact would find that often hundreds of corporations, each owning one or two taxicabs and each with only the minimum bond or insurance required by law, operated as the "fleet."[22] In these cases, New York courts recognised the public interest, concluded that the use of the corporate structure had been abused, and that equity should not permit this to defeat the plaintiff's claims. The apprehension about responsibility of such businesses to the public and the clear underinsurance led the courts to permit a complaint against the individual investor as well as the parent company in one fleet enterprise.[23]

In the widely publicised *Amoco Cadiz* case,[24] the court, in an

---

[17] See generally, *Blumberg, Substantive Law*, Chap. 12 and p. 229, 689. See Craig, n. 43 above.

[18] *Blumberg, Substantive Law*, Chap. 12 and p. 232.

[19] *Pennsylvania RR* v. *Jones*, 155 U.S. 333 (1894); *Lehigh Valley R. Co.* v. *Dupont*, 128 Fed. 840 (2d Cir. 1904).

[20] See *Berkey.* v. *Third Avenue Railway*, n. 34 above, discussed in 50 A.L.R. 599 and *Blumberg, Substantive Law*, 235. See more recent cases applying piercing approaches in railway cases in 7 A.L.R. 3d 1343 at 1380.

[21] See generally *Blumberg, Substantive Law*, at 248; *Henn and Alexander* at 349 and footnote 25; *Mull* v. *Colt Co.*, 31 F.R.D. 154 (SDNY 1962). *Mull* allowed a suit by a pedestrian and denied a motion to dismiss. Clearly, pedestrians do not rely on the group identity for reliability or quality of service or financial responsibility. See *Zubik* v. *Zubik*, n. 43 above at 273. See *Blumberg, Substantive Law*, at 254.

[22] *Mull* v. *Colt Co.*, above; *Teller* v. *Clear Serv. Co.*, 9 Misc. 2d 495, 503, 173 N.Y.S. 2d 183, 190 (Sup. Ct. 1958). Both are cases involving pedestrians and pre-trial motions. *Mull* contains an interesting discussion of the effect of undercapitalisation as a factor in piercing the veil cases.

[23] *Walkovsky* v. *Carlton* 18 N.Y. 2d 414, 223 N.E. 2d 6 (1966); and *Walkovsky* v. *Carlton*, 29 A.D. 2d 763, 287 N.Y.S. 2d 546 (2d Dept.), aff'd 23 N.Y. 2d 714, 244 N.E. 2d 55 (1968).

[24] Page 20, n. 1 above. Juric "A review of Liability Issues Arising from the Grounding of the Oil Tanker Amoco Cadiz," 31 Trial Law. Guide 297 (1987). See Rosenthal and Raper, "Amoco Cadiz and Limitation of Liability for Oil Spill Pollution:

exhaustingly detailed 1984 memorandum opinion, in essence employed piercing the veil approaches to find intragroup liability for the oil spill as a result of the grounding of the supertanker off the French coast.

The court found that the vessel-owning subsidiary, its parent company and the ultimate parent of the corporate group were all individually liable. Despite some statements that appear to be statements of "enterprise" liability, it is submitted that the decision is a piercing the veil approach to the extent that it deals with intragroup liability, as opposed to instances where individual entities directly assumed individual duties.

Damages were assessed in the case in January, 1988, and further proceedings and appeals are continuing.

As to tort law generally, Blumberg concludes that entity law still largely renders intragroup liability the exceptional result.[25] This is so despite many cases found which have imposed liability on affiliates (as opposed to imposing liability on individual investor shareholders for corporate torts). Piercing the veil jurisprudence still would appear to be the usual approach.

Bank holding companies

For some time the Board of Governors of the Federal Reserve System has asserted that it has the authority to require a bank holding company to assist financially troubled subsidiary banks. Regulation Y of the Board which deals with bank holding company matters contains a provision that a bank holding company should be a

---

Domestic and International Solutions," 5 Va. J. of Nat. Res. Law 259 (1985). See *In re Barracuda Tanker Corp.*, 281 F. Supp. 228 (SDNY 1968), *rev'd. on other grounds*, 409 F. 2d 1013 (2d Cir. 1969), commented on in Gilmore & Black, *The Law of Admiralty* s.10–10 at 843 (2d ed. 1975).

[25] *Blumberg, Substantive Law*, at 229. See *Henn and Alexander* at 349 and 354; Craig, n. 43 above. In *A L Laboratories Inc.* v. *Phillips Roxane*, 803 F. 2d 378 (8th Cir. 1986), a parent corporation was held not liable for punitive damages where a controlled subsidiary misappropriated proprietary information of the plaintiff. The court applying Missouri law, applied the following piercing of the veil principle to deny liability:

> "Corporate forms may be disregarded and separate entities treated as one only where a two-prong test is met: 'Not only must the corporation be controlled and influenced by one or a few persons, in addition, the evidence must establish that the corporate cloak was used as a subterfuge to defeat public convenience, to justify wrong or to perpetuate fraud.' *Fairbanks* v. *Chambers*, 665 SW 2d 33, 37 (Mo. Ct. App. 1984). Thus full ownership, with concomitant dominance and control, is insufficient to justify 'piercing the corporate veil'; rather a plaintiff must prove that equity requires that the parent and subsidiary be treated as one ..." *Ibid.* at 385 (citing other Missouri cases).

This is a traditonal formulation reminiscent of the test applied in the New York instrumentality cases of *Lowendahl*, page 20 n. 3 above at 76, and of *Fisser* v. *International Bank*, n. 3 above at 76 and n. 66 above at 238, except that these cases also added a third factor—proximate cause. See *American Protein*, n. 46 above at 60. The court's language here of treating the corporations as one is a use of *alter ego* rather than instrumentality theory. See *Fletcher* s.41.10.

"source of strength" to its subsidiary banks.[26] The Board interprets this to require a bank holding company to "use available resources to provide adequate capital funds to its subsidiary banks during periods of financial stress."[27]

In *MCorp Financial Inc. et al and Official Creditors' Committee of MCorp et al* v. *Board of Governors of the Federal Reserve System*,[28] the Board alleged that MCorp had not complied with Regulation Y, and engaged in unsound banking practices, because it had not contributed additional cash to financially troubled subsidiary banks. In May, 1990, the Fifth Circuit Court of Appeals held that the Board exceeded its statutory authority in attempting to force MCorp to make contributions and that to interpret the failure to do so as an unsound practice (which would give the Board authority under other banking laws) was an unreasonable and impermissible use of the term.

The Court thus rejected the use of the source of strength doctrine in the circumstances where the Board attempted to force the holding company to transfer funds to its banks without statutory authority or prior commitment. The decision does not involve the statutory rights of the Federal Deposit Insurance Corporation to assert claims resulting from the failure of a subsidiary bank against solvent subsidiary banks of a holding company under the cross guaranty provision contained in Section 206 of the Financial Institutions Reform, Recovery and Enforcement Act of 1989. The Board will likely appeal the decision.

For our purposes the case can also be seen as an example of entity law being applied even in the highly regulated banking atmosphere, protecting the position of creditors of a bank holding company against the claims of bank regulators on funds of the holding company. The court stated:

> "Such a transfer of funds would require MCorp to disregard its own corporation's separate status; it would amount to a wasting of the holding company's assets in violation of its duty to its shareholders. Also, one of the fundamental purposes of the FBCA [sic] is to separate banking from commercial enterprises. That purpose is obviously not served if the Board is permitted to treat a holding company merely as an extension of its subsidiary bank ..."[29]

CONCLUSION

Of course, there are many legal issues relevant to the operations of corporate groups which have not been included here. There is a great

---

[26] 12 C.F.R. s.225.4(a)(1).

[27] Policy Statement, April 24, 1987, 52 Fed. Reg. 15707, 15708; Fed. Res. Reg. Service Vol. 1 at para. 4–878.

[28] No. 89–2816, slip op. (5th Cir. May 15, 1990); reprinted CCH Fed. Bank L. Rep. para. 88,153.

[29] Ibid. at p. 96, 501.

deal of case law in the United States dealing with piercing the corporate veil. Professor Blumberg, while critical of the manner in which the technique is perceived and applied in general and in cases involving affiliated companies in particular, recognises that it is the primitive vehicle through which a more coherent law of corporate groups may emerge.[30]

In commercial transactions, courts traditionally try to find the intention of the parties to a transaction and to take into account their reasonable expectations.

In tort cases, the relationships of involved parties in a damage suit are non-consensual. This perhaps gives courts more scope for questioning established principles in such cases. Still, in tort cases generally traditional entity law is manifest.

Observing settled distinctions between corporations and their shareholders is at the base of corporation law and practice. It is of great economic significance and affects investment decisions, domestic and international. These distinctions must not be disregarded lightly.

Whether concepts of enterprise law which Professor Blumberg sees developing in various bodies of law will ultimately supplement or supplant entity law in general is a fascinating and important question.

In reviewing the authorities mentioned above, the reluctance of courts to ignore the separate identity of corporation is apparent. Nevertheless, piercing the corporate veil concepts, while perhaps imperfect, are available where equity requires.

---

[30] *Blumberg, Substantive Law*, 682. See *Gower*, at 138.

III

Legal Problems in the Management of a Group of Companies

James Keir Q.C.*

1. INTRODUCTION

The approach to the topic in this chapter is an empirical one, based on experience in a complex multi-national group, and so what is said will be largely free of references to authorities and learned writing in the field. In drawing a distinction between an academic approach and an empirical approach I do not seek to make any value judgement as to their relative merits. Indeed, I think there is an over-emphasised tendency amongst English lawyers to maintain too sharp a division between the academic approach and the empirical approach. The importance of academic thought and contribution within the subject under discussion are underrated. Hard working practitioners may lack the temperament and the scholarship and the time to look objectively at principles and development of the law and practice in the relevant field and it would be beneficial to them if they spent more time listening to or reading what is said or written by the academic thinkers or even taking a little time to do more academic thought themselves.

Employee representation in groups of companies

My experience of the systems of law with which I have come into contact relating to the management of groups of companies is that the similarities, at any rate of principle, are more striking than the differences. That is not to say that there are no differences and indeed these differences can relate to what properly belongs to the field of corporate governance. For example, much thought and effort has been given to the question of the rights, powers and duties in the field of corporate governance which should be possessed by the employees of companies. It may be added parenthetically that this is a question which poses very special problems in *groups* of companies. If there are employee representatives on the boards of subsidiary companies within the group, it may be difficult to achieve the necessary strategic coherence for the group as a whole. If, on the other hand, there are no such representatives except at the parent company level then it may be felt that "industrial democracy," to use an over-worked and rather inaccurate phrase, is found wanting at the subsidiary company level.

* Former Company Secretary, Unliver plc.

Employee representation is a matter which has been greatly debated and written about in the last 20 years or so. Actual progress has been limited. There was the much discussed but now, I think, largely forgotten Bullock Report. There is the European Commission draft Fifth Directive on Employee Participation and Company Structure. This remains in draft form, and is unlikely to be adopted in the immediate future. The Germans, with characteristic persistence, devised a detailed system for providing for employee representation, which has been embodied in legislation and which has worked effectively for a considerable number of years. The Dutch have a system which is ingenious and seems to work but which does not involve anything like the German system of employee participation at board level. What the Dutch system does is to give the Works Council a right to make recommendations for appointment to, and to disapprove new appointments to, membership of a self-perpetuating supervisory board. Such objections may be upheld or rejected by the Social and Economic Council of the Netherlands, which is a body consisting of representatives of government and of both sides of industry.

The German and Dutch systems would seem to be the most developed ones within the European Community. Compulsory employee participation at board level is provided for under Luxembourg and Danish legislation. Other Member States have systems of employee councils etc., but most of these bodies have merely a consultative role. It may be worth mentioning in passing the rather remarkable proposal for the so-called Vredeling draft Directive of the European Commission which was very much concerned with international trade union rights in multi-national groups of companies. It aroused enormous opposition on many grounds but principally because of its unsatisfactory drafting and its impracticability. It now seems unlikely that this proposal will be revived.

Legislative measures relating to groups

Apart from industrial democracy there have been a certain number of initiatives in relation to the corporate governance of groups of companies as distinguished from single companies. United Kingdom Company Law makes some provision for groups of companies, particularly in relation to accounting and other information which they are required to publish. The Germans, once again, are the leaders in actually having got a carefully thought out and detailed system embodied in legislation and put into operation. The European Commission, spurred on by this good example, produced the draft Ninth Directive which in its own way raised as big a furore as the Vredeling Directive. This was probably because the draft was very obviously based on German Law and did not appear to have taken account of the way in which the matter was dealt with in other Member States, nor to have addressed its mind sufficiently thoroughly to exactly what the purpose of the proposed Directive was. We must not, however, overlook the successful steps that have been taken in the European Community in relation to groups of companies, notably the Seventh Directive on Group Accounts. This has now been implemented in nearly all the Member States.

2. THE GOVERNANCE OF THE UNILEVER GROUP

It might be useful and interesting to examine a practical example of the way in which a fundamental problem was dealt with (and continues to be dealt with) by the multi-national group for which I worked for nearly 30 years. This was Unilever and I am proposing here to try and summarise the system of group co-ordination which it operated. Unilever is an atypical organisation because it has two parent group companies, one Dutch (Unilever NV) and one British (Unilever PLC). The reasons for this are partly historical and partly fiscal.*

There are two basic principles which underlie the arrangements which Unilever has made. The first is so far as possible to conduct the businesses of the two groups as if they formed a single group with a single parent. The second is to ensure that the shareholders of each of the two parent companies have rights to the profits and assets of the two groups combined which are equalised fairly as between the shareholders of each parent company. The way in which the first of these principles is implemented is to ensure that the boards of the two parent companies are composed of the same individuals. They consider it their function to carry out their duties as directors in relation to the combined operations of the two groups viewed as a whole rather than separately. In order to ensure the identical composition of the two boards, there are special provisions in the articles of association of each parent company. These ensure that only persons nominated by the holders of specially designated shares of the two parent companies can be elected to be directors of those two companies. The companies holding these specially designated shares are themselves beneficially owned as to 50 per cent. by each of the two parent companies. The actual election of directors of the parent companies is, however, made by the voting shareholders of the two parent companies as in an ordinary public company.

It is worth noting, however, that NV does not have a supervisory board although normally under Dutch Law an NV must have a supervisory board. A special exception has been made for NV because the existence of the supervisory board would not be compatible with the arrangements that I have just been describing. It is also worth noticing that there are currently no non-executive directors of either of the two parent companies, despite the recent enthusiasm for such appointments. Once again, this is because such appointments

---

* For a detailed account, see the published history of Unilever by Charles Wilson, formerly Professor of Modern History at the University of Cambridge, which is published by Cassell in three volumes.

would not fit in with arrangements outlined above. There are, however, advisory directors who fill in practice something of the same role as non-executive directors. The enthusiastic supporters of non-executive directorships, however, would regard the advisory directors as a pale shadow of the real thing because they are not directors in the sense of having the legal rights and obligations which ordinary directors of a company have. They are very distinguished people but their authority is a moral one rather than a legal one.

The Unilever Agreements

There are also several agreements which support the arrangements that set out above the principal being The Equalisation Agreement. The Equalisation Agreement has as its purpose to ensure that in principle it makes no difference to a shareholder whether he holds shares in the NV or the PLC. The present Equalisation Agreement was made in 1946 and replaced two previous ones, the first dated 1927 and the second 1937. The current one was amended slightly in 1951 and more substantially in 1981. It provides that the two parent companies are to have identical financial periods and accounting principles. It goes on to provide that dividends are to be declared or recommended on the same day for both companies, that the dividends are to be decided in relation to the aggregate profits of both groups and that the dividends are to be equal as defined in The Equalisation Agreement with certain special exceptions which have so far never happened in practice. The Agreement also provides that if one of the parent companies does not have sufficient profits to enable it to pay the declared or recommended dividend, and if the two boards think it appropriate, then the company with a shortfall comes under an obligation to require a subvention from the other one, which is under an obligation to give it. Analogous arrangements are made in relation to a liquidation of one of the parent companies alone or of both the parent companies.

The 1981 Amendment to the Equalisation Agreement gives an interesting example of ad hoc problem solving. At that time the Dutch guilder was very strong and sterling was very weak. Circumstances were arising in which the appropriate dividend, having regard to the aggregate profits of the whole group, could result in a dividend which seemed unjustifiably low in relation to the profits of the NV taken alone and unjustifiably high in relation to the profits of the PLC taken alone. It was foreseen that this situation might develop to the stage where it was no longer acceptable for both companies to declare the same dividend. However, the principle of equalisation had to be maintained and so an amendment was devised which allowed different dividends to be declared by the two parent companies in special circumstances and which provided for equalisation to be maintained by the use of so-called "equalisation reserve."

The opportunity was also taken to deal with the situation in which statutory dividend control exists. This did exist in the United

Kingdom for a long period which ended in 1979 and Unilever dealt with it by the simple expedient of obtaining permission from the Bank of England to declare a higher dividend than the statutory maximum on condition that the difference between the dividend and statutory maximum was not paid until either the regulation had been removed or the Bank of England gave permission for it to be paid. This meant that the PLC shareholders had a bonanza in 1979, or at any rate what appeared to be a bonanza. The exchange rate problem has never developed to the stage where use has had to be made of the new provisions and I dare say they never will have to be used.

Other specific agreements set out arrangements for defining the spheres of influence of the two companies, and for ensuring a policy of co-operation and common approach in terms of exchanging information, developing products and industrial processes, and mutual financial undertakings.

It is interesting to note that all these agreements are written in English and are by their terms expressed to be construed in accordance with English law.

The operational management of the Unilever Group

This is an outline of how Unilever operates as a unitary group. I see it as an interesting example of a tailor-made solution (some might say a home-made solution) to an important "problem." On the question of how Unilever actually manages its world-wide operations, as with all multi-national groups, there is a very wide range of interests to be taken into account. First of all there are the shareholders of the parent companies and of course according to what some would see as the pure doctrine, they are the principal interest to be taken into account. Next, and, it must be stressed, not in any order of importance, are the outside shareholders in companies which are controlled within the group. It is worth saying that this situation arises more frequently than might be supposed. Next are the employees, the people who work for the companies within the group or companies where the group has a significant influence; others include: trade unions, both national and international; the legal regimes in the countries where Unilever companies operate; legal and quasi-legal regimes of supranational bodies; political and cultural attitudes and situations throughout the world; international, fiscal and financial factors.

The broad principle which governs the group operation is to establish a coherent and well understood commercial policy and within that policy to give wide flexibility of action to individual management and boards. The operational management has ample opportunity to contribute to the formation of the group strategy. The group policy makers are in constant touch with operational managements by way of established management information systems, by visits of the policy makers to operational areas and by operational managers to the group headquarters. It is a strength rather than a weakness that many managers see work in Unilever as a career or part of a career rather than a job. Thus individuals within the group are well known to one another and a strong group culture develops which is constantly modified in relation to changing circumstances but contains an important element of fundamental stability.

Within this broad principle Unilever seeks to carry it into effect in accordance with a number of other guiding principles. It regards it as important to be and to be seen to be commercially and socially worth while to each operation in which Unilever has an interest. This means carrying on the business in such a way as to cause it to be seen as positively beneficial to each society where it operates. It will be seen as contributing to employment on fair terms, to the economic wealth of the country where it operates, to the revenue of that country and to the fabric of society generally. It perhaps goes without saying that it is seen as vitally important to be law abiding in the broadest sense of the words and a good corporate citizen wherever an operation may be carried on.

There a number of cases where there are outside shareholders in group companies. Sometimes their participation was deliberately invited. For example, in Nigeria Unilever had a substantial shareholding and management interest in Nigerian Breweries Limited, the first brewery to be established in Nigeria. It was decided as long ago as 1958 to invite shareholding participation from Nigerian distributors who were seen to have played an important part in the commercial success which the company achieved. This participation was a resounding success and has been greatly appreciated by the company itself and by the Nigerian shareholders.

However, in a number of other cases the outside participation has been to a greater or lesser extent imposed as part of an express "indigenisation" policy. It should perhaps be said that participation from local shareholders might well have been invited voluntarily had it not been for the legislative intervention. However, the outside shareholding has come about and there are many ways besides those I have mentioned in which it may happen. The policy is always to give the closest possible attention to the interests of the outside shareholders both in compliance with the applicable legislation and in compliance with the spirit and practice of fair dealing. Further, it is very important to be careful to observe the most correctly formal corporate procedures in wholly-owned companies as well as in those with outside shareholding interests. My experience is that if this is not done, sloppy habits ensue and mistakes are made which cause problems out of all proportion to the apparent importance of the original error. It is also true to say that I have never found the corporate formalities in any country too serious an obstacle to achieving a sensible commercial purpose. Of course one sometimes finds particular detailed requirements tiresome and the volume of paper, notably in the United States of America, which has to be produced seems unending. It may even be questioned whether sometimes the sheer volume of information called for has the result that the recipient is so

51

swamped with information that the really important items do not make any impact on his mind.

Special topics

I shall now describe one or two particular topics in this field which used to occupy quite a lot of my time in my working life. I have already touched upon compulsory shareholding participation legislation. This I have encountered in a number of countries and it is a very understandable element in the nationalism which accompanies the break-up of former colonial empires which we have seen since the end of the Second World War. The principal problems in my experience arose out of the construction of the governing legislation. It was obviously a defined field to which the shareholding participation applied and not infrequently there were problems in defining whether a particular operation fell into a class where compulsory participation was required and, if so, into which particular class. The other major problem related to the price which was to be paid for the shares floated to the indigenous public. It goes without saying that the prices offered were always considered too low by the seller and many shareholders must have picked up wonderful bargains in those circumstances. These problems had to be dealt with partly on a financial and legal basis, but principally on a diplomatic basis and whilst we never achieved the improvement in the prices that we hoped for, we often made very worthwhile improvements on the starting price. It is worth mentioning that in all these situations where there was an outside shareholding, whether majority or minority, it was always the policy, and a very important policy, to ensure that we as a group went on being really useful to the organisation in which the outside shareholding participation existed. If we continued to be seen as a valued adviser and provider of useful services and a fair dealer, it enabled us to preserve the value of our existing interest while increasing the worth of the enterprise as a whole.

I have already touched on the question of so-called industrial democracy and indeed I spent a lot of time discussing draft legislation of various kinds intended to give employees of an enterprise some say in the way it is run. On the whole few of these initiatives have been successful or made much progress until recently except perhaps in Germany and in an ingenious form in the Netherlands. To my mind the reason why comparatively little progress has been made has been the complete lack of a reasonably common conceptual basis for action. Unless there is some common ground as to the objectives to be achieved and the interests to be protected, progress is not likely to be made and supposed solutions which are imposed against the will of one of the major interests involved are likely not to work out in practice because the necessary common objective does not exist. One of the outstanding examples of this was the proposed Vredeling Directive which would have imposed very serious burdens upon the enterprises to which it applied to their considerable economic detriment and would almost certainly not have achieved the purpose which it was claimed to be intended to effect. It may be that there is possible scope for fresh ingenious solutions to this problem such as the Dutch have achieved, but as I see it they have to be rooted in the culture and history of the society in which they have to work. I have great doubts as to whether they can be imposed in the first instance in a supra-national form until, for example in the EEC, the member states have made greater progress in developing systems which suit their own sociological background.

A further matter that has engaged a lot of attention and on which I found myself busy from time to time was that of special regimes for groups of companies. Here too, the provision in national legislation is infinitely diverse; until recently Germany was the only country which possessed a specially designed and fully developed legislative system. German legislation seems to be based on premises which would not be universally shared. The purpose of the German legislation and in consequence the apparent purpose of the EEC proposed 9th Directive seems to be to protect the interests of minority shareholders in group companies and creditors. It seems to be assumed in both these systems that groups are likely to be operated in a way which would be detrimental to those two particular interests. I can only say that within my experience those have not necessarily been the obvious interests which required to be protected. Another topic in this field which has been much studied and developed is that of internal regulating machinery such as audit committees and non-executive directors. I think there is much more chance of making progress along these lines and some success has attended the introduction of systems of this kind. The difficulties that I foresee arising in the development of such arrangements relate to the possible difficulty of finding suffi- cient suitable candidates for offices as non-executive directors; the problem of what powers such directors or committees should have and the extent to which the establishment of audit committees and the appointment of non-executive directors should be a matter of obligation under legislative provisions or whether such appointments should be allowed to become more frequent by informal means and be enforced where necessary by such arrangements as appropriate pro- visions in the conditions for stock exchange listings.

3. CONCLUSION

If I were to summarise these comments, it will have been readily gathered that I am not a radical in this field. I have a feeling that improvements in structures and practice should be allowed and encouraged to grow organically. Reactions to particular events or states of affairs need to be carefully controlled. The French say, I believe, of their company law "Chaque article a son scandale." That is perhaps not the ideal way for company law to develop, though in practice in may be difficult to avoid. Violent reaction to supposedly outrageous events leads to disjointed legislation out of tune with true conceptual growth.

I cannot emphasise too much the importance of continuing conceptual thought by those who have to operate or work with groups of companies, whether as businessmen, accountants, lawyers or in any other capacity and by those who study these matters in a more scholarly way. There are examples of very useful work being done in this way. Though I am no expert in it, it seems to me that the growth of the recent financial services legislation may well be a good example of the profitable application of experienced academic thought to a practical system of legislation. It is however at all times important to remember that what we are about is the effective regulation of wealth-creating enterprise and that regulation which restricts enterprise or inhibits the creation of wealth will defeat the principal objective. The other thought that I would like to conclude with is the importance of not confusing matters of corporate governance with considerations which properly lie in another field of socio-legal development. Of course, a major commercial enterprise has to take account of an enormous range of social and economic factors but in legislating and regulating it is important to be sure at all times at which particular objective we are aiming.

IV

Group Indebtedness

Prof. D. D. Prentice*

A. INTRODUCTION: THE GROUP AS DEBTOR

For the purpose of this chapter a group will be taken to exist where there is a relationship of parent and subsidiary between one company and another.[1] Obviously there will be situations where this does not provide a sufficiently comprehensive definition of when the group phenomenom can be said to exist since control can be exercised with less than a de iure holding. This is, for example, recognised with respect to accounting for controlled non-subsidiaries and this problem has been addressed in connection with the United Kingdom's obligations to implement the Seventh Directive on Consolidated Accounts.[2]

---

* D. D. Prentice, Fellow, Pembroke College, Allen & Overy Professor of Corporate Law, University of Oxford. Since this chapter was first written a number of texts have appeared which have illuminated nearly every aspect of the issue addressed in this article. They are referred to in the footnotes but full justice has not been done to them in the somewhat hasty revision of this text for publication. Also, as the material was substantially prepared prior to the Companies Act 1989, the pre- and post-1989 versions of the law relating to corporate capacity and director's authority have been given.

[1] By the Companies Act 1985, section 736 (*i.e.* the predecessor to the current definition introduced by the Companies Act 1989) a parent-subsidiary relationship existed where one company was a member of and controlled the composition of the board of another company, or held more than half of the nominal value of its equity share capital. The latter part of this definition was somewhat anomalous in that "equity share capital" was defined not in terms of voting rights but in terms of capital and dividend rights: see, for a criticism, Jenkins Committee Report 1962, (Cmnd. 1749), at paras. 148–150. The definition of subsidiary and holding company for non-accounting purposes has been altered by section 144 of the Companies Act 1989 (introducing a new section 736) which defines the relationship in terms of control of voting rights at board or shareholder meetings. However, the old definition is preserved for documents or deeds executed before the new definition came into operation: see section 144(6). A new definition of parent and subsidiary undertaking has been also introduced for the purpose of determining when consolidated accounts have to be prepared. This definition relies on the concept of de facto control and treats unincorporated entities as subsidiary undertakings see *Buckley on the Companies Acts—Special Bulletin—The Companies Act 1989* (eds. Mary Arden Q.C. and D. D. Prentice), at pp. 66–71 and 279.

[2] *The EC Seventh Company Law Directive On Consolidated Accounts* (DTI, Consultative Document, 1985); *Implementation of the EEC Seventh Company Law Directive on Consolidated Accounts: Definition of a Subsidiary* (Law Society, 1988); Companies Act 1985, sections 259–260 (as introduced by the Companies Act 1989); see also n. 1.

When compared with some Continental systems, for example the German which has specific legal provisions dealing with groups, it might be claimed that English company law does not possess a law relating to groups of companies. But this would be a somewhat facile conclusion. As was stated in connection with the Seventh Directive, which lays down requirements for consolidated accounts,

> "This [the definition of a group] is not a question solely for accounting law—labour law, tax law, competition law, bankruptcy law, all to a greater or lesser extent, have their definitions of groups in each Member State. For the most part these definitions differ even within the same Member State: it would appear that in this matter, legal science is suffering from an excess of quantity rather than from any shortage."[3]

This statement is very much applicable to the United Kingdom. It is proposed in this chapter to examine one aspect of the group phenomenon, that is, group indebtedness. This chapter is divided into two parts. The first part deals with the situation where the liability for the indebtedness of the group is assumed, that is, there is an agreement or undertaking to answer for the debts of the group. The second part will deal with liability imposed, that is, the circumstances in which the law imposes a liability or a disability on some members of a group for the debts of the other members of the group.

B. LIABILITY ASSUMED

The starting point for any analysis of the assumption of liability for group indebtedness is that hoary old chestnut, *Salomon* v. *Salomon & Co. Ltd.*[4] For the present purposes, there are certain features of the case which need to be highlighted. Mr. S had incorporated his business by selling it to S Ltd. in return for shares and a secured debenture. The company was wound up insolvent and the significant issue before the court was the validity of the debenture which, of course, if enforceable, had the effect of giving its holder priority to the unsecured creditors. The House of Lords held that the company (S Ltd.) was an entity separate from its members and as such was capable of contracting with its principal shareholder. And, as there were no other grounds for holding Mr. S liable for the debts of the company, or for invalidating the debenture, the debenture was enforceable.[5] This decision had two very important long term

---

[3] Petite, *The Conditions For Consolidation Under The 7th Company Law Directive* (1984) 21 C.M.L.R. 81, at 84.

[4] [1897] A.C. 22. On the implications of this case for the topic under discussion see Schmitthoff, *The Wholly Owned and the Controlled Subsidiary* [1978] J.B.L. 218.

[5] Admittedly Mr. S had assigned the debenture, but the assignee could take no better title than that possessed by Mr. S. As was stated by Professor Diamond, "Meanwhile Mr. Salomon scooped the pool with his floating charge in 1897" (*Security Interests In Property Other Than Land, A Consultative Document, 1986, H.M.S.O.*), at p. 38. For the final report see *A Review Of Security Interests In Property* (H.M.S.O., 1989).

implications for company law. First, it entailed that incorporators of a company could structure its capital so as to minimise the risk to them of the company's failure by taking some form of secured debenture; there is no explicit requirement that the investment of the incorporators in a company must necessarily to a significant extent be in the form of equity.[6] Secondly, the possibility of merely subordinating the debenture of Mr. S so that he would only be paid after the other creditors had been paid was not raised. The case was argued on the basis that the debenture was fully enforceable, or alternatively that Mr. S should be liable in full for the debts of the company. The issue of subordination, which in many situations would produce a fairer result, was simply never canvassed.[7]

It follows from *Salomon* v. *Salomon & Co. Ltd.* that any legal relationship between a creditor and "the group" will have to be effected with the individual corporate members of the group: "the separate legal existence of the constituent companies of the group has to be respected."[8] In the typical situation involving a loan to a company in a group, one of the members of the group will be the borrower (hereafter referred to as the principal debtor company) and the other company or companies (hereafter referred to as the secondary debtor company) will undertake some type of "secondary" liability. For example, the secondary debtor company may execute a guarantee or grant some type of security with respect to the liability of the principal debtor company. Thus there will be at least two separate and distinct legal relationships, and almost invariably a third. There will be a legal relationship between (i) the principal debtor company and its creditor; (ii) the secondary debtor company and the creditor; and (iii) the principal debtor company and the secondary debtor company. It would be possible, but highly unlikely, and legally extremely suspect, for this third legal relationship to be jettisoned.[9] It is proposed to deal with these three legal relationships in order.

C. RELATIONSHIP BETWEEN PRINCIPAL DEBTOR COMPANY AND CREDITOR

A creditor will obviously want to ensure that its claim, and where relevant any security, are valid and enforceable against the principal

---

[6] The only exception to this is that a public company must have an authorised minimum capital of £50,000: Companies Act 1985, s.118.

[7] There are precedents for this: see Insolvency Act 1986, s.74(2).

[8] *Ford & Carter Ltd.* v. *Midland Bank Ltd.* (1979) 129 New L.J. 543, at 544 *per* Lord Wilberforce (guarantee given to bank to cover the debts of the group did not cover a company which joined the group subsequently as a fresh guarantee covering the company had not been executed). See also *Adams* v. *Cape Industries plc* [1990] 2 W.L.R. 657 at 749–764.

[9] *Brown Shipley & Co. Ltd.* v. *Amalgamated Investment (Europe) B.V.* [1979] 1 Lloyd's L. Rep. 488 (parent guarantees debts of its subsidiary without there being apparently any contract between the parent and the subsidiary). This type of arrangement could give rise to difficulties with respect to section 238 of the Insolvency Act 1986 (transactions at an undervalue); this section will be examined later.

debtor company. Also, the liability of the secondary debtor company will often be dependent on their being a valid and presently enforceable claim against the principal debtor company. A transaction between the principal debtor company and a creditor could be challenged on the grounds that (i) the principal debtor company lacked capacity to enter into it; (ii) the directors of the principal debtor company in entering into the transaction did so for improper reasons and not for the purpose of furthering the interests of the principal debtor company or simply exceeded their authority; (iii) the transaction is not what it purports to be (the issue of sham transactions); (iv) that the conditions for the enforcement of the obligations of the principal debtor company have not been satisfied; or lastly, (v) the transaction is unenforceable because of the Insolvency Act 1986.

(i) Lack of capacity—the "pre-1989 position"

As regards the argument of want of capacity, any transaction between a creditor and the principal debtor company will prima facie only be enforceable against the latter if authorised by its objects. Normally a company's objects will authorise it to borrow money and execute security, and in the case of a trading company the court will imply these powers.[10] Also, many of the problems relating to a company's want of capacity were substantially eliminated by section 35 of the Companies Act 1985; this broadly provided that any transaction decided on by the directors was binding on the company unless the company could prove, in a situation where the transaction was not authorised by the company's objects, that the other party to the transaction had not acted in good faith.[11] The courts were disposed to give section 35 a broad interpretation so as to protect creditors against having their transactions declared unenforceable on the grounds of ultra vires. A good example of this was the recent decision of Sir Nicolas Browne-Wilkinson V.-C. in *TCB* v. *Gray*.[12] In that case, the seal of the company was affixed to a debenture by a person appointed by a power of attorney to act for a director of the company, although under the company's articles of association its seal had to be affixed by a director personally as there was no provision for doing this through an attorney. It was argued by the company that "since [the company] never sealed the debenture in the only way authorised by the articles" there was no transaction to which the company was a party and therefore the debenture was not enforceable against the

---

[10] See generally *Palmer's Company Law* (24th ed., Stevens & Sons, 1987), at pp. 661–664.
[11] On the definition of "good faith" see *Barclays Bank Ltd.* v. *TOSG Trust Fund Ltd.* [1984] BCLC 1, at 18: "a person acts in good faith if he acts genuinely and honestly in the circumstances of the case." The court also stressed in that case that good faith was not to be equated with reasonableness.
[12] [1986] BCLC 113 (the case involved section 9(1) of the European Communities Act 1972 which was reproduced in section 35 the Companies Act 1985). The decision was upheld on appeal but the *ultra vires* point did not have to be dealt with by the court: [1987] Ch. 458.

company. This argument was rejected by the court on the grounds that section 35 "applies to transactions which a company purports to enter into and deems them to be validly entered into."[13] In other words, appearances were all important and a person dealing with a company is, unless not acting in good faith, entitled to rely on something which the directors represent as being valid. Added to this, section 35(2) provided that a person dealing with a company was "not bound to enquire as to the capacity of the company" and thus a company's objects clause was further diluted as regards its "external effect" on transactions between a company and a third party.

(ii) Lack of capacity—the post-1989 position

The Companies Act 1989 section 108 replaces section 35 of the 1985 Act with three new provisions; sections 35, 35A and 35B. The new section 35 deals with the issue of the validity of acts which exceed the capacity of a company and its broad effect is to provide very wide protection to third parties who deal with a company in circumstances where a company enters into a contract not authorised by its objects clause. Section 35(1) provides that the "validity of an act done by the company shall not be called into question on the ground of lack of capacity by reason of anything in the company's memorandum." This, if anything, is more protective than old section 35.[14] In addition, new section 35B provides that a party to a transaction with a company is not "bound to enquire as to whether it is permitted by the company's memorandum" and thus precludes any possible argument that a person dealing with a company is deemed to have constructive notice of the company's articles or memorandum.[15]

(iii) Breach of director's duties—the pre-1989 position

It is trite law that directors in exercising their powers must act bona fide in the interests of the company. In the context of groups, this requires the directors of each company in a group to consider whether a given transaction is in the interests of that company.[16] Undoub-

---

[13] The court also decided that (i) the provision in the company's articles as to how it could seal its document constituted a limitation on the power of the directors but nevertheless section 35 deemed them to have the necessary authority to enter into the transaction, and (ii) although no formal meeting of the directors had been held, since all the directors had agreed to the transaction and the company had put forward what purported to a minute of the board, the company was bound by the transaction. On this latter point see also *International Sales & Agencies Ltd.* v. *Marcus* [1982] 3 All E.R. 551.

[14] For commentary see Furey, *The Companies Act 1989, A Practitioner's Guide*, (Jordans, 1990) Chap. 4.

[15] Note also the abolition of deemed notice by s.142 of the 1989 Act (inserting a new s.711A into the 1985 Act). It is submitted that there will be no need to invoke s.711A(2) with respect to limitations on a company's capacity since s.35B explicitly removes the duty of enquiry.

[16] See *Charterbridge Corporation Ltd.* v. *Lloyds Bank Ltd.* [1969] 2 All E.R. 1185, at 1194: "Each company in the group is a separate legal entity and the directors of a particular company are not entitled to sacrifice the interest of that company."

tedly, it will often be the case that the interests of a company, which is part of a group, will be so inextricably bound up with the welfare of the group, that what is in the interests of the group is in the interests of the company. This will almost invariably be the case with respect to a parent as regards its subsidiary. A subsidiary may not have the same compelling interest in preserving the other members of a group, but where a subsidiary is threatened by the failure of one of the members of a group then it will have an interest in preserving it. This for example would be the case where a member of a group supports another group member which markets the group's products. Where directors breach their duty by entering into a transaction without considering the interests of the company, this does not render the transaction void, but only voidable; the other party to the transaction will be able to enforce it unless he has actual knowledge, or is put on notice, that the directors are acting in breach of duty. In *Rolled Steel Products (Holdings) Ltd.* v. *British Steel Corporation*,[17] the Court of Appeal held that a guarantee and debenture executed by one company to secure the debts of another was unenforceable by the creditor company in whose favour they had been created as it "had actual knowledge of facts which showed that the giving of the guarantee and the debenture was an abuse of powers by the directors."[18]

The *Rolled Steel* decision created something of a frisson, but the reaction was probably exaggerated in so far as it was seen as a serious challenge to the validity of standard group guarantees. In a number of respects the facts were exceptional:

(i)   the case did not involve a group of companies in the strict sense; the principal and secondary debtor companies were controlled by the same individual but there was no other interrelationship (other than that of debtor and creditor) between them;

(ii) the debenture and guarantee were not executed in order to secure new monies but were in reality designed to secure a past indebtedness[19]; and

---

[17] [1986] Ch. 246. There have been a number of Australian cases in which guarantees within a group have been successfully challenged: see *Northside Developments Pty. Ltd.* v. *Registrar-General* (1990) 2 ACSR 161; *Seabird Corporation Ltd.* v. *Sherlock* (1990) 2 ACSR 111.

[18] Ibid., at 307.

[19] This is an important feature of the case for which a fuller statement of the facts is necessary. Somewhat simplified the facts were as follows: S controlled both RS Ltd. (the plaintiff company) and SS Ltd. RS Ltd. owed SS Ltd. £400,000. SS Ltd. owed C Ltd. £820,000, which was personally guaranteed by S. To protect the position of C Ltd. (and to reduce S's exposure on the guarantee), the following scheme was implemented. C Ltd. loaned £400,000 to RS Ltd. to enable it to repay its debt to SS Ltd. and SS Ltd in turn used this to repay part of its debt to C Ltd. In fact C Ltd.'s loan to RS Ltd. simply circulated through the parties' bank accounts back to C Ltd. on the same day. RS Ltd. executed a guarantee and debenture to secure SS Ltd.'s outstanding debt to C Ltd. This type of arrangement, which is really designed to secure an existing indebtedness and not to inject new money into a company, invariably gives rise to acute problems in company law: see, for example, *Re GT*

(iii) throughout the negotiations setting up the arrangement considerable misgivings were expressed as to its propriety.

Also, to concentrate on the ultimate decision in *Rolled Steel*, that the guarantee and debenture were unenforceable, is to miss the positive aspects of the judgment which strongly favour upholding the principle of security of transactions entered into by companies. As was stated by Slade L.J., "if something is *capable* of being performed as reasonably incidental to the attainment or pursuit" of a company's objects, the transaction will not be rendered *ultra vires* "merely because in a particular instance [the company's] directors, in performing the act in its name, are in truth doing so for purposes other than those set out in its memorandum."[20] Coupled with this, a person dealing in good faith is entitled to assume that the "directors are properly exercising such powers for the purposes of the company as set out in its memorandum."[21] What *Rolled Steel* indicates is that a person dealing with a company is entitled to rely on appearances; a position, as we have aleady seen, also arrived at in *TCB* v. *Gray* with respect to section 35 of the Companies Act 1985 and the issue of corporate capacity.

Section 35 of the 1985 Act also has a bearing on the question of the validity of transactions which exceed the authority of the board of directors (and this would include a limitation on such an authority which flows from the objects clause). This section provided that in favour of a person dealing with the company in good faith the powers of the directors to bind the company were deemed to be free of any limitation in the company's articles or memorandum. A third party dealing with the company was not bound to enquire as to any limitation of the powers of the directors.[22] Once a person dealing with a company knows that a transaction is outside the powers of the directors (whether the limitation is imposed by the articles or the memorandum), the presumption created by section 35 did not operate.

As was stated earlier, a person dealing with a company will not be able to enforce a transaction where he is put on notice that the directors are acting improperly in the sense of not pursing the company's interests. Even though involving a commercial setting, notice for this purpose includes some variant of "constructive notice." A person will have constructive notice where there are reasonable

Whyte & Co. Ltd. [1983] BCLC 311; *Re Destone Fabrics Ltd.* [1941] Ch. 319. It is unclear the extent to which these transactions are affected by s.245(2)(b) of the Insolvency Act 1986. Stewart, *Administrative Receivers and Administrators* (CCH, 1987), at 203 asserts that it may reverse the *Whyte* decision. It is difficult to see how this is the case. In a *Whyte* type of situation there is as a matter of substance no reduction or discharge. See Fletcher, *The Law Of Insolvency*, (Sweet & Maxwell, 1990) at 516 who interprets the subsection as covering the provision of "new" moneys.

[20] [1986] Ch. 246, at 295.
[21] *Ibid.*
[22] s.35(2).

grounds putting him on notice that the directors are abusing or exceeding their authority.[23]

(iv) Breach of director's duties—the post-1989 position

The structure of the 1989 reforms of ultra vires doctrine are more sophisticated than those of section 35 of the 1985 Act in that the 1989 legislation draws a clear distinction between on the one hand invalidity caused by lack of capacity on the part of the company, and on the other hand invalidity caused by lack of authority on the part of the board of directors. Section 35A deals with the latter issue (the sidenote to the section reads "Power of the directors to bind the company"). This section provides that in favour of a person dealing with a company in good faith the power of the directors will be deemed to be free of "any limitation under the company's constitution."[24] Obviously central to the operation of this provision is the concept of "good faith." Section 35A(2)(b) provides that a person "shall not be regarded as acting in bad faith by reason only of his knowing that an act is beyond the powers of the directors under the company's constitution."[25] The adverb "only" is crucial as it is designed to make it clear that knowledge of the fact that a transaction exceeds the directors' authority will not by itself constitute bad faith. However, this protection does not extend to other situations involving an abuse of authority by directors; for example where the directors are abusing their authority and not acting in the best interests of the company.[26]

(v) Sham transactions

The validity of a transaction entered into by a company can be challenged on the grounds that it is not the type of transaction authorised by the company's objects clause. Thus, for example, although a company may have capacity to pay salaries, a particular payment may nevertheless be challenged on the grounds that it constitutes a gift rather than payment of a salary for services rendered. The proper classification of a transaction will be determined by the courts and not by what the parties call it. As Oliver J. stated in *Re Halt Garage (1964) Ltd.*,[27] in connection with the question whether a

---

[23] See Bowstead, *The Law of Agency* (15th ed., Sweet & Maxwell, 1985), at 303–305; Elias, *Explaining Constructive Trusts*, (O.U.P. 1990), at 119–125.

[24] s.35A(1).

[25] Under the 1989 Act (as with the 1985 Act) the onus of showing want of good faith is on the company: s.35A(2)(c).

[26] This is designed to ensure compliance with Article 9(2) of the First Directive Dir. 68/151 (J.O. 1968, L 65/8; O.J. 1968(I), 41 which precludes limits on the "powers of the organs of the company" being invoked against a third party but obviously does not extend to abuse of its powers by an organ of the company.

[27] [1982] 3 All E. R. 1016, at 1042. See also *Aveling Barford Ltd.* v. *Perion Ltd.* [1989] BCLC 626 (purported sale an improper return of capital to a member of the company).

particular payment to a director constituted remuneration for services or merely a gift,

> "But of course what the company's articles authorise is the fixing of 'remuneration' which I take to mean a reward for the services rendered or to be rendered; and, whatever the terms of the resolutions passed and however described in the accounts or the company's books, the real question seems to me to be whether the payments really were 'directors' remuneration' or whether they were gratuitous distributions to a shareholder of capital dressed up as remuneration."

(vi) Conditions for enforcement

Even though a transaction giving rise to liability may be validly created, it will always be open to the principal debtor company to argue that the conditions giving the creditor the right to enforce the transaction have not arisen. One of the principal characteristics of security is the right of enforcement and, to the extent that this is in any way circumscribed, then to that extent it cuts down the quality of a creditor's security. Whether a transaction is enforceable in a given situation will depend primarily on the terms of the agreement between the parties. There have been two important recent developments which facilitate a creditor's right of enforcement against a defaulting debtor company. The first of these is the decision of Walton J. in *Bank of Baroda* v. *Panessar*.[28] In that case a debenture in favour of the plaintiff bank provided for the repayment on demand of all moneys secured by it.[29] The bank made a demand and when its demand was not met it appointed a receiver. The validity of the appointment was challenged on the grounds that (i) the demand did not specify the exact sum due and (ii) the company was not given a reasonable time in which to raise the moneys to pay off the debt. Both points were rejected by Walton J. As regards (i), he held that the validity of the notice was not dependent on it stating the exact amount due, or for that matter stating any figure at all.[30] As regards (ii),

---

[28] [1986] BCLC 497; [1987] Ch. 335.
[29] To be repayable on demand, it is necessary for the loan agreement to provide for this expressly. A loan made subject to "normal banking terms and conditions" will not be treated as being payable on demand: see *Cryne* v. *Barclays Bank plc* [1987] BCLC 548, 552, 556–557.
[30] Followed in *N.R.G. Vision Ltd.* v. *Churchfield Leasing Ltd.* [1988] BCLC 624. (Knox J. appeared to leave open the question as to whether an excessive demand would be valid: at p. 638). While the validity of the notice may not be dependent on it stating the exact sum due, an argument might be made that a notice stating an excessive figure that has been compiled negligently could give rise to liability given the relationship between the parties. Such a duty could be excluded and the exclusion would not be subject to the Unfair Contract Terms Act 1977 (see Sched. 1 (1) (e)); *Micklefield* v. *S.A.C Technology Ltd.* [1990] 1 W.L.R. 1002. Also, if the company is insolvent then it would be difficult to show that the defective notice caused any damage to the company; the problems of causation where a creditor improperly enforces a claim against an insolvent company have not as yet been fully worked out: see *Alexander* v. *Cambridge Credit Corporation Ltd.* (1987) 12 ACLR 202 for a related

Walton J. held that English law adopted the "mechanics of payment test" by which he meant that the debtor should be given a reasonable time in which to put into operation the normal machinery for discharging a debt. Given what Walton J. referred to as the "modern conditions... available for the transfer of money," the amount of time which the mechanics of payment test would require a creditor to give a debtor to enable the debtor to comply with the creditor's demand for payment (at least as regards a demand made during normal banking hours) would be extremely short. It was found to have been satisfied in *Bank of Baroda* v. *Panessar*[31] where the time allowed was between one and two hours.[32]

The second development of some importance as regards the right of enforcement relates to the situation where a receiver is appointed on grounds that are improper but after his appointment facts are unearthed that would have justified the original appointment. In *Byblos Bank SAL* v. *Al-Khudhairy*[33] a bank, in whose favour the company had issued a debenture, apparently made a premature demand for payment and appointed a receiver on the grounds that the company had breached the terms of the charge by failing to produce accounts and by making a loan to an associated company. The receiver discovered that the company was insolvent within the terms of section 223(d) of the Companies Act 1948 (inability to pay debts as they fell due)[34] and in these circumstances the bank was entitled by the terms of its debenture to appoint a receiver. The court held that the bank could rely on the company's insolvency to justify the appointment of the receiver although this was not the original basis on which the bank had initially sought to justify the appointment of the receiver.[35] A creditor will often discover new facts after the appointment of a receiver and it follows from *Byblos Bank* that if these

discussion on whether an auditor's negligence caused the loss to the company. Lastly, it is arguable that the debtor company is in as good a position as the creditor to assess the state of account between the parties (this would not necessarily be the case where payments were paid directly into the company's account by a third party).

[31] There was a lapse of about one hour between the demand and the appointment of the receiver in *Cripps (R.A.) & Son* v. *Wickenden* [1973] 1 W.L.R. 944 and the appointment was also held to be valid. In a number of Commonwealth jurisdictions the courts have held that the debtor company should be allowed a reasonable time in which to try to raise moneys to pay off the debt: *Ronald Elwyn Lister Ltd.* v. *Dunlop Canada Ltd.* (1982) 135 D.L.R. (3d) 1 (Canada); *Bunbury Foods Pty. Ltd.* v. *National Bank of Australasia* (1984) 51 A.L.R. 609 (Australia).

[32] An acceleration clause making a loan immediately repayable on failure to pay an instalment when due is not a penalty clause: *The Angelic Star* [1988] 1 F.T.L.R. 94; Pennington, *Bank Finance for Companies*, (Sweet & Maxwell, 1987) at p. 17.

[33] [1987] BCLC 232.

[34] See now s.123 of the Insolvency Act 1986.

[35] The proceedings in *Byblos Bank* were for summary judgment under Ord. 14. The court held that it would be futile to refer the matter to a full trial if the bank could show that it had grounds on which to justify the appointment of a receiver.

would have justified the appointment of a receiver then they can be relied upon.[36]

(vii) The Insolvency Act 1986

There are a range of provisions in the Insolvency Act 1986 that permit transactions to be challenged if a company goes into insolvent liquidation. These relate to (a) transactions at an undervalue, (b) preferences, and (c) defective floating charges. These will be dealt with in the next section. A transaction can also be challenged under section 244 as an extortionate credit transaction. This requires the terms of the transaction to be grossly exorbitant in terms of the risk being undertaken or otherwise grossly contravene, in the light of the risk being undertaken, the ordinary principles of fair dealing.[37] Given the difficulties of proving such a transaction,[38] it will seldom be successfully invoked and it is not proposed to deal with it in any detail.

D. RELATIONSHIP BETWEEN CREDITOR AND SECONDARY DEBTOR COMPANY

A significant aspect of consensual group indebtedness is the relationship between the creditor and the secondary debtor company. It will be assumed for the purpose of this part of the chapter that the debt owed by the principal debtor company is valid and has become payable, or alternatively the liability of the secondary debtor company is autonomous and independent of the liability of the principal debtor company.[39] The creditor, in its relationship with the secondary debtor company, will want to ensure that: (i) the transaction between it and the secondary debtor company is, as *created*, valid and enforceable and does not give rise to any counterclaims; (ii) that the right to *enforce* the secondary debtor company's liability is not in some way qualified; this will involve at least two separate issues: (a) the creditor, because of the manner in which its claim is enforced against the

---

[36] It has also been held that where a company acquiesces in the appointment of a receiver which is defective and does not challenge the appointment with reasonable promptness, it may be subsequently estopped from doing so: *Bank of Baroda* v. *Panessar* [1986] BCLC 497, at 511–514. In that case the alleged defect in the appointment was capable of being put right by the creditor if the company had timeously challenged the validity of the appointment. This, however, is not essential for the operation of the estoppel doctrine which is based on the inequity of allowing the representor to go back on his representation. See the decision of Morritt Q.C. (sitting as an acting High Court judge) in *Save Acoustics Ltd.* v. *Pimms Furnishing Ltd.* (January 11, 1985, unreported) in which he cited the dictum of Goff J. in *The Post Chaser* [1982] 1 All E.R. 19, at 26 on the nature of estoppel as that being applicable in this context.

[37] s.244(3).

[38] Although note the presumption that the transaction is extortionate if an application is made: s.244(3).

[39] See Goode, *Commercial Law*, (Penguin, 1982) at pp. 875–876 on the distinction between dependent and independent liability.

principal debtor company, may incur some liability towards the secondary debtor company, or (b) the enforcement of the creditor's claim may be impugned or constrained under the Insolvency Act 1986; and lastly, (iii) the creditor will not want to compete with any member of the group in the insolvency of another group member. It is proposed to deal with these issues in that order.

(i) Challenges to validity of transaction as created and counterclaims

The validity of a transaction can be challenged, as we have seen from the last section, on the grounds that it is outside the capacity of the company, or because it had been entered into by the directors not in the interests of the secondary debtor company but in order to further the interests of the parent company or those of the group. To have capacity to secure or guarantee the debts of a third party, a company will have to have a specific provision in its objects clause empowering it to do so.[40] However, a creditor will be able to rely on the reforms of the *ultra vires* doctrine in dealing with the secondary debtor company.

A more serious potential challenge to the validity of a transaction entered into by a secondary debtor company is that the directors did not consider the interests of the company but rather considered the interests of the group, or of some member within the group. This matter has to a large extent already been dealt with in the previous discussion of *Rolled Steel*. All that needs to be emphasised in the present context is that it will often be in the interests of the members of a group to guarantee the debts and liabilities of the other members of the group on the basis that they will all sink or swim together.

There is also the possibility that the circumstances of the creation of the charge could result in the secondary debtor company having a counterclaim against the creditor. Obviously any creditor runs the risk that the secondary debtor company, like any debtor, will raise a defence to its action. The question arises as to whether there are any special features of group indebtedness that give rise to unique problems. It will often be the case that the creditor will have acquired information with respect to the affairs of the principal debtor company and an issue of some importance is whether this can affect its legal relationships with the secondary debtor company. Assume, for example, that the information reveals that, as regards the secondary debtor company, the transaction is extremely imprudent. There are

[40] *Re Friary, Holyroyd and Healy's Breweries Ltd.* [1922] W.N. 293 (the obvious implication of this decision is that, in the absence of a provision empowering the company to guarantee its subsidiary's debentures, the transaction would have been *ultra vires*). It may be that a "general commercial company" will be deemed to have this power. This depends on whether or not it is incidental or conducive to the carrying on of trade or business generally. It is submitted that it should be so treated as to do otherwise is simply to ignore the realities of group trading activity. For the nature of the general commercial company see Companies Act 1989, s.110(1) (the (1) is omitted from the Queen's Printers copy).

two ways in which this information could be relevant to the liability of the creditor. It might give rise to a claim in negligence by the secondary debtor company, or it might indicate that, because of the transaction's imprudence, the directors of the secondary debtor company could not really have independently considered the interests of the secondary debtor company.[41]

As regards liability for negligence, the starting point is that intending contracting parties do not normally owe a duty of care to each other and thus, for example, "a stranger invited to sign a guarantee ... by a third party—perhaps a bank" is not owed a duty by the other party.[42] Accordingly, the creditor will have no duty to advise on the prudence of the loan and will owe no duty of care giving rise to liability. However, in many situations, the creditor and secondary debtor company will not be "strangers," and will often have had a long term business relationship. Where this is the case, the creditor could be held to owe a duty of care to the secondary debtor company where the latter has relied on the former for advice.[43]

The other way in which knowledge of the principal debtor's affairs might affect the rights of the creditor, is that it could indicate that the transaction was so imprudent that no reasonable board of directors could possibly have considered that it could be in the interests of the secondary debtor company. As a transaction can be rendered voidable where a person dealing with directors has been put on notice that they are not acting in the interests of the company, there may well be situations where knowledge of the principal debtor's affairs could affect the validity of the transaction between the creditor and the secondary debtor company.

---

[41] Other difficult issues could arise. For example, the information may be confidential and therefore the creditor would be under an obligation not to reveal it to the secondary debtor company. The point being discussed in the text is not, however, whether the information should be revealed but merely as to whether it should deter the creditor from entering into a transaction with the secondary debtor company. On other aspects of this problem see *Standard Investment Ltd.* v. *Canadian Imperial Bank of Commerce* (1985) 22 D.L.R. (4th) 410; noted (1986–87) 12 C.B.L.J. 211; *Marcel* v. *Commissioner of Police of the Metropolis* [1991] 1 All E.R. 845; Watts, *The Companies Amendment Acts 1983 and 1985—the need for further reform* in *Contemporary Issues in Company Law* (ed., Farrar, 1987) at 9.

[42] *O'Hara* v. *Allied Irish Banks Ltd.* [1985] BCLC 52; see also *Redmond* v. *Allied Irish Banks plc* [1987] F.L.R. 307.

[43] The possibility has been mooted of there being a duty of care where a bank makes an imprudent loan to a customer who has relied on it for advice: *Butterworths Encyclopedia of Banking Law*, (Butterworths, 1990) at C35. There may be a duty of the part of a bank to explain the essential nature of the transaction ([1987] 3 J.I.B.L. 181, at 182) and if the contract contains an unusually onerous clause a duty to draw it to the attention of the other party may exist: *Interfoto Picture Library Ltd.* v. *Stiletto Visual Programmes Ltd.* [1988] 1 All E.R. 348; Cranston, *The Banker's Duty of Disclosure* (1990) J.B.L. 163. See also *Bank of Baroda* v. *Shah*, (1988) 138 New L.J. 98, C.A., in which a surety unsuccessfully attempted to challenge the validity of a guarantee because of the undue influence of the creditor.

(ii) Creditor's right to enforce its claim

Often the right of the creditor to enforce its claim against the secondary debtor company will be dependent on it having a claim that is enforceable against the principal debtor company. Any restriction on the right of, or the manner in which a creditor can enforce its claim against the principal debtor company, will have a knock on effect as regards its rights against the secondary debtor company. The only development of importance with respect to the right of enforcement is the clear recognition of the duty owed by a mortgagee in exercising his power of sale "to take reasonable care to obtain the true market value of the property at the time when he chooses to sell."[44] A similar duty is owed by a receiver and the duty extends to the guarantor of the mortgagor's debt.[45] There is nothing in the context of group indebtedness which appears to give rise to any unique difficulty in applying these rules.

Of greater significance with respect to a creditor's right to enforce its rights with respect of group indebtedness is the Insolvency Act 1986 which contains a number of provisions which have the effect of upsetting certain transactions between a company and its creditors in the event of the company being wound up insolvent.[46] Liquidation is a collective procedure designed to provide a class remedy for the distribution of company's assets on its liquidation. As a general principle, the order in which the claims of a company's creditors are paid off in a liquidation will mirror the pre-liquidation entitlement of the creditors. There are a number of provisions in the Insolvency Act 1986 which depart from this principle and which are designed to prevent one creditor obtaining an unfair advantage over other creditors in circumstances where a company's insolvency is imminent.[47] As was stated earlier, these provisions also have relevance to any claim that a creditor may have against the principal debtor company. But probably they have a greater significance for the creditor's claims against the secondary debtor company. The relevant provisions are those dealing with (a) transactions at an undervalue, (b) preferences, (c) and defective floating charges. In the following sections it will be assumed that the transaction is between a company and a person not connected with it within the meaning of section 249 of the Insolvency Act 1986.

---

[44] *Predeth* v. *Castle Phillips Finance Co. Ltd.* (1986) 279 Estates Gazette 1355.

[45] These rules are set out succinctly in Stewart, *Administrative Receivers and Administrators*, *op. cit*, at pp. 75–78; on the exclusion of such duties see *Bishop* v. *Bonham* [1988] BCLC 656. Earlier cases suggested that the duty involved an extension of negligence to supplement equity but more recent cases see it as flowing from the mortgagor/mortgagee relationship: *Parker-Tweedale* v. *Dunbar Bank (No. 1)* [1990] 2 All E.R. 577; *China and South Sea Bank Ltd.* v. *Ton* [1990] 2 W.L.R. 56.

[46] In this context insolvency includes administration under Part II of the Insolvency Act 1986.

[47] For the underlying rationale of these principles see Prentice, *The Effect of Insolvency on Pre-Liquidation Transactions* in *Company Law In Change* (1987, Stevens & Son, ed. B. G. Pettet).

(a) *transactions at an undervalue—section 238*

Where a company goes into liquidation, or an administration order is made, and during the "relevant time" it had entered into a "transaction at an undervalue," and at that time the company was insolvent or the transaction rendered it insolvent,[48] the liquidator or administrator can apply to have the position restored to what it would have been had the transaction not been entered into. "Relevant time" is defined in section 240 as being "at a time in the period of 2 years ending with the onset of insolvency." A transaction at an undervalue is one where the company makes a gift or receives no consideration, or the consideration received by the company in "money or money's worth, is significantly less than the value, in money or money's worth, of the consideration provided by the company."[49] The court, however, cannot make an order restoring, to the extent that it thinks fit, the former status quo if it is satisfied that the company entered into the transaction in good faith and for the purpose of its business, and there were reasonable grounds for believing that the transaction would benefit the company.[50] Thus, broadly speaking, gratuitous transactions entered into by an insolvent company within a period of two years preceding its insolvent winding up will prima facie fall within the section 238.

There are a number of aspects of this section that need to be highlighted:

(i) the two year period runs from the time the transaction was "entered into,"[51] and thus the date of performance will not be relevant in assessing the application of section 238. This could be important for "security"[52] provided by a secondary debtor company under an agreement that is to endure for a considerable period of time;

(ii) in determining whether a transaction at least prima facie falls within the section the "consideration" provided by the other party to the secondary debtor company has to be measured against the consideration provided by the secondary debtor company. What this requires is a "comparison to be made between the value obtained by the company and the value of the consideration provided by the company. Both values must be measurable in money or money's worth and both must be considered from the company's point of view."[53] "Considera-

---

[48] This is a combination of s.238 and 242. The definition of insolvency is that set out in s.123 of the Act.

[49] s.238(4)(b).

[50] s.238(5).

[51] s.238(2); "transaction" is defined in section 436.

[52] This is a somewhat question—begging concept and will be developed later.

[53] *Re MC Bacon Ltd.* [1990] BCLC 324 at 340. Section 238(4)(b) does not refer to consideration "received" by the company although it does refer to consideration "provided" by the company. From this it could be argued that if the consideration (in the sense of executed benefit under the contract) is provided to the primary

tion" in the context of section 238(4)(b) is probably used in its common law contractual sense and not in the wider sense attributed to it in the context of defective floating charges where it means "because of the existence of."[54] In many situations the actual benefit to the secondary debtor company will be very difficult to value and where the "material" benefit of the transaction is enjoyed by the primary debtor company there will be a greater likelihood that the transaction will be treated as one at an undervalue. Also, as the dictum of Millett J. cited above makes clear, both sides of the transaction must be capable of valuation in money or money's worth. If this is not possible then the transaction will be treated as a transaction at an undervalue; any other interpretation would enable the section to be evaded by the use of derisory consideration.[55]

(iii) broadly speaking, a transaction, although at an undervalue, will not be impeachable if the "company" entered into it in "good faith and for the purpose of carrying on its business" and there were "reasonable grounds for believing" that it would benefit the company.[56] The good faith and the belief appear to be those of the company and therefore a creditor could be prejudiced even though it had acted in all good faith.[57] These mental acts (*i.e.* good faith and belief) on the part of the company will be provided by its directors. If the directors dissemble, there is little likelihood that some type of estoppel will operate to protect the third party. First, because it is difficult to see how an estoppel could override the express provisions of a statute (estoppel prevents you from denying something of which you are otherwise capable). Secondly, as section 238 operates in the context of a liquidation or administration, the acts of the directors would not normally estop the liquidator or administrator.[58] The right to bring an

---

debtor company rather than the secondary debtor company then this can be taken into account in determining if the transaction falls within section 238. An example of this would be loan which the secondary debtor company guarantees. However, such an interpretation would enable the section to be evaded and it would also run contrary to the normal meaning of consideration which imports a relationship between two parties. Accordingly, it is submitted that the interpretation put forward in the text is the correct one.

[54] *Re Yeovil Glove Co. Ltd.* [1965] Ch. 148.

[55] See Treitel, *The Law Of Contract* (7th ed., Sweet & Maxwell, 1987) at 68. For other difficulties in connection with valuation see Goode, *Legal Problems of Credit and Security* (2nd ed., Sweet & Maxwell, 1988) at 206–209.

[56] s.238(5). The burden of proof is probably on the other party and this will require him to prove something that is not within his knowledge. But since the administrator and liquidator are officers of the court, the court can probably seek their assistance if the issue is raised.

[57] This appears to be a variant of the test in *Re Lee Behrens & Co.* [1932] 2 Ch. 46. See also the defence provided in section 241(2) broadly in favour of bona fide transferees who give value.

[58] *cf. Re Exchange Securities and Commodities Ltd.* [1987] BCLC 425. There is always that argument of last resort, the rule in *Ex. p. James* (1874) L.R. 9 Ch. 609 which could give

action with respect to a transaction at an undervalue is vested in the liquidator and nothing the directors do can deprive him of it. If absence of good faith is proven, the *Rolled Steel* doctrine could also come into operation and section 241(4) provides that section 238 does not prejudice the "availability of any other remedy."[59] Because of this, it is arguable that section 238 was not really needed; however there are differences between section 238(5) and *Rolled Steel*.[60] The major differences between *Rolled Steel* and section 238(5) would appear to be: (a) *Rolled Steel* is not dependent on liquidation for its operation and a transaction rendered voidable by it is not subject to a two year period of challenge; (b) if a trust of the company's property is imposed where *Rolled Steel* is invoked, the court may have to recognise the proprietary right of the company and will have no discretion about making any other type of order; (c) *Rolled Steel* could cover a situation where the company obtains equivalent consideration; a diminution in the company's assets is not a *sine qua non* to showing breach of duty by the directors[61]; (d) the court has a wider range of remedies to deal with a section 238 transaction than it would have to deal with a transaction caught by *Rolled Steel*; (e) in *Rolled Steel* the good faith of the person dealing with the company is relevant whereas, as we have seen, under section 238 it is the good faith of the company that is relevant; (f) *Rolled Steel* does not involve any test of reasonableness whereas section 238(5)(b) does; (g) lastly, recovery under section 238 would probably, at least prima facie,[62] not benefit secured creditors whereas recovery under the *Rolled Steel* doctrine would probably enure for their benefit and the court would have no jurisdiction to order otherwise.[63]

rise to an argument that it is inequitable to permit the liquidator to invoke section 238 where the directors had misled the creditor. However, it is difficult to see how the liquidator would be acting in a way that is inequitable by invoking the section on behalf of the creditors who have been prejudiced. Also, this rule only applies to a court ordered winding up: *Commissioners of Customs and Excise* v. *T.H. Knitwear Ltd.* [1988] BCLC 195.

59 The subsection also applies to transactions with respect to which the company has no capacity to enter into.

60 Another possible justification for s.238(5) is that of symmetry to bring corporate insolvency and personal bankruptcy into line: see section 339.

61 This is not as far fetched as it appears as a "company is entitled to the unbiased judgment of every one of its directors": *per* Vinelott J., *Movitex Ltd.* v. *Bulfield* [1988] BCLC 104 at 118.

62 Whatever the prima facie position, the court can under section 238(3) make such order as it thinks fit for restoring the position to what it would have been had the transaction not taken place. However, in *Re MC Bacon Ltd. (No. 2)* [1990] BCLC 607 at 612 the court held that section 239(3), a subsection similar to section 238(3), was not intended "to be exercised to enable a debenture holder to obtain the benefit of the proceedings brought by the liquidator."

63 For a general discussion of this issue see Prentice, *Creditor's Interests and Director's Duties* (1990) 10 OJLS 265 at 271–273; Oditah, *Wrongful trading* (1990) L.M.C.L.Q. 205. See also *Re a company (No. 00359 of 1987)* [1988] Ch. 210 at 221 (possible recovery

71

(iv) As regards the transactions at an undervalue at least one special problem arises in the context of groups; this relates to the granting of security by the secondary debtor to secure the debts of principal debtor. In *Re MC Bacon Ltd.*[64] Millett J. held that the granting of security by a company in favour of its bank (that is a two party situation) to secure an existing indebtedness did not constitute a transaction at an undervalue since the transaction did not "deplete its assets or diminish their value."[65] All it did was readjust the rights of creditors. At first blush this seems counterintuitive, but on examination it is respectfully submitted that it is correct. Where assets are encumbered the company has an equity of redemption which is less valuable than assets in an unencumbered form. However, the balance sheet position of the company remains unaltered and the enforcement of the security to pay off the debt cannot constitute a transaction at an undervalue.[66] The reasoning in *Re MC Bacon Ltd.*, however, would not apply to the hypothetical situation being discussed. Where security is given to secure the debts of another person, a new liability is created and, although admittedly contingent, it nevertheless is capable of constituting a transaction at an undervalue. This may create valuation difficulties and of course if valuation cannot be made then, as was stated earlier, the transaction would be treated at an undervalue.

(v) As regards remedies, section 238(3) empowers the court to make such order as it thinks fit for restoring the position to what it would have been had the transaction not taken place. The commentary as to the court's remedial power in paragraph (iii)(g) also applies here. Section 241 then spells out in greater detail the type of specific orders that the court may make. The court can for example revive the obligation of a guarantor which was discharged by the transaction at an undervalue or order that security be provided for any order made under the section.[67]

(b) *preferences—section 239*

This section, like section 238, applies where a company goes into insolvent liquidation or an administrator is appointed. The section strikes at preferences given during the "relevant time." In the case of a person not connected with the company (the situation under discus-

---

under sections 213 or 214 of the Insolvency Act 1986 could not constitute assets for the purpose of conferring jurisdiction to wind up a foreign company).

[64] [1990] BCLC 324.

[65] *Ibid.*, at 340.

[66] See Goode, *Principles of Corporate Insolvency Law* (Sweet & Maxwell, 1990) at p. 144 who points out that payment of a debt cannot constitute a transaction at an undervalue since the diminution in the company's assets is matched by a corresponding reduction in its liabilities.

[67] s.241(1)(e) and s.242(2)(f) respectively.

sion) "relevant time" is "the period of 6 months ending with the onset" of the company's insolvency.[68] A preference occurs where a company does anything that puts a creditor "or a surety or guarantor" for the company's debts into a better position than he would have been had it not been done and in doing the act the company was "influenced . . . by a desire" to put him in this position. It is important to note that it is not the fact of preference which is dispositive, but this fact coupled by a desire on the part of the company to bring about this state of affairs. This could obviously catch transactions between a creditor and a secondary debtor company. However, it is of significance that it is a desire of the insolvent company to prefer its creditor that is caught, and if the secondary debtor company wants to prefer the creditor of the principal debtor company which, for example, subsequently goes into insolvent liquidation, the section will have no bearing on that transaction. If of course the secondary debtor company goes into liquidation then the payment to the creditor company could constitute a preference if it discharges a liability of the secondary debtor company.

The unfair preference provisions present obvious difficulties in situations where, for example, a company is indebted to another company and as a condition of continued support the creditor company requires additional security.[69] In *Re MC Bacon Ltd.*[70] the court emphasised that a major requirement of section 239 was the desire on the part of the debtor company to "produce the effect mentioned in the subsection" (*i.e.* subsection (4)(b)),[71] and also that the company must have "positively wished to improve the creditor's position in the event of its own insolvent liquidation."[72] This interpretation of the section, particularly the strong emphasis placed on the subjective desire to effect a preference, should make it easier to provide financial support for a company that is in financial difficulties. It will also make it more difficult for the transaction to be challenged as a preference.

(c) *defective floating charges—section 245*

A floating charge created in favour of person not connected with the company within a period of 12 months preceding the onset of a company's insolvency will be invalid except to the extent of any

---

[68] s.240(1)(b).
[69] If the security takes the form of a floating charge then this would be caught by the "new monies" requirement of s.245. See also Wood, *English and International Set-Off*, (Sweet & Maxwell, 1989), at para. 7–29 dealing with the issue of preference in the context of set-off in a group context.
[70] [1990] BCLC 324, the first case to deal with the meaning of s.239. Millet J. made it clear that because of the altered language of the section the old case law on fraudulent preferences was no longer of assistance (at 325b).
[71] *Ibid.*, at 335f.
[72] *Ibid.*, at 336a–b. Such a desire merely had to be present and did not have to be the factor which tipped the scales or that without it the company would not have entered into the transaction (at 336b–d).

money, goods or services[73] that swell the assets of the company. Thus a floating charge executed by a secondary debtor company to secure the debts of the principal debtor company, will only be valid to the extent that the *secondary debtor company's* assets are increased. However, section 245(2)(b), despite the recommendation of the Cork Committee to the contrary,[74] also provides that the charge is valid to the extent that any debt of the company is reduced or discharged. This could be of significance to the relationship between the secondary debtor company and the creditor.

E. COMPETITION BETWEEN CREDITOR AND GROUP MEMBERS

A creditor will not want to compete, in the winding up of a member of the group, with other group members. There are a number of ways in which the interests of the creditor can be or are protected against having to compete with the other members of the group in the insolvency of one of the group members. Protection can be provided by (i) agreement, (ii) the principle of double proof, or (iii) by the Insolvency Act 1986.

(i) Agreement

The creditor, to protect its position *vis á vis* other group members, may enter into an agreement with members of the group whereby they agree to subordinate their claims to those of the creditor. Assuming that the arrangement is not carried out by means of some type of subordination trust, the question arises as to whether a straightforward subordination agreement would be enforceable. There is high authority for the proposition that creditors cannot contract out of the *pari passu* principle of distribution in a winding up. For example, in the *British Eagle* case Lord Cross stated that contracting out of the *pari passu* principle must "be contrary to public policy."[75] But the facts in that case were quite different from the situation where, for example, two creditors agree simply to re-arrange the order of their claims in the insolvency of a mutual debtor. *British Eagle* involved the situation where A (which was insolvent) agreed that debts owed to it by B and C could be set off against debts owed by it to B and C. This could confer a preference if B or C was a creditor and the other was a debtor of A. More importantly, it would have the effect of prejudicing the other creditors of A not parties to the agreement. Where there is no question of preference or prejudice then there is no reason why a

---

[73] This is a very loose interpretation of section 245(2) which also covers the discharge of any debt. For the detailed operation of the section see Sealy and Milman, *Annotated Guide to the 1986 Insolvency Act* (2nd ed., CCH, 1988) at 271–273.

[74] Cmnd. 8558 (1982), at para. 1564.

[75] *British Eagle International Airlines Ltd.* v. *Compagnie Nationale Air France* [1975] 1 W.L.R. 758 at 780; *Carreras Rothmans Ltd.* v. *Freeman Mathews Treasure Ltd.* [1984] BCLC 420 at 432.

subordination agreement should not be enforced. In *Horne* v. *Chester & Fein Property Developments Pty. Ltd.*,[76] an Australian case, the court held that an agreement between creditors departing from the *pari passu* principle would be enforced in the winding up of an insolvent company provided it did not affect creditors who were not a party of the agreement and, it was on this latter basis, that the *British Eagle* case was distinguished.

(ii) The principle of double proof

One of the consequences of the *pari passu* principle is that there can only be one dividend with respect to a given debt and this precludes proof being lodged in the liquidation of a company for what is in substance the same debt. This operates to preclude a surety from lodging proof in the liquidation of the principal debtor if the creditor has not been paid off. If the "guarantor pays [the creditor] in *full* prior to the time that the principal creditor *has lodged his proof against the principal debtor*",[77] then the guarantor can lodge proof. This rule is of obvious importance in the context of group liability as, where there are cross-guarantees, it will preclude the guarantor company from proving in the insolvency of the principal debtor company unless the creditor has been paid off.

(iii) The Insolvency Act 1986

The provisions of the Insolvency Act 1986, dealing with preferences, and defective floating charges (which have already been dealt with) can operate to preclude competition between a creditor and a secondary debtor company in the winding up of the principal debtor or to swell the assets of the primary debtor company. Where a transaction is between "connected persons," and this would cover companies that are part of the same group,[78] then the sections are more far reaching in their effect than when this relationship does not pertain. A combination of techniques are used: the time periods within which the transaction can be challenged is extended, sometimes there is a presumption that the transaction is tainted, and the need to show that the company was insolvent at the time of the transaction is entered into is jettisoned. First as regards transactions at an undervalue, there is a rebuttable presumption that the company was insolvent at the time the transaction is entered into.[79] Second, as regards preferences, the period within which a transaction can be challenged is two years prior to the insolvency; there is a rebuttable presumption of insolvency,[80] and, more importantly, a preference will

---

[76] (1987) 11 ACLR 485; Wood, *English and International Set-Off* at pp. 222–224.
[77] Wood, *The Problems of Set-Off: Contingencies, Build-Ups and Charge-Backs* (1987) 8 Com. Law. 262, at 263; see also Derham, *Set-Off*, (O.U.P. 1987) at pp. 86–93; *Seabird Corporation Ltd.* v. *Sherlock* (1990) 2 ACSR 111.
[78] Insolvency Act 1986, ss.249 and 435.
[79] s.240(2).
[80] s.240(1)(a) and 240(2) respectively.

be presumed, "unless the contrary is shown."[81] In other words, where connected persons are concerned, the fact of preference is sufficient to bring the transaction within section 239.[82] As regards floating charges covered by section 245, a floating charge in favour of a connected person can be challenged within a two year period and there is no need to show that the company was insolvent at the time the charge was effected.[83]

F. RELATIONSHIP BETWEEN THE GROUP MEMBERS

It is not proposed to deal with this in any detail. Normally the group members will have entered into some type of legal arrangement with respect to their liability for group indebtedness. The factors bearing on the validity of these arrangements are not dissimilar to those affecting the validity of any transaction with the creditor. Where one member of the group enters into a transaction with the creditor for another member of the group but receives nothing from that member, this will be a gratuitous transaction and could give rise to difficulties.[84] Such a transaction could be challenged under section 238 as a transaction at an undervalue. The special rules relating to transactions between connected persons have already been dealt with. Also of relevance to intra-group claims is section 74(2) of the Insolvency Act 1986 which precludes a member from competing with a creditor in a winding up with respect to any sum due to the member, by "way of dividends, profits or otherwise."[85]

G. OBLIGATIONS IMPOSED

In this section it is proposed to deal with the issue of obligations imposed, that is, situations where the law imposes on one of the members of the group liability for the debts of another member even though there is no agreement on its part to answer for that other member's liability. For the purposes of discussion, it will be assumed that it is the parent on whom liability is sought to be imposed.[86] There are two principal devices that could be used to impose such liability: piercing the corporate veil of the subsidiary so as to make the parent liable for the debts of its subsidiary and liability for wrongful trading under section 214 of the Insolvency Act 1986. Also of relevance, is

---

[81] s.238(5).
[82] In the poorly reported case of *Re Allen Fairhead & Sons Ltd.* (1971) 115 S.J. 244, concerning a transaction between two companies controlled by the same persons, Brightman J. held that a person could not negotiate with himself any more than he could put pressure on himself and therefore the payment of one company to the other should be treated as a fraudulent preference under the pre-1986 law.
[83] s.245(3)(a) and s.245(4).
[84] See *Brady* v. *Brady* [1988] BCLC 20, on appeal [1989] A.C. 755.
[85] See *Re LB Holliday & Co. Ltd.* [1986] BCLC 227.
[86] This could at the end of the day make the other subsidiaries also answerable if the parent is wound up.

liability for fraudulent trading under section 213 of the Insolvency Act 1986, and the recent decision of the Court of Appeal in *West Mercia Safety Ltd.* v. *Dodd.*[87]

(i) Piercing the corporate veil

In certain circumstances the courts will ignore the separate identity of a company and hold its members liable for its debts. There are a number of cases where the courts have done this in the context of groups so as to make a parent liable for its subsidiary's debts.[88] The starting point is, however, the principle in *Salomon* with the consequence that prima facie a parent will not be answerable for the liabilities of its subsidiary. Also, as we have seen, the incorporators of a company do not have to inject into a company any minimum amount of equity and there has been no attempt, in the United Kingdom, to develop any doctrine which would subordinate the debts of a parent in the winding up of its subsidiary. The only qualification to this is the requirement in section 118 of the Companies Act 1985 that a public company possess an authorised minimum capital of £50,000. This figure is derisory.

Although the courts do pierce the corporate veil, the case law does not permit any confident prediction as to when they will do so; the cases tend to hunt in packs of two, each case reaching a different result on almost identical facts. In so far as generalisation is possible, there is a likelihood that the court will pierce the corporate veil in a parent-subsidiary situation where: (a) the subsidiary is grossly under-capitalised, (b) the affairs of the parent and the subsidiary are commingled, and (c) the subsidiary is set up to enable the parent to perpetrate a fraud, although as regards this aspect of the rule the desire to limit liability does not constitute fraud.[89] However, piercing the corporate veil is very much the exception to the rule and probably in the majority of situations the courts will refuse to do so.

(ii) Wrongful trading—section 214 of the Insolvency Act 1986

Of greater importance as regards a parent's liability for the obligations of its subsidiary, is section 214 of the Insolvency Act 1986. Under this section directors of a company which goes into insolvent liquidation can be ordered to "make such contribution (if any) to the company's assets as the court thinks proper."[90] Such an order can be made where the director knew or ought to have concluded that there was no reasonable prospect that the company could have avoided going into insolvent liquidation and the director failed to take every

---

[87] [1988] BCLC 250.
[88] It is important to note that when the parent is made liable by this device the principle of limited liability is not jettisoned but merely comes into operation at a different point.
[89] See generally Gower, *Principles of Modern Company Law* (4th ed. (Stevens & Sons)), Ch. 6; *Adams* v. *Cape Industries plc* [1990] 2 W.L.R. 657.
[90] s.214(1).

step that he ought to have reasonably have taken to minimise potential loss to the company's creditors.[91] In determining whether a director did take every step which he ought to have taken, the director will be deemed not only to possess the actual skill and knowledge which he has but also to possess the "general knowledge, skill and experience that may reasonably be expected of a person carrying out the same functions."[92]

An important feature of section 214 is that it applies not only to *de iure* directors but also extends to a "shadow director," defined as a person in accordance with whose "directions or instructions the directors of the company are accustomed to act"[93] but excluding those who advise the directors in a professional capacity. The definition of shadow director will in many situations cover a parent company as it will be extremely difficult for the parent, particularly where the subsidiary is wholly owned, to rebut the inference that the subsidiary acted in accordance with its instructions. For example, it is arguable (but far from clear) that *Re Augustus Barnett & Son Ltd.*,[94] a case dealing with the fraudulent trading section in the 1948 Act,[95] would be decided differently under section 214. In that case Augustus Barnett was the wholly owned subsidiary of Rumasa and it had consistently traded at a loss. The accounts of Augustus Barnett contained a "letter of comfort" to the effect that Rumasa would continue to "provide such additional working capital as is necessary to enable the company to continue to trade at its current level of activity for a period of not less than 12 months" from the date on which the letter of comfort was given. Rumasa went into liquidation on the grounds of insolvency and the liquidator sought an order making Rumasa liable under the fraudulent trading section of the 1948 Act. It was argued that (i) by giving the auditors letters of comfort, (ii) by providing subsidies and (iii) by making statements of continued support, Rumasa had induced the board of Augustus Barnett to continue trading and this was sufficient to make the Rumasa liable as a person who has carried on the business of Augustus Barnett. The argument was unsuccessful as the court found that there was no fraudulent intent on the part of those who actually carried on the business of the Augustus Barnett, namely the directors of Augustus Barnett, and therefore there was no basis for invoking the section. The question arises as to what the outcome of a case like *Augustus Barnett* would be under section 214. The crucial factors in answering this are (i) would Rumasa be treated as a shadow director and, if so, (ii) did it take every step that it ought to have taken to minimise loss to the creditors of Augustus Barnett? As to the first question, one can only speculate, but it is difficult to imagine that a

---

[91] s.214(2) and (3).
[92] s.214(4).
[93] s.251.
[94] [1986] BCLC 170; noted Prentice, (1987) 103 L.Q.R. 11.
[95] s.332; now s.213.

parent would not exercise detailed control over the affairs of a subsidiary which it had over the years supported to the tune of £4,000,000. Assuming that the parent was a shadow director, the second question is whether it would have satisfied the defence in section 214(3): had it taken every step it ought to have taken with a view to minimising the loss to Augustus Barnett's creditors? The answer to this is probably no. It could be argued that since the letter of comfort did not legally oblige Rumasa to compensate in any way the creditors of Augustus Barnett from their point of view it had done nothing and the doing of nothing can hardly constitute the taking of every step with a view to minimising the potential loss to the company's creditors.[96] But there may be situations where it is reasonable to assume that the steps which the directors have taken, although not providing legal protection to the creditors, will enable a company to sort out its problems and be in a position to satisfy the claims of its creditors. If a parent company which is a shadow director were to be made liable under section 214 for failing to take steps which legally protected the subsidiary's creditors, it would be difficult to resist the extension of this reasoning to cover individuals who are directors. Such a standard it is submitted is unrealistically demanding.

(iii) Fraudulent trading—section 213 of the Insolvency Act 1986

Also of relevance is section 213 of the Insolvency Act 1986 which provides that those who carried on the business of the company so as to defraud its creditors may, on the application of the liquidator, be ordered to contribute to the assets of the company. In view of section 214, it is difficult to see when this section would be invoked.[97]

(iv) Director's duties to creditors

In *West Mercia Safety Ltd.* v. *Dodd,*[98] the Court of Appeal held that directors owed a duty to creditors where a company was insolvent and they continued to carry on business. Dillon L.J. cited with approval the dictum of Street C.J. in the Australian case of *Kinsela* v. *Russell Kinsela Pty. Ltd. (In Liquidation)*[99]:

> "In a solvent company the proprietary interests of the shareholders entitle them as a general body to be regarded as the

---

[96] A more plausible argument would be that the *de iure* directors of Augustus Barnett are within the defence of s. 214(3) since it would be reasonable for them to assume that the parent company would stand behind its subsidiary.

[97] Criminal sanctions can be imposed under section 458 of the Companies Act 1985 for fraudulent trading. In the recent decision of *R.* v. *Kemp* [1988] BCLC 217 the court held that the phrase "for any fraudulent purpose" could cover the defrauding of the company's customers.

[98] [1988] BCLC 250.

[99] [1986] 4 N.S.W.L.R. 722, at 730; see Sealy, *Directors' "Wider" Responsibilities—Problems Conceptual, Practical and Procedural* (1987) 13 Mon. U.L. Rev. 164; Prentice, *Creditor's Interests and Director's Duties* (1990) 10 O.J.L.S. 265.

company when questions of the duty of directors arise. If, as a general body, they authorise or ratify a particular action of the directors, there can be no challenge to the validity of what the directors have done. But where a company is insolvent the interests of the creditors intrude. They become prospectively entitled, through the mechanism of liquidation, to displace the power of the shareholders and directors to deal with the company's assets. It is in a practical sense their assets and not the shareholders' assets that, through the medium of the company, are under the management of the directors pending either liquidation, return to solvency, or the imposition of some alternative administration."

This could obviously have a bearing on intra-group dealings. If the directors of one of the companies do something to the prejudice of the company's non-group creditors at a time when the company is insolvent then the transaction may be set aside by the liquidator or the directors could be made personally liable.

CONCLUSION

It is clear that in many situations a parent will be liable for the debts of its subsidiary if the latter goes into insolvent liquidation. Liability will arise either because of agreement or because it has been imposed by the law. Although the principle in the *Salomon* case is the starting point for determining liability of members of a group for each other's debts the reality is that in many situations the principle will either be contracted out of by the parties or circumvented by rules of law.

V

Legal Elements and Policy Decisions in Regulating Groups of Companies

Professor Klaus J Hopt*

1. THE PROBLEM

A. Facts

By 1965 when for the first time West Germany enacted special rules of law governing groups of companies (*Konzernrecht*: para. 291 *et seq.* of the *Aktiengesetz* or Stock Corporation Act of 1965) it was estimated that 70 per cent. of all German corporations and 20 per cent. of the limited liability companies (GmbH) were no longer independent enterprises.[1] Since then, *economic concentration* has progressed steadily as the regular inquiries of the German Monopolies Commission reveal, even though recently the rate of increase of such concentration appears to have diminished.[2] According to a recent survey the autonomous corporate enterprise belongs largely to the past and at least 40 per cent. of the GmbHs representing 90 per cent. of the capital of all such companies belong to groups.[3] This is not a special German characteristic; in all other Western industrialised countries, groups of companies are not only a reality but, economically speaking, the rule.[4]

It is true that *merger control* legislation has helped to slow down this economic concentration process, at least in Germany where the rules are stricter than in all other European countries, and today probably even stricter than in the United States.[5] However, it was true in the

---

* Institute for International Law, University of Munich.

[1] Gessler "Les groupes de sociétés en droit allemand," Rev. prat. des sociétés (Bruxelles 1972), 41, 45.

[2] The latest figures can be found in Monopolkommission, Achtes Hauptgutachten 1988/89, BT-Drucksache 11/7582, 16.7.1990. As to economic concentration *cf.* Emmerich, Sonnenschein, *Konzernrecht*, (3rd ed., München 1989), s.1 III; Kübler, R. H. Schmidt, *Gesellschaftsrecht und Konzentration*, (Berlin 1988). The best economic introduction regarding the phenomenon and its causes is still Lenel, *Ursachen der Konzentration*, (2nd ed., Tübingen 1968). See also Kaufer, *Konzentration und Fusionskontrolle*, (Tübingen 1977).

[3] Ordelheide, "Der Konzern als Gegenstand betriebswirtschaftlicher Forschung," (1986) Betriebswirtschaftliche Forschung und Praxis (B.F.U.P.) 293, 294 *et seq.*

[4] For example for Great Britain see Prentice, "Groups of Companies: The English Experience," in Hopt, ed., *Groups of Companies in European Laws*, (Berlin, New York 1982), 99.

[5] *cf.* Hopt, "Restrictive Trade Practices and Juridification: A Comparative Law Study," in Teubner, ed., *Juridification of Social Spheres: A Comparative Analysis in the Areas of Labor, Corporate, Antitrust and Social Welfare Law*, (Berlin, New York 1987), 291.

past that economic forces were stronger than law and in the immediate future, the political and economic events attendant on German reunification, which has resulted in an acute need for the rescue of thousands of East German enterprises, may be expected to accelerate the concentration process considerably. As for European merger control, which after nearly two decades of debate was finally introduced in 1989, it remains to be seen what impact it will have in the different Member States, given the political compromises which were needed to bring it about.[6]

As it stands, the European merger control system, which became operative from the end of September 1990, will extend to probably no more than 40 to 50 mergers. Some of them have already arisen or will arise from German economic reunification. The complaint of British Airways plc concerning the merger plans of Deutsche Lufthansa AG and East German Interflug is of interest in the present connection. The EC Commission has already indicated that it wishes to obtain more extensive jurisdiction by 1993.

Between the different groups of companies there are considerable variations as to *size* (*i.e.* number of members), *form* and *organisation*. Some are huge; the fourth largest German enterprise, the VEBA AG, is parent of more than 1,000 subsidiaries.[7] As far as the parent company is concerned, most of the groups have chosen the legal form of a stock corporation, even though there are also a considerable number of holding companies which are not stock corporations (*i.e.* public limited companies). In Germany, by the end of 1988, there were only 2,373 stock corporations[8] as compared with about 400,000 GmbH[9] and probably considerably more than 60,000 GmbH & Co.[10]: more and more subsidiaries take a form other than that of a stock corporation, for example that of a GmbH or even a partnership. One

---

[6] EC Reg. 4064/89 (O.J. L 395/1, 30.12.1989). Note the first German commentaries by Koch, "Die neuen Befugnisse der EG zur Kontrolle von Unternehmenszusammenschlüssen," (1990) Europäisches Wirtschafts & Steuerrecht (E.W.S.) 65, and Niederleithinger, "Grundfragen der neuen europäischen Zusammenschlußkontrolle," (1990) E.W.S. 73. The first draft of the regulation dates from July 20, 1973 (O.J. C 92/1, 31.10.1973).

[7] Lutter, "Stand und Entwicklung des Konzernrechts in Europa," (1987) ZGR 324, 333.

[8] As of December 31, 1988. In France there are some 135,000 stock corporations and Belgium has some 35,000 stock corporations. For figures relating to other EC member States see Peltzer, "Übernahmeangebote nach künftigem Europa-Recht und dessen Umsetzung in deutsches Recht," in Assmann, Basaldua, Bozenhardt, Peltzer, *Übernahmeangebote*, (Berlin 1990), 179, 186.

[9] See Deutsche Bundesbank, Jahresbericht 1989, 52.

[10] The GmbH & Co. is a typically German legal hybrid between the GmbH and a limited (commercial) partnership. In many other countries this mixture is forbidden, for example in Switzerland and in France. In Germany it is allowed, but creates many legal problems. Statistics are not available, since the GmbH & Co. is legally speaking a partnership and not a limited liability company. For a short introduction see Baumbach-Duden-Hopt, *Handelsgesetzbuch*, (28th ed., München 1989), Anhang s.177 a: "GmbH & Co. (mit Publikumsgesellschaft)"; Hopt, "L'expérience allemande: Le succès de la 'S.A.R.L. en commandite' (GmbH & Co. KG)," La Semaine juridique, (J.C.P. édition entreprise 1984, no. 14371) 640.

of the reasons for this may be that German *Konzernrecht* of 1965 (paras. 291–337 of the German *Aktiengesetz*) is applicable only to stock corporations; when subsidiaries take the form of a stock corporation, the legal form of the parent does not matter. A law of groups applicable to other companies is emerging only more recently from case law. As to the organisation, one of the more obvious differences is the one between the groups with a rather loose internal structure and others which involve close relationships. In German legal literature the latter are called qualified groups of companies (*qualifizierter Konzern*) and special rules are applied to them.[11] It has been observed that horizontal groups of companies are a European phenomenon whilst the vertical group prevails in the United States and Japan.[12] However, recently bi-national horizontal groups of companies have lost ground. Despite increased economic integration of the markets, there seems to be less horizontal group structuring, the fate of Hoesch-Hoogovens being just one example.[13] On the other hand most contemporary groups of companies are transnational in the sense that the parent has subsidiaries abroad.

B. Diversity of laws

The economic reality of groups of companies and the fact that they present certain challenges for the law have been recognised for a long time. Groups of companies have been observed already in the 19th century and transnational enterprises were active in world trade in the second half of the last century.[14] In *Germany*, legal discussion of groups of companies began in 1910 and was particularly intense between the two world wars. The German *Konzernrecht* of 1965 has to be seen against this background. It is not a sudden original postwar invention. Legal development did not cease in 1965. German courts and authors have discovered serious shortcomings in the 1965 Act as far as stock corporations are concerned. Furthermore, they no longer

---

[11] *cf.* Hoffmann-Becking, "Der qualifizierte faktische AG-Konzern—Tatbestand und Abwehransprüche," and Koppensteiner, "Über die Verlustausgleichspflicht im qualifizierten AG-Konzern," both in Ulmer, ed., *Probleme des Konzernrechts: Symposion für Schilling* (Heidelberg 1989), 68 and 87; Lutter, "Der qualifizierte faktische Konzern," (1990) AG 179; Kropff, "Konzerneingangskontrolle bei der qualifiziert konzerngebundenen Aktiengesellschaft," in *Bilanz-und Konzernrecht, Festschrift für Goerdeler*, (Düsseldorf 1987), 259. *Cf.* also Hommelhoff, *Die Konzernleitungspflicht*, (Köln 1982).

[12] Böhlhoff and Budde, "Company Groups—The EEC Proposal for a Ninth Directive in the Light of the Legal Situation in the Federal Republic of Germany," 6 Journal of Comparative Business and Capital Market Law 163 (1984) 172. But see also Wiedemann, *Die Unternehmensgruppe im Privatrecht*, (Tübingen 1988), 12.

[13] Bayer, "Horizontal Groups and Joint Ventures in Europe: Concepts and Reality," in Hopt, *Groups of Companies* (*op. cit.*, n. 4, *supra* 3–17).

[14] P. Hertner, G. Jones, *Multinationals: Theory and History* (Brockfield, Vermont 1986); Großfeld, "Die rechtspolitische Beurteilung der Aktiengesellschaft im 19. Jahrhundert," and same, "Zur Kartellrechtsdiskussion vor dem Ersten Weltkrieg," in Coing and Wilhelm, eds., *Wissenschaft und Kodifikation des Privatrechts im 19. Jahrhundert*, (vol. IV, Frankfurt 1979) 326 *et seq.* and 255 *et seq.*; Nörr, "Die Entwicklung des Aktien-und Konzernrechts während der Weimarer Republik," (1986) ZHR 150, 155.

accept that the German legislator has enacted a law of groups for stock corporations only, leaving aside other forms of companies such as the GmbH and commercial partnerships. In addition there is an important body of leading cases[15] relating both to the situation where the dependent enterprise is a stock corporation, and where it is a GmbH or commercial partnership. Legal developments in the latter area are far more dynamic than in the field of traditional stock corporation law.[16] German case law on groups of companies has been

[15] *cf.* the following (not exhaustive) list of landmark cases:

ZVN (1975): 65 BGHZ 30: joint venture for sales treated as cartel;

VEBA (1977): 69 BGHZ 334; Federal Republic of Germany considered as dominant enterprise; domination even by a shareholder with less than 50 per cent. of the share capital held to be possible;

Gervais/Danone (1979): BGH, (1980) NJW 231: liability of parent for losses of subsidiary (limited partnership) in case of enterprise contract and *de facto* integration between parent and subsidiary;

Süssen (1981): 80 BGHZ 69: dependency in the sense of para. 17(1) of the Stock Corporation Act of 1965, law of groups where one or more of the dependent companies is a GmbH;

Hoesch/Hoogovens (1981): 82 BGHZ 188: transfer of (all) assets according to para. 361 of the Stock Corporation Act;

Holzmüller (1982): 83 BGHZ 122: transfer of important plant to subsidiary held to be a matter to be decided by the general assembly under para. 119(2) of the Stock Corporation Act 1965;

Heumann/Ogilvy (1983): 89 BGHZ 162 unlawful competition by dominant company and its parent company, law of groups where one or more of the dependent companies is a GmbH & Co. KG;

BuM/WestLB (1984): 90 BGHZ 381, 394; 1984, WM 625: economic dependency held not sufficient for legal dependency under para. 17 of the Stock Corporation Act; also held no dominating influence by bank on whose credit a corporation is dependent;

Autokran (1985): 95 BGHZ 330: no piercing of corporate veil, but parent held liable for losses of creditor of subsidiary (GmbH) by analogy to paras. 303 and 322(2) and (3) of the Stock Corporation Act, law of groups where one or more of the dependent companies is a GmbH;

OAM (1985): 96 BGHZ 69, 86: so-called cooperative joint ventures held subject to merger control as well as to control over cartels under the Law Against Restraints on Competition;

Familienheim (1987): 103 BGHZ 1: a defective control agreement and agreement to transfer profits treated as *de facto* company; law of groups where one of the dependent companies is a GmbH;

Linotype (1988): 103 BGHZ 184: fiduciary duty of shareholders towards each other going beyond the principles of good faith under paras. 226, 242 and 826 of the Civil Code;

HSW (1988): 105 BGHZ 168, 182: responsibility of a member of a GmbH and of its parent company (bank) for adequate financing of the GmbH under paras. 32(a) and 32(b) of the Companies Act 1978;

Supermarkt (1988): 105 BGHZ 324: enterprise contracts between two GmbH;

Tiefbau (1989): 107 BGHZ 7: liability of parent for losses of creditor of subsidiary (GmbH) in analogy to para. 302 of the Stock Corporation Act, law of groups where one or more of the dependent companies is a GmbH.

[16] For the law of groups enshrined in the Stock Corporation Act of 1965 see the execellent survey by Krieger, "Konzernrecht des Aktiengesetzes," in Hoffmann-Becking, ed., *Münchener Handbuch des Gesellschaftsrechts*, vol. 4, *Aktiengesellschaft*, (München 1988/Ch. XII.

For the law of groups where one or more of the dependent companies is a GmbH,

set out and analysed by several recent studies.[17] Thus it should be evident that if a foreign lawyer simply examined the 1965 Act, he would have a very misleading picture of the German law of groups. In some *other countries*[18] the prevailing opinion is that the problems of the groups of companies can be solved by traditional civil law. In some of them not only specific legislation is lacking, but the courts have not had the opportunity or the courage to develop their own rules for group problems. Most textbooks of company law neglect the group of companies almost entirely. As a foreign observer one almost has the impression that sometimes the phenomenon is virtually ignored. The separate entity doctrine is usually not challenged, to the detriment of the creditors of the (closely held) subsidiary. The interest of the outside shareholders are treated as being adequately provided for by the doctrine that account may not be taken of the group interest. Even in *France* where modern doctrine is well aware of these problems,[19] the concepts of the *action en comblement du passif* and the liability of the *dirigeant de fait* (de facto director) have only rarely been made applicable to groups of companies.[20]

As to the situation in *Great Britain*, the 1982 report of Prof. Prentice[21] has been taken note of in Germany. It opened with the statement:

note for example Zöllner in Baumbach-Hueck, *GmbHG*, (15th ed., München 1988), Schlußanhang I; Fischer-Lutter-Hommelhoff, *GmbH-Gesetz, Kommentar*, (12th ed., Köln 1987); Hommelhoff, ed., *Entwicklungen im GmbH-Konzernrecht*, (Berlin, New York 1986). See also Winter, *Mitgliedschaftliche Treuebindungen im GmbH-Recht*, (München 1988).

    For the law of groups where one or more of the dependent enterprises is a commercial or limited partnership (*Offene Handelsgesellschaft* and *Kommandit-gesellschaft* or limited partnership), see for example Ulmer in Staub, *Großkommentar zum HGB*, (4th ed., Berlin 1989) Anhang §105, Rdn. 59 *et seq.* and same, "Grundstrukturen eines Personengesellschaftskonzernrechts," in Ulmer, ed., *Probleme des Konzernrechts* (*op. cit.*, n. 11, *supra*) 26; Baumgartl, *Die konzernbeherrschte Personengesellschaft*, (Köln 1986); Schießl, *Die beherrschte Personengesellschaft*, (Köln 1985); Löffler, *Die abhängige Personengesellschaft* (Heidelberg 1988).

[17] *cf.* Fleck, "Die Rechtsprechung des Bundesgerichtshofes zum Recht der verbundenen Unternehmen," (1986) WM 1205; M. Lutter, "100 Bände BGHZ: Konzernrecht," (1987) ZHR 151 444; Hopt "Le droit des groupes de sociétés—Expériences allemandes, perspectives européennes," (1987) Rev. soc. 371; see most recently Bälz, "Verbundene Unternehmen—Konzernrecht als Speerspitze eines fortschrittlichen Gesellschaftsrechts?" in *40 Jahre Bundesrepublik Deutschland 40 Jahre Rechtsentwicklung*, (Tübingen 1990) 176 at 194 *et seq.* More generally for important cases in the field of German company law, see Ulmer, *Richterrechtliche Entwicklungen im Gesellschaftsrecht 1971–1985*, (Heidlleberg 1986).

[18] For comparative law governing groups *cf.* Hopt, ed., *Groups of Companies in European Laws* (*op. cit.*, n. 4 *supra*); Immenga, "Company Systems and Affiliation," *Int.Enc.Comp.L.* (Tübingen 1985) vol. XIII ch. 7; Wooldridge, *Groups of Companies: The Law and Practice in Britain, France and Germany* (London 1981); most recently Sugarman, Teubner, eds., *Regulating Corporate Groups in Europe*, (Baden-Baden 1990).

[19] *cf.* for example Guyon, *Droit des affaires*, (5e éd., Paris 1988), tome 1, 552 *et seq*; Cozian, Viandier, *Droit des sociétés*, (Paris 1987), 3e partie, 415 *et seq*; see also Ohl, *Les prêts et avances entre les sociétés d'un même groupe* (Paris, 1982).

[20] *cf. infra* pp. 103–104.

"To a large extent this is an essay in speculation and synthesis."

On the other hand one remembers the bold prognostic statement by Lord Denning made in 1976:

"There is an evidence of a general tendency to ignore the separate legal entities of various companies within a group, and look instead to the economic entity of the whole group.[22]"

The obvious diversity of laws in the various European countries, in particular in Germany, France and Great Britain, is best shown by the fate of the draft Ninth EC Directive which goes back to early efforts of the *EC Commission* at the beginning of the 1970's. The far-reaching plans of group law harmonisation which were conceived by Directorate General III had failed conspicuously by 1985. They did not find enough support even within the EC Commission itself because they were considered too burdensome and probably because they were too closely styled on the model of the German Stock Corporation Act which, after 20 years of existence, has shown weaknesses and lacunae. However, the projected version of this Ninth Company Law Directive on Groups of Companies,[23] illustrates what purposes a law of groups might have and what provisions it might contain for the purpose of protecting creditors and outside shareholders. The future of group law harmonisation is doubtful. While company, banking and capital market law harmonisation are increasing in significance with 1992 in sight,[24] the law governing groups is so difficult to handle conceptually and the development of law and practice in the Member States is so diverse that the matter will probably have to be left to the Member States. It remains to be seen whether the courts, both national and European, will reach solutions which are more uniform than at present.

---

[21] Prentice, *op. cit.* (n. 4 *supra*) 99.

[22] *D.H.N. Food Distributors Ltd.* v. *Tower Hamlets* [1976] 1 W.L.R. 852.

[23] First version of 1974/75, Doc. No. XI/328/74, Doc. No. XI/593/75, later Doc. No. XI/215/77: amended version of 1984/85, Doc. No. III/1639/84; the text (without the comments) can also be found in (1985) ZGR 446. As to the latter see Hommelhoff, "Zum revidierten Vorschlag einer EG-Konzernrechtsrichtlinie," in *Festschrift für Fleck*, (Berlin, New York 1988) 125. See most recently the "swan song" by Gleichmann, "The Law of Corporate Groups in the European Community," in Sugarman, Teubner (*op. cit.* n. 18, *supra*) 435.

[24] *cf.* for example Goerdeler, "Überlegungen zum künftigen Gesellschaftsrecht in der EG," in *Festschrift für Steindorff*, (Berlin, New York 1990) 1211; Hopt, "Legal Harmonization on the Way to Europe 1992: Banking and Capital Markets," (1990) 4 Banking & Finance Law Review 309.

More generally see Buxbaum and Hopt, *Legal Harmonization and the Business Enterprise*, (Berlin, New York 1988); Buxbaum, Hertig, Hirsch, Hopt, eds., *European Business Law: Legal and Economic Analyses on Integration and Harmonization* (Lugano Symposium), (Berlin, New York 1991).

C. Purposes of a law governing groups of companies

(1) *The position in sectors of the law*

The international discussion on the law of groups tends to concentrate only on the commercial and company law side. This will also be the focus of this chapter. Yet it should be clear that in Germany and elsewhere there are many legal devices concerning groups of companies in other sectors of the law. This is true, for example, of labour law (and its specialised branch governing the workers' codetermination both at plant level and in the boardroom at enterprise level),[25] in bank supervision law,[26] in bankruptcy law[27] and particularly in tax law.[28] As far as the latter is concerned, the specific purposes of a sectoral law of groups of companies is most apparent. The national tax authorities have long since reached beyond the individual enterprises belonging to the group, for example, by developing a doctrine of transfer pricing at arm's length in order to uphold the national tax interest against transnational enterprises and against the tax interests of other countries.[29] Somewhat surprisingly there has been rather little cross-fertilisation between these different fields so far as the development of rules governing groups of companies is concerned.

(2) *Special considerations applicable in commercial and company law*

Originally the commercial and company law applicable to groups had been of an empowering nature. The specific dangers which groups of companies gave rise to only became apparent at a later stage. Thus the public interest came to be seen as being jeopardised by "trusts." This led to the development of antitrust law and specifi-

---

[25] *cf.* Wiedemann (*op. cit.* n. 17, *supra*) 91–128; Birk "The Group Enterprise as a Problem for German Labour Law," in Sugarman, Teubner (*op. cit.* n. 18, *supra*) 335; Hoffmann-Becking, "Arbeitsdirektor der Konzernobergesellschaft oder Konzernarbeitsdirektor?," in *Festschrift für Werner*, (Berlin, New York 1984) 301.

[26] *cf.* Dietz, *Bankkonzernrecht nach der Novelle zum Kreditwesengesetz* (Dissertation, Tübingen 1988); major parts of this thesis now appear in (1990) AG 269, 333 and 376; Mülbert, "Bankenaufsicht über internationale Bankkonzerne—Informationsrechte und-pflichten nach der KWG-Novelle 1984," (1986) AG 1. See also Colloque international, *L'avant-projet de loi fédérale sur les banques*, (Geneva 1983) with a broad comparative law basis.

[27] See for example, Albach "Betriebswirtschaftliche Überlegungen zur rechtlichen Neugestaltung bei Insolvenz von Konzernen," (1984) ZFB 773; Lutter, "Der Konzern in der Insolvenz," (1984) ZFB 781; Hopt "Das Unternehmen in der Krise," in Birk, Kreuzer, eds., Das Unternehmen in der Krise: Probleme der Insolvenzvermeidung aus rechtsvergleichender Sicht (Frankfurt 1986) 11, 66–68. The draft of the new German law on insolvency of November 1, 1989, adheres to the traditional concept of insolvency of each single juridical person whether it belongs to a group of companies or not. *cf.* Bundesministerium der Justiz, Referentenentwurf, Gesetz zur Reform des Insolvenzrechts, Stand: 1. November 1989.

[28] See generally Kluge, *Das Internationale Steuerrecht der Bundesrepublik* (2d ed., München 1983).

[29] OECD, *Transfer Pricing and Multinational Enterprises, Report of the Committee on Fiscal Affairs* (adopted by the Council) (Paris 1979).

cally to *merger control*. In the United States this took place as early as 1914 with the enactment of section 7 of the Clayton Act. In Europe it took place first of all in Great Britain in 1965 with the passing of the Monopolies and Mergers Act. This legislation was followed by German legislation in 1973, and by French legislation in 1977.[30] Subsequently, the public interest aspect of the law of groups of companies has been treated as being of secondary importance in comparison to the private interests of creditors and shareholders. This recognition of different interests to be protected by separate statutes governing antitrust matters on the one hand and the law of groups on the other has also resulted in a rather different approach. The majority opinion in Germany is that the law governing groups of companies should not be concerned with free markets, and it affirms the "neutrality" of corporate law and the law governing groups.

The private interests which need protection against the group interest and its pursuit by the parent are primarily those of the creditors of the subsidiary and of the so-called outside shareholders of the subsidiary. It is now generally required that, by entering a group of companies, an enterprise changes its character. The recognition of the separate legal entity of the subsidiary does not then accord with the economic realities reflected in relations between the parent and the subsidiary. In such an event the decision making centre has radically changed. The dangers for the *creditors and outside shareholders of the subsidiary* arising from the resulting dependency are obvious, and the protective purposes made manifest in the traditional rules of law governing groups of companies take account of them.

In modern times, the question has been asked whether these protective purposes should be extended to take into consideration the *minority shareholders*, or even the creditors, *of the parent company*. The former point has been answered positively by the German *Bundesgerichtshof* in its famous (or according to many commentators notorious) *Holzmüller* decision of 1982 which will be dealt with later on.[31] The answer to the latter point depends on whether the existence of a group relationship may expose the creditors of the parent company to danger as well. This has not yet been fully tested in practice. However, in the field of banking, it is taken for granted that banks which have banking and non-banking subsidiaries will go a long way to help them out in situations of financial difficulty. If they fail to do so, serious difficulties for the group and the parent company may well arise. The subsidiary will usually be sacrificed only if it is a matter of life or death for the parent as well. The specific danger for creditors of the parent company consist of the risk that the parent company misjudges the situation of the subsidiary and provides funds for the latter for too long or that the parent cannot escape the effects of the crisis of confidence which the failure of the subsidiary initiates for it irrespective of the separate legal entities of these companies. The

---

[30] Hopt, ed., *European Merger Control*, (Berlin, New York 1982).
[31] See *infra* 3 A(2).

German *Herstatt* case of 1974 illustrates this point even though it was not a simple bank case. The dominant shareholder was practically forced to answer for the debts of the Herstatt bank with half of his insurance business in order to save the other half. This was because the crisis of confidence caused by the failure of the bank threatened to have further ramifications.

D. Tasks

In the previously mentioned report, Dr. Prentice has concluded that the two key issues of the law governing groups are the underlying economic purposes of limited liability and the nature of the shareholders' interest, *i.e.* whether the latter owns property in a significant sense or rather a fungible money claim.[32] In a theoretical sense these are questions of central importance. Indeed, they are so fundamental that general answers are bound to be controversial, if not impossible. A recent survey of the development of groups undertaken from an economic standpoint has served to somewhat diminish the hope that ready insights will be derived from as economic approach.[33] Nevertheless further thought should be given to the question under what conditions creditors and outside shareholders can make adequate provision for themselves through the market[34] by demanding a risk premium from the subsidiary of the parent company. The nature of the shareholders' interest remains a rather philosophical question unless considered in the light of concrete circumstances, as in the question governing the constitutional guarantee of property rights which was decided by the German Supreme Court (*Bundesverfassungsgericht*) in the 1978 workers' codetermination case.[35] Even then the answer seems to be dependent partly on the analysis of national legal materials, and partly on judicial value judgments. The question of how to shape a rational law of groups will probably have to be answered by adopting an approach which is intermediate between the use of philosophical and of legal and economic concepts.

The question remains as to whether national law of groups will be shaped by the future Community legislation or as appears more likely at present, by the legislatures of Member States and by their courts. The prerequisite for such an answer involves insight into the various elements of a possible law of groups and their combination in a system of such law which is conceived in response to the full range of

32 Prentice (*op. cit.* n. 4, *supra*) 128–129.
33 Kirchner, "Ökonomische Überlegungen zum Konzernrecht," (1985) ZGR 214.
34 The same questions arise for the harmonization of law in general and are debated very much between lawyers and economists; *cf.* Starbatty, ed., *Europäische Integration: Wieviel Wettbewerb—wieviel Bürokratie?* (Essen 1990); Hopt, ed., *Europäische Integration als Herausforderung des Rechts: Mehr Marktrecht—weniger Einzelgesetze*, (Hanns Martin Schleyer-Stiftung, Essen 1991).
35 Judgment of March 1, 1979, 50 BVerfGE/90 and (1979) NJW 699. For a summary of this decision see (1980) 28 Am.J.Comp.L. 88. See also Hopt, "New Ways in Corporate Governance: European Experiments with Labor Representation on Corporate Boards," (1984) 82 Mich.L.Rev. 1338.

regulatory problems presented by such groups. This kind of systematic approach which is advocated by modern German literature in the field[36] may help to compare and evaluate different possible answers and regulatory patterns and to improve possible harmonisation proposals. This approach should not be misunderstood as a plea for uniform solutions for regulating all kinds of groups of enterprises, *i.e.* irrespective of the legal form of the single members. It may very well be that different rules are preferable for stock corporations, for limited liability companies and for commercial and limited partnerships. Nevertheless, recent German experience of different concepts of group law and legal provisions concerning groups in all three of these sectors shows that the basic elements and their combination in a system are the same or rather similar. Furthermore, it is by no means certain that this German classification of the law governing groups according to the legal form of the enterprise will be followed in other Member States. To a certain extent the German method is a result of the sectoral codification of stock corporation law undertaken in 1965, in contrast to the codification of the law of commercial companies as whole, which took place, for example, in France by the law of July 24, 1966.

2. IMPORTANT ELEMENTS RELEVANT TO THE SYSTEMATIC LEGAL REGULATION OF GROUPS OF COMPANIES

A. The notion of an enterprise

(1) *Private shareholders*

One of the problems of a law governing groups of companies is the concept of an enterprise. Under German law as well as under the projected Ninth EC Directive only enterprises are subject to the specific duties and liabilities of a law of groups. In most cases, the term presents no difficulties. However, the situation is different where either a private shareholder or a public enterprise is at the head of a group of companies. According to unanimous German opinion purely private shareholders should not be treated as an enterprise in the sense of the law of groups. This is true even for controlling shareholders. Control by a private shareholder gives rise to the difficult problems of minority protection. But these problems and the problems which occur within a group of companies are not necessarily the same. This regulatory distinction is unknown to the law concerning groups as developed in most other countries, for example in the United States of America,[37] in Great Britain or in France.

---

[36] Note, for example Lutter (*op. cit.*, n. 7, *supra*) 344 *et seq.*; Wiedemann (*op. cit.*, n. 2, *supra*) 39 *et seq.*

[37] Short surveys are given by Vagts, "Konzernrecht in den Vereinigten Staaten," in Druey, ed., *Das St. Galler Konzernrechtsgespräch*, (Bern, Stuttgart 1988) 31, and by Kübler, Schmidt (*op. cit.*, n. 2, *supra*) ch. B III.

While the German approach may seem more refined theoretically and more flexible in practice, the overall results do not differ substantially because it is also true that under German law, private majority shareholders rarely fall outside the ambit of the law applicable to groups.[38] As pointed out above, the character of a company itself changes at the time when it becomes a dependent member of a group because from then on the group interest prevails at least *de facto*. According to this rationale even a private shareholder must be deemed to be an enterprise in the sense of the law if he has participations in more than one company which he holds for business reasons and not only for investment purposes (so-called *entrepreneurial participations*). This is usually the case where he has substantial holdings in two or more companies. Obviously this theory can have far-reaching consequences. In Germany, for example, the trade unions which belong to the trade union federation (*Deutscher Gewerkschaftsbund*) have representatives on the supervisory boards of all the major enterprises. Under the quasiparitative system of worker participation on the boards of companies introduced by the Codetermination Act 1976, one half of the seats are filled by workers who usually belong to these unions. The question could arise under what circumstances must the trade union federation be regarded as an enterprise in the sense of the law governing groups.

(2) *Public enterprises*

In all Western European countries their are frequent cases in which the state, a community or a "public" enterprise under its control is at the head of a group. For Germany the above mentioned *VEBA* presents a good example. The German *Bundesgerichtshof* in the well known *VEBA-Gelsenberg* decision of 1978[39] held that such public enterprises (in the instant case the Federal Republic of Germany itself) might very well be enterprises in the sense of the law governing groups. One of the consequences might be that the annual accounts of a subsidiary belonging to such a group may not be audited any longer by a state-owned auditing company, since the latter would not be independent in the sense of auditing law. The practical consequences of all this on public enterprises have not yet been fully explored. However, there is general agreement that public enterprises may also be subject to at least certain rules of the law of groups of companies. Similar developments can be found in other European countries, for example in Belgium under the *action en comblement du passif* which was based upon a French model although it has a narrower ambit and differs in certain other ways. In one judgment the Belgian State was held liable as a *de facto* director for negligent conduct in the context of

---

[38] See Koppensteiner, in *Kölner Kommentar zum Aktiengesetz*, (2d ed., Cologne 1986), § 15 comments 6 *et seq.*, 21 *et seq.*
[39] 69 BGHZ 334.

granting a rescue credit.[40] More generally there is a healthy tendency of treating private and public enterprises alike not only in the law governing groups, but also in antitrust law, unfair competition law and elsewhere. This helps to reduce the market imbalances created by the entry of public enterprises which have access to very considerable resources (deep pocket doctrine).

B. Dependency and control

(1) *Formal as opposed to substantive criteria: the example of the seventh EC directive*

The Seventh EC Directive on consolidated accounts illustrates the difficulty of defining the concept of control (by the parent company) or dependency (of the subsidiary). The decision of the Community legislators was finally to adopt a formal concept of control and dependency. The parent company has to prepare consolidated accounts if it has the majority of votes or if it has the right (alone or by a voting agreement with fellow shareholders) to nominate or remove the majority of the members of the board of the subsidiary, provided it holds shares or parts of the subsidiary.[41] The advantage of such formal control criteria consists of their relative ease of application which, at least as far as determining whether enterprises must consolidate their accounts is concerned, may lead to clear answers. However, both in this and other relevant areas, for example antitrust law and merger control law, it is well known that enterprises may fall just slightly below the threshold required by such criteria and may thus avoid the regulation. The Seventh EC Directive has taken account of the latter fact by allowing Member States to apply in addition a substantive criterion, namely actual control or dependency where the parent has a participating interest in the subsidiary, which is entrepreneurial in the sense explained above. Such an interest will be presumed in the event of a participation of more than 20 per cent. (the figure may be reduced under the national legislation of Member States). As a result under the German law governing group accounts there are now two different concepts of control, a formal one and a substantive one,[42] whilst in accordance with the general law of groups under commercial and corporation law as well as in other sectors of law the substantive concept prevails. If one looks beyond company law to banking law, a further concept of control can be found.[43] It seems doubtful whether such a diversity is necessary and useful. On the other hand it becomes apparent that in modern

---

[40] Tribunal de commerce de Bruxelles (October 22, 1982), (1982) Revue pratique des sociétés 244.

[41] Art. 1(1) of the Seventh Directive of June 13, 1983, (O.J. 1983 L 193/1).

[42] See para. 290(2) of the Commercial Code and, briefly, Baumbach-Duden-Hopt (*op. cit*, n. 10, *supra*), para. 290, comments 2 and 3; Ulmer, "Begriffsvielfalt im Recht der verbundenen Unternehmen als Folge des Bilanzrichtlinien-Gesetzes," in *Festschrift für Goerdeler*, (*op. cit.*, n. 11, *supra*) 623.

[43] *cf.* Dietz, (*op. cit.*, n. 26, *supra*) Chap. 6 part A.

commercial and economic law the search for uniform concepts in different areas of law leads to increasing frustration. Functional approaches to individual problems prevail, with the result that sometimes the same concept will be interpreted differently under different provisions of one and the same statute.

(2) *Legal as opposed to economic concepts of control*

Where a substantive concept of control is employed, it sometimes is very difficult to give clear answers to particular questions. This may be illustrated by considering the practical examples discussed below. Let us assume that a Bavarian bank rescues a brewery corporation by extending substantial credits to it, and that the bank acquires a major participation in it, and also exercises surveillance over the major policy decisions taken by the corporation. The question then arises as to what is necessary before the bank can be treated as a parent company in the sense of the law governing groups of companies? Actual influence on the enterprise policy of the brewery on the basis of a major participation is certainly enough. The same is true if the bank secures the appointment of its own managers on the board of the brewery and thereby can get its way on the board. However, the question arises whether the position is the same if the bank, which does not have a major shareholding in the brewery company and does not appoint persons to its board, has the final say as the major supplier of credit or because of other non-corporate legal relationships with the brewery. The clear majority opinion in Germany answers this question in the negative. If this were not the case a great number of situations where some kind of economic control existed, which type of control is common among modern businesses, would fall under the law governing groups. Accordingly substantive control in the legal sense exists only if the economic control is reinforced by an influential position as shareholder of the company.[44]

While this view is now widely shared in Germany, many questions remain. Does a small shareholding, for example, less than 10 per cent. establish enough for legal (and not only for economic) control, if the rest of the shares are widely dispersed amongst the public? The answer should be in the affirmative. Can there be legal control by a minority shareholder if such a shareholder can secure a majority vote in a general meeting but only on specific occasions? The answer to this question is in the negative. The same is true also for what has been called negative control, *i.e.* a blocking participation. One may also ask, on the other hand, whether a major shareholding of perhaps 30 per cent. held by a business enterprise with the intention of contributing to its business is a controlling participation when there are two or three other major shareholders, whose holdings are simply for the purpose of investment. The answer is probably that it depends on the

---

44 BGH (1984) WM 625, 628; Koppensteiner (*op. cit.*, n. 38, *supra*) para. 17, comment 50, with further references.

circumstances. A special German problem is worth mentioning. This is whether an individual majority shareholder of a (parent) company who himself has an entrepreneurial interest in this company, may be regarded as a controlling enterprise, even though the supervisory board of the (parent) company consists of 50 per cent. of workers under the legal provisions governing employee participation at board level. The latter problem has arisen under US securities law when the German parent company intended its American subsidiary to go public. The risks involved were considered such that the subsidiary refrained from doing so, and thus no litigation ensued.

Joint ventures are very commonly used, both nationally and across the borders. Although the usual position is that two parent companies each hold 50 per cent. of the shares in the subsidiary company, on occasions there may be more than two parent companies, for example three parent companies each holding 33⅓ per cent. of the shares in the subsidiary. The question arises whether a subsidiary may be *dependent on more than one controlling parent* company. There is a temptation to answer this question in the negative, because then one or more partners may block one another. However, it is noteworthy that from the viewpoint of the subsidiary, there is no real autonomy, and this perspective should be decisive for protective purposes. Therefore, if there is no clear evidence of actual blocking, multiple control should be held possible. In the German *Seitz* case, the *Bundesgerichtshof* affirmed this view provided that the coordination of the two parents could be seen as based on their previous behaviour and their common economic interests.[45] Similar problems come up in family corporations when legal control depends on whether the combined holdings of spouses or family members can be taken account of. It is interesting to note that family quarrels may not only be relevant for family law and divorce, but also for the purposes of law of groups of companies.

C. Contractual and *de facto* groups of companies

(1) *Experience with German "Konzernrecht"*

Under the German *Konzernrecht* of 1965 (para. 291 *et seq.* of the Stock Corporation Act of 1965) the distinction between contractual and factual groups of companies is paramount. In contractual groups the creditors of the subsidiary are protected by the legal obligation of the parent towards the subsidiary to make good the losses at the end of the year. Outside shareholders of the subsidiary have a right to periodic compensation payments and must be offered the opportunity of selling their shares to the parent as against equitable indemnity. Why should a parent company conclude an enterprise contract voluntarily? The choice was intended to be made attractive by the legislator by including provisions governing contractual groups which legalise the pursuit of the interests of the group. Thus under

---

[45] *cf. Seitz* case, 62 BGHZ 193 and *WAZ* v. *Brost & Funke*, 74 BGHZ 359, both decided under merger control legislation.

German law the parent company is expressly allowed to induce the subsidiary to act against its own interest if the basis of the group is a contractual one. This full entrepreneurial freedom on the side of the parent company appears a remarkable incentive to the conclusion of control contracts. However, it is clear that the legislator's intention has not been fulfilled very successfully. It has been estimated that between 1970 and 1980 enterprise contracts (*i.e.* control agreements or agreements to transfer profits) were concluded in respect of 130 corporations.[46] A more recent example of a business decision to form a contractual group is that of the agreement between Daimler-Benz and AEG.[47] Nevertheless, it is clear that the great majority of parent companies have chosen "cohabitation without marriage certificates."

Despite these negative experiences the projected Ninth EC Directive of 1985 still adheres to the German model by creating two different regimes for contractual and *de facto* groups,[48] but without giving sufficient incentives for enterprises to choose the contractual solution. This has been criticised even by German authors and is one of the reasons for the political failure of the draft.[49]

The consequences to be drawn from the German experience are quite obvious. There are two choices. The first one consists in dropping the legal distinction between contractual and *de facto* groups, at least as a central element in the enactment of systematic legal regulations governing groups of companies. Instead the protective legal rules should be attached to the existence of a *de facto* group of companies.[50] How these legal rules and mechanisms could be shaped is treated below together with other major policy issues. Nevertheless, it should be emphasised here that there is also some legitimate scope for rather different approaches to the manner of defining a group. Whilst in certain contexts dependency and control should be enough for the application of the law governing groups, it remains true that under German law a *Konzern* only exists if there is not just control, but one or more controlled enterprise is subject to the uniform management of the controlling enterprise. It is true that under German law there is a legal presumption that such uniform management by the controlling parent exists. However, at least in theory, this presumption may be rebutted.[51]

---

[46] Wiedemann (*op. cit*, n. 12, *supra*) 13.

[47] "Daimler-Benz bietet 200 DM je AEG-Aktie," FAZ Nr. 89 (16.4.1988) 13; Jeske, "Ein Stück von Daimler Benz, Zum Unternehmensvertrag mit AEG," FAZ Nr. 90 (18.4.1988) 13; "Der Beherrschungsvertrag mit Daimler ist für die AEG nur konsequent," FAZ Nr. 145 (25.6.1988) 16.

[48] Art. 6 *et seq.*, art. 13 *et seq.* of the projected Ninth Directive (n. 23 *supra*); critical comment by Immenga, "L'harmonisation du droit des groups de sociétés: La proposition d'une directive de la Commission de la C.E.E.," (1986) Giurisprudenza commerciale XIII 846, 848.

[49] See *supra* 1 B at the end.

[50] This solution is advocated for example by the German Monopolies Commission, 7th Hauptgutachten, BT-Drucks. 11/2677, (July 19, 1988), comment 839 *et seq.*

[51] Para. 18(1) sentence 3 of the Stock Corporation Act. See Koppensteiner (*op. cit*, n. 38, *supra*) s.18 comments 30 *et seq.*

The second choice many lead to better results. In accordance with this approach, the distinction between contractual and *de facto* groups of companies is maintained, which ensures that the enterprises have a choice of whether and how to organise their group status contractually. However, the view is taken that the treatment of the *de facto* groups should not be more favourable than the treatment of contractual groups. If, as under the German approach, the "normal" case for legal purposes is considered to be the contractual group then the legal treatment of *de facto* groups should be such as to make it more imperative for the parent company to enter into an enterprise contract. The German legislator has tried to make a *de facto* group relationship burdensome for the parent company, but obviously the burden imposed is not onerous enough. Detailed consideration of the latter point follows in the next main section of this chapter, which deals with the major policy decisions which have to be taken in formulating a law governing groups.

(2) *Priority of the interests of the subsidiary or legitimacy of the interests of the group*

The traditional solution which is found especially in systems of Roman law is to *deny any legitimate interest of the group* as such. The parent company thus may not give orders to the board of the subsidiary which would be prejudicial to the interest of the latter. Sometimes there are even provisions for the imposition of penal sanctions on the board members of the subsidiary if they follow such orders. This approach results in the fact that the problems which group relations give rise to for shareholders and for creditors are effectively denied, but evidently not solved. Reports from Italy indicate that in order to avoid these penal sanctions parent companies sometimes give orders directly to the personnel of the subsidiary.[52] Since breaches of the prohibition imposed on the parent company of giving prejudicial orders to the subsidiary are rarely sanctioned this prohibition tends to have the status of a "paper law" only, and fails to reflect the realities of the group. But even if it were enforced more frequently, the situation might still be similar. Experience shows that the managers of the subsidiaries in a group will be tempted to act in the way they are expected by the parent even without orders, and they will do so openly or covertly. Furthermore it is quite difficult for a court to establish that a business decision made freely by the management of the subsidiary in ex ante against the long-term interests of this corporation.

Another legislative approach is to treat the *interests of the group as*

---

[52] Lutter (*op. cit*, n. 7, *supra*) 352. As to the situation in Italy *cf.* Vanetti "Die Diskussion über die Konzerne und ihre Regelung in Italien," (1989) ZGR 396, and also Abbadessa, "I gruppi di società nel diritto italiano," in Pavone la Rosa, ed., *I gruppi di società*, (Bologna 1982), 103. See also Alessi, *La disciplina dei gruppi multinazionali nell' ordinamento societario italiano*, (Milano 1988).

legitimate provided that there is adequate protection for the creditors and the shareholders. This answer is certainly nearer to every day practice. In the long run divergences between reality and the law are prejudicial to the legal order in general. Indeed the real problem seems not the legitimacy of actions against the interest of the subsidiary provided they are in the interest of the group at large, but the adequacy of the protection of the creditors and the outside shareholders of the subsidiary. This view entails that management can choose the policy for the group as it seems fit. This implies that the parent is also free to prefer the interests of the subsidiary which could not happen in accordance with the alternative solution mentioned above.[53]

D. Participation, cross-participation and integration

The particular problems of participation, cross-participation and integration into a 100 per cent. subsidiary can only be mentioned briefly. The definition of participation is rather controversial. However, different levels of participation will have different legal consequences. As for the concepts of dependency and control there is the difficult choice between formal and substantive criteria. While in certain contexts clear percentages are helpful and even necessary, the basic concept should probably be a substantive one combined with a presumption as is contained in the Fourth EC Directive (Accounts Directive).[54]

Cross-participation must be regulated in order to avoid the possibility that the management of each corporation act together so as to diminish the influence (if any) of the general meeting. This problem has been noticed and regulated with particular care for example in France.[55]

The major legal problem of the 100 per cent. integration of a subsidiary into the parent company is under what conditions the parent may exclude the remaining perhaps five or ten per cent. minority shareholders even against their will.[56]

3. MAJOR POLICY DECISIONS WHICH HAVE TO BE TAKEN IN FORMULATING A LAW GOVERNING GROUPS

In the following part some of the major policy decisions which have to be taken in structuring a system of the law of groups of companies will

[53] *cf.* Prentice (*op. cit.*, n. 4, *supra*) 112.
[54] Art. 17 of the Fourth Directive of July 25, 1978, (O.J. 1978, L 222/11; *cf.* para. 271 of the German Commercial Code. The presumption is valid for shareholdings of more than 20 per cent. of the shares.
[55] Guyon (*op. cit.*, n. 19, *supra*) 560 *et seq.*; *cf.* also Mestre, Florès, La réglementation de l' autocontrôle, (1985) Rev. soc. 775. For Germany see para. 328 of the Stock Corporation Act.
[56] See art. 36 of the projected Ninth Directive (n. 23, *supra*): 10 per cent.; para. 320 of the German Stock Corporation Act: 5 per cent. Note also Immenga, (*op. cit.*, n. 18, *supra*), Ch XI: Elimination of minority shareholders by integration.

be mentioned. It should be clear however that already the method of treating the elements of the system mentioned above (including concepts and definitions) implies such policy decisions. Furthermore, the following policy choices are necessarily incomplete and based on a personal, albeit not only German background of experience with groups of companies.

A. The stage of formation of the groups of companies

(1) *Disclosure*

While German *Konzernrecht* contains innovatory legal provisions governing the organization and operations of groups of companies, until recently it has rather neglected the important prior stage of the formation of the group (*Konzernbildungskontrolle*).[57] Other laws have done more. A first option is early disclosure of the building up of controlling blocks of shares. There is agreement that the acquisition of relevant controlling interests in another company must be notified to the latter. The German 25 per cent. threshold is very high in comparison to other countries; in France the critical legal margin may be as low as 10 per cent.[58] The projected Ninth EC Directive adopted the 10 per cent. threshold, and required notification of each succeeding 5 per cent. for all corporations, including those which are not listed.[59] In the meantime the Block Trading Disclosure Directive of December 12, 1988[60] has tackled the problem from the side of capital market law, yet it reaches only companies with officially quoted securities.

(2) *Formal requirements applicable to the member companies*

Under the German legal regime applicable to contractual groups all enterprise contracts (*i.e.*, the formation of a contractual group) must be approved by a 75 per cent. majority by the general meetings of both the parent and the subsidiary company. However, if the contractual group remains the exception as has been shown above, this is seldom helpful.

Some years ago, in 1982, the famous *Holzmüller* decision of the German *Bundesgerichtshof* made an important step forward in the

---

[57] *cf.* Lutter, Timm, "Konzernrechtlicher Präventivschutz im GmbH-Recht," (1982) NJW 409; Ebenroth, *Konzernbildungs- und Konzernleitungskontrolle—Ein Beitrag zu den Kompetenzen von Vorstand und Hauptversammlung,* (Konstanz 1987); same, "Die Kompetenzen des Vorstandes und der Aktionärsschutz in der Konzernobergesellschaft," (1988) AG 1; Timm, "Grundfragen des 'qualifizierten' faktischen Konzerns im Aktienrecht, Bemerkungen zur 'Banning'—Entscheidung des OLG Hamm vom 3.11.1986," (1987) NJW 977; Kropff, "Konzerneingangskontrolle bei der qualifiziert konzerngebundenen Aktiengesellschaft," in *Bilanz- und Konzernrecht, Festschrift für Goerdeler (op. cit.,* n. 11, *supra)* 259.

[58] Para. 20 of the German Stock Corporation Act; art. 356–1 of the French Company Act of July 24, 1966 as revised.

[59] Art. 3 of the projected Ninth EC Directive (n. 23, *supra*).

[60] Dir. 88/627, (O.J. 1988 L 348/62).

development of a case-law of groups of companies in the process of formation.[61] The facts were as follows. The plaintiff was a minority shareholder in the defendant, a Hamburg based corporation which carried on the business of the storage of wood. Under its articles of incorporation, the defendant was allowed to acquire interests in other enterprises and to transfer all or part of its business to other companies. In 1972 the managing board of the defendant constituted a subsidiary taking the legal form of a limited liability company and transferred to it all its activities in the sea port of Hamburg. The plaintiff claimed that these activities amounted to the most valuable and promising part of the defendant's business and that therefore the transfer needed the consent of the defendant's general meeting. Without considering the legal intricacies of German corporation law, the result of this decision may be summarised by saying that the managing board has the duty to ask for the consent of the general meeting if a subsidiary is to be formed and a substantial part of the corporate assets are to be transferred to it. In the words of the court's decision, the shareholders' consent is necessary "for all fundamental corporate decisions which affect so deeply the rights of the shareholders as members of the corporation and their interests as quasi-owners represented by their shares that a reasonable board cannot take such decisions solely under its own responsibility."[62] Furthermore in the context of group relationships, a parent company must submit the decision on a capital increase in a 100 per cent. subsidiary to its general meeting if this increase may be prejudicial to the membership rights of the parent's shareholders including their financial interests.

This landmark decision has received much criticism which has been directed not so much at its result in the instant case (since there is agreement that the shareholders of the parent company also need some protection under the law of groups of companies) but instead at its dogmatic reasoning and particularly at the practical uncertainties raised by it. What are the "fundamental decisions" referred to in this case and when are the shareholders of the parent company and their financial interests affected by such decisions to such a degree that the managing board must place the matter before the general meeting? Overall, one may ask whether groups of companies are still manageable in a quick and flexible way if in all financially important group matters the board must first ask for the consent of the general meeting. Meanwhile, German corporate practice has tried to adjust to the new rule,[63] and legal theory has tried to formalise what is meant by "fundamental decisions" by introducing the concept of a *de facto* amendment of the articles of the incorporation.[64]

---

[61] 83 BGHZ 122.
[62] *Ibid.* 131.
[63] *cf.* Ebenroth (*loc. cit.*, n. 57, *supra*) (1988) AG 1, 7.
[64] Note for example Heinsius, "Organzuständigkeit bei Bildung Erweiterung und Umorganisation des Konzerns," (1984) ZGR 383; Lutter, "Organzuständigkeit im Konzern," in *Festschrift für Stimpel*, (Berlin, New York 1985) 825.

(3) *Compensation payments and mandatory bids*

Outside shareholders of the subsidiary of a German contractual group must be adequately compensated, *i.e.* they have a right on an annual dividend which is calculated according to the value of their shares at the time of the formation of the contractual group and the likelihood of such dividends without the formation of the group. Furthermore, the parent must offer to buy their shares from them against adequate indemnity either in kind or, if the parent is a corporation, against shares of the parent. Whilst the policy decision for periodic compensation payments belongs to the operative stage of the group, the requirement of a mandatory bid is an important formal provision governing the formation of groups of companies, if it is applied not only to contractual groups, but also and already to the formation of *de facto* groups.

Nevertheless, both the provision of adequate compensation and adequate indemnity present rather thorny problems. The decisions of the German courts show that it is very difficult to establish the fairness of these payments.[65] The true value of an enterprise and its shares can only be estimated, and the different certified public accountants often come to astonishingly different figures. At least in Germany the methods of determining the value of an enterprise are already very controversial indeed, both in theory and in practice. On the procedural level it suffices to mention that litigation may go on for years with an uncertain outcome. In addition to this there are considerable disputes as to the correct interpretation of the relevant provisions of the German *Aktiengesetz*..

(4) *Special rules for take-over bids and for sales of control*

Here English law as well as the laws of other European countries are ahead of German law. Curiously enough, even though in Germany quite a lot of mergers and acquisitions are taking place, there are only very few public take-over bids and the number of hostile take-over bids up to 1990 was practically nil. It is not easy to explain this phenomenon. In part it may be due to the German multi-purpose banking system in which sales of controlling blocks often take place with the bank acting as an intermediary. There are, however, certain other reasons for the position in Germany about which one may only speculate, such as tradition, a relatively closed corporate share market, and the influence of the multi-purpose banks on the supervisory boards of the major corporations and the importance of their votes as depositaries, the strength of the legal provisions concerning minority protection and the existence of workers codetermination,

---

[65] *cf.* Wiedemann, "The German Experience with the Law of Affiliated Enterprises," in Hopt, ed., *Groups of Companies*, (n. 4, *supra*) 22, 34–35. For the legal problems see Koppensteiner (*op. cit.*, n. 38, *supra*) comments on paras. 305 and 306 of the law of 1965.

etc.[66] Accordingly German law on take-over bids is not particularly developed.[67] It remains to be seen whether the plans of the EC to enact a harmonising directive concerning take-over bids will be successful. The draft directive of February 16, 1989,[68] (which has recently been revised) has not been received well by German banks and businesses, particularly because of proposed Article 4, which embodies a mandatory take-over bid rule which would apply from $33\frac{1}{3}$ per cent. upwards.[69] Yet this critique is made from a purely national German viewpoint, and the question of whether such a mandatory take-over bid rule fits comfortably into the German law of groups may be less relevant for other Member States.[70] In the meantime arguments in favour of such a rule have been put forward from the standpoint of the economic analysis of law.[71] On the other hand it is quite clear that in the long run it is hardly satisfactory to harmonise the law governing take-over bids, whilst leaving aside the law of the sales of controlling blocks, another area which is completely unregulated in Germany, and which may be even more sensitive. The German

B. The stage of operation of groups of companies

(1) *Disclosure, with particular reference to the special dependency report*

Disclosure is a useful tool for protecting outside interests also in an operating group of companies. This is particularly true for the dependency report which has to be distinguished from the normal annual group accounts.[72] Under German law and Article 7 of the projected Ninth EC Directive, the board of the subsidiary has to give a report on all transactions, measures and omissions during the past year which result from its membership in the group. The ambit of the German and of the proposed European dependency reports differ in several aspects. The European dependency report, for example, would only cover the parent-subsidiary relationship, but not that between other members of the group. Since this amounts to an invitation to evasion, German law has been more demanding in this respect. The German

---

[66] Note, for example, Werner, *Probleme "feindlicher" Übernahmeangebote im Aktienrecht*, (Berlin 1989), 17 *et seq.*; Peltzer, "Hostile Takeovers in der Bundesrepublik Deutschland?" (1989) ZIP 69; Hopt, "Übernahmeangebote im europäischen Recht," in *Festschrift für Rittner*, (München 1991), 187, 189 *et seq.*

[67] The voluntary Guidelines of January 1979 are reprinted in Baumbach-Duden-Hopt (*op. cit.*, n. 10, *supra*) 1481: (18) Übernahmeangebote.

[68] (O.J. 1989, C 64/8); for the revised September 10, 1990, (O.J. 1990, C 240/7).

[69] See, for example, Association of the German Banks, Annual Report 1987/89, 40 *et seq.*; Mertens, "Förderung von, Schutz vor, Zwang zu Übernahmeangeboten," (1990) AG 25.

[70] Hopt, (*op. cit.*, n. 66, *supra*) 201.

[71] Reul, "Übernahmeangebote in der ökonomischen Analyse, Zur Kritik des aktuellen Richtlinienvorschlags der EG," in *Veröffentlichungen der Gesellschaft junger Zivilrechtswissenschaftler*, Vol. 1 (lecture July 18, 1990 in Hamburg).

[72] As to para. 312 of the Stock Corporation Act see Emmerich-Sonnenschein, (*op. cit.*, n. 2, *supra*) § 21: Dependency report.

dependency report needs to be audited by a certified public accountant.[73] Under certain conditions the shareholders are even granted the right to a special audit. All this is burdensome for the parent company.[74] This is one of the reasons why some German enterprises have chosen to "legalise" their group relationship with their subsidiaries by means of an enterprise contract as mentioned above.[75]

Another question is whether the shareholders of the parent company have a right to information concerning the subsidiaries not only as against their own board, but directly as against the subsidiary. This has been correctly answered in the negative. There should be no exception even for a 100 per cent. subsidiary.[76]

(2) *Capital and liquidity: the case of banking groups*

The experience with banking groups has clearly shown that capital and liquidity requirements lose their sense if they are applied only to the single enterprise within the group. Already in 1978 the Basle Committee or Cooke Committee had made proposals for supervising banks on a consolidated basis. These proposals influenced the EC which made the Council Directive of 1983 on the supervision of credit institutions on a consolidated basis.[77] Under this directive consolidation is required where a credit institution has a participation of 50 per cent. or more in another credit or financial institution. The enactment of more stringent national supervisory laws is optional. In Germany, for example, since 1985 consolidation as to proper funds is mandatory for banks from a 40 per cent. threshold upwards and for large credits consolidation is mandatory from a 50 per cent. threshold upwards. The reasons for this curious divergence and the details of the consolidation cannot be treated here.[78]

As for non-banking corporations the financial requirements are of course different. But basically the same rationale for a consolidated treatment of the financial situation of the group of companies applies here as well. In Germany the discussion of the latter matter is already fairly developed.[79] In part, this concerns the question of liability of the parent for losses made by the subsidiary.

(3) *Patterns of liability of the parent company*

For groups of companies the separate entity doctrine cannot

[73] Again this audit, according to paras. 312 and 313 of the Stock Corporation Act, has to be distinguished from the audit of the annual group accounts under para. 321 of the Commercial Code. For the latter *cf.* Weirich, "Der Konzernprüfungsbericht nach dem Bilanzrichtlinien-Gesetz," in *Festschrift für Goerdeler* (*op. cit.*, n. 11, *supra*) 649.

[74] Para. 312 *et seq.* of the German Stock Corporation Act.

[75] Krieger (*op. cit.*, n. 16, *supra*) s.69, comment 1; in particular the present uncertainty of the law for factual groups is disturbing for enterprises.

[76] Wiedemann (*op. cit.*, n. 12, *supra*) 72.

[77] Directive of June 13, 1983, (O.J. 1983, L 193). See also *supra* note 16.

[78] See Dietz (*op. cit.*, n. 26, *supra*) and Mülbert *ibid.*

[79] Schneider, "Das Recht der Konzernfinanzierung," (1984) ZGR 497.

remain the final answer. It is safe to say that this general statement is true at present for quite a number of European countries. Yet the extent to which liability of the parent requires specific regulation and the conditions of such a specific group liability are very controversial indeed. Three different types of liability of the parent can be discerned.

(a) In the case of "normal" (*i.e.*, *de facto*) groups of companies there is a tendency to hold the *parent liable for* damages inflicted to the subsidiary provided that there was *fault*. In Germany for example under the legal rules applicable to the *de facto* group the controlling enterprise may not use its influence to induce the subsidiary to enter into transactions disadvantageous to it or to take or refrain from taking measures to its disadvantage unless compensation is granted for such disadvantage usually within the same fiscal year. If compensation is not granted, the controlling enterprise and its legal representatives are liable to the subsidiary for the damages incurred. They are exonerated however, if a diligent and prudent executive of an independent company would have acted similarly.

This may seem impressive in theory, but the practical difficulties of establishing the responsibility and of substantiating the damage are considerable. This is true particularly for long-term transactions and for contracts concerning goods which do not have a market with a functioning pricing mechanism, for example if the goods or services are specially made for the subsidiary or parent company, or if the market for them is monopolistic, so that the parent can manipulate prices. The problem is even more acute for "measures" as opposed to legal transactions, for example decisions taken by the subsidiary on research and development, on new investments or on entering a foreign market.

Even if the damage can be established it is still necessary to show that it is caused by the parent. If the members of the management board of the subsidiary make a credible statement that they have acted without having been ordered or induced to act by the parent, this is often the end of the matter.

Another interesting approach is the use of the concept of the *dirigeant de fait* (*i.e.*, *de facto* director) which can be found in France, Belgium and the Netherlands and is applied in the context of insolvency (*action en comblement du passif*).[80] The *de facto* director has to bear all or part of the losses if he is unable to prove that he has not been at fault. It appears that although this concept has been of relevance in a number of decisions, few of these decisions have concerned groups of companies. Nevertheless, it scarcely seems impossible that this concept could be employed for the purpose of holding the parent company liable towards the subsidiary.

The same approach was followed in the projected Ninth EC Direc-

[80] Zahn, *Geschäftsleiterhaftung und Gläubigerschutz bei Kapitalgesellschaften in Frankreich*, (Frankfurt 1986); Hopt (*op. cit.*, n. 27, *supra*) 32; Lutter (*op. cit.*, n. 7, *supra*), 358, 363 *et seq.*; Wiedemann (*op. cit.*, n. 12, *supra*), 35–36, 79 *et seq.*, 84 *et seq.*

tive on Groups of Companies. This draft contains a provision that an enterprise which takes a decisive influence on the decisions of the board of another company is considered to be a *de facto* director and as such is liable to that company like a *de jure* director for faults in management including the disregard of the interests of that company.[81]

As far as Great Britain is concerned, a foreign observer has speculated whether similar results could not be achieved by employing the English concept of "agency" and treating the subsidiary company (at least under certain circumstances) as an agent of the parent company.[82]

(b)   A second pattern of liability is the *assumption of the subsidiary's losses by the parent* at the end of the year. In Germany this is the consequence of the conclusion of an enterprise contract and part of the legal price for being granted the liberty to pursue the interests of the contractual group instead of the interests of the single member enterprises. Nevertheless, as shown above, the linking of the assumption of losses to the conclusion of an enterprise contract has not produced very convincing results.

In the meantime the German *Bundesgerichtshof* in the *Autokran* decision of 1985[83] has gone further in developing the law of groups in which one or more of the dependent companies is a limited company (GmbH). In this case the defendant was the majority partner of seven GmbHs. The other partners were members of his family or other companies belonging to him. The defendant had full control over these GmbHs not only by his interests, but also because he himself or others who were doing exactly what he wanted were the managing directors of most of these seven GmbHs. Accounting and financing was done by still another company belonging to the same group. By factoring contracts between this latter company and the seven GmbHs, the defendant was able to receive the profits and obtain control of all the liquid assets of the GmbHs. In 1974, the plaintiff concluded leasing contracts with the seven GmbHs and delivered 39 crane cars. In 1979 the seven GmbHs went bankrupt. The plaintiff sought to recover his losses from the defendant personally.

The court held the defendant liable, but not on the basis of piercing the corporate veil. Under German law this concept is only applied by way of exception, and is reserved, for example, for cases where there is confusion of the assets of two companies or persons, or where other clear abuses exist. Instead the court based its decision on principles of the law of groups which it developed freely when deciding the case. Accordingly a controlling enterprise is liable for the debts of a bankrupt GmbH which it controls if it has managed the business of the GmbH in a lasting and comprehensive way unless it can prove

---

[81] Art. 9 of the draft Ninth EC Directive (n. 23, *supra*).
[82] Lutter, (*op. cit.*, n. 7, *supra*), at 364, referring to Schmitthoff, "The Wholly Owned and the Controlled Subsidiary," (1978) J.B.L. 218.
[83] 95 BGHZ 330.

that a diligent and prudent director of an independent GmbH would have acted similarly.

The decision has been criticised more for the contents of its reasoning than for its results. Indeed an analogy to the law of contractual groups of corporations is hardly convincing in case of a *de facto* group of GmbHs. However, what counts is the practical outcome and this is the assumption of losses of closely-held subsidiaries by the controlling parent, *i.e.* in the so-called *qualified factual group*. Indeed, under such a group relationship the normal method of compensating individual disadvantages imposed on the subsidiary by the parent (under the first pattern of liability examined above) is bound to fail. As stated in *Getty Oil Co.* v. *Skelly Oil Co.* it "is, of course, obvious that it is impossible, as between parent and subsidiary, to approximate what would have been agreed upon at arm's length"[84]; this is true at least in the case of qualified factual groups. While this is now more or less accepted for the qualified group (of GmbHs), it is still very controversial whether for this assumption of losses, fault is really necessary. There is a considerable body of opinion that this loss-bearing by the parent is the simple consequence of close control in a qualified group.[85]

(c) It appears that only in very exceptional cases should there be a *direct and joint liability of the parent towards the creditors of the subsidiary*, *i.e.* a full disregard of the corporate entity (piercing the corporate veil) since the principle of acknowledging juridical persons without imposing personal liability of their members is an economic necessity.[86] Such an exception occurs in the 100 per cent. integration, *i.e.* the procedure made available under paragraphs 319 *et seq.* of the Stock Corporation Act of 1965.

(4) *Fiduciary duties and the balancing of interests*

The legal concepts of fiduciary duties and of balancing of interests are often used as between parent and subsidiary. While they are useful for their flexibility, they are only open to meaningful discussion once they have assumed concrete form as was the case in the German *ITT* case of 1975.[87] The facts were the following. In the multinational group ITT America the American parent corporation imposed on its

---

[84] *Getty Oil Co.* v. *Skelly Oil Co.* (1970) 267 A. 2d 883, 886; *cf.* also Wiedemann (*op. cit.*, n. 12, *supra*), 46–47.

[85] See, for example, Zöllner, in Baumbach-Hueck, *GmbH-Gesetz* (*loc. cit.*, n. 16, *supra*), Schlußanhang I comment 29; Schmidt, "Konzernhaftung oder mitgliedschaftliche Haftung des privaten GmbH-Gesellschafters?" (1986) ZIP 146, 147 *et seq.*

[86] *cf.* Stimpel, "Durchgriffshaftung bei der GmbH: Tatbestande, Verlustausgleich, Ausfallhaftung," in *Festschrift fur Goerdeler* (*loc. cit.*, n. 11, *supra*), 601. See now also Teubner, "Die 'Politik des Gesetzes' im Recht der Konzernhaftung, Plädoyer für einen sektoralen Konzerndurchgriff," in *Festschrift für Steindorff*, (Berlin, New York 1990) 261; Hofstetter, "Multinational Enterprise Parent Liability: Efficient Legal Regimes in a World Market Environment," 15 N.C.J. Int'l L. & Com. R. 299 (1990); same, "Parent Responsibility for Subsidiary Corporations: Evaluating European Trends," 39 I.C.L.Q. 576 (1990).

[87] 65 BGHZ 15.

subsidiaries a charge of one per cent. of their turnover for general services allegedly rendered to them on a continuous basis by the parent. This charge was payable to ITT Industries Inc., a 100 per cent. subsidiary of ITT, according to service contracts which the subsidiaries of ITT had to conclude with ITT Industries Inc. The plaintiff was a minority shareholder of the German group G. This group of companies consisted of a GmbH at the head of which ITT held 85 per cent. and the plaintiff 15 per cent., and of several limited partnerships (*Kommanditgesellschaften*) in which ITT held 60 per cent. and the plaintiff 40 per cent. The plaintiff claimed that the services were not worth the value placed on them and that nearly two million DM had to be paid back to the limited partnerships by ITT.

The court held that the majority shareholder in the group has a fiduciary duty not to induce the subsidiaries of the GmbH to pay charges without adequate consideration. The case was therefore remanded to the court of appeal for further factual investigation. The legal details of this case are very controversial owing to the complicated structure of the group involved. Nevertheless, the decision is commonly accepted at present, namely that the minority shareholders of a GmbH need protection against the parent in a *de facto* group.

While the *ITT* decision at least in its final outcome may have been a rather clear-cut case, there remain major problems. One of these is the concept of fiduciary duties. In a recent landmark case, the *Linotype* case,[88] the *Bundesgerichtshof* has finally acknowledged the existence of fiduciary duties as between shareholders in a stock corporation. This approach has generally been welcomed by commentators[89] and opens up very interesting possibilities for legal development, especially, but not solely as far as the behaviour of majority shareholders is concerned. The concept of illegal competition by a dominating shareholder,[90] which has been developed in many court decisions, is very much akin to the concept of fiduciary duty. Some observers hold that a group law based primarily on the concept of fiduciary duties is far superior to the traditional German stock corporation law.[91] While it is true that this concept is more flexible than the other instruments discussed above, the recognition of fiduciary duties does not solve all problems since such duties do not constitute more than a general concept, which has to be formalised; *i.e.* the real difficulty is under what circumstances and with what content the courts should impose such duties in the context of the law governing groups of companies.[92] It thus seems that in regulating groups of companies, the whole range of available instruments should be used. It is doubtful whether these

[88] 103 BGHZ 184.
[89] See Lutter, "Theorie der Mitgliedschaft", (1980) 180 AcP 84; for the GmbH *cf.* Winter, *Mitgliedschaftliche Treuebindungem im GmbH-Recht*, (München 1988).
[90] Note, for example, Raiser, "Wettbewerbsverbote als Mittel des konzernrechtlichen Präventivschutzes," in *Festschrift für Stimpel*, (Berlin, New York 1985) 855.
[91] Kübler, Schmidt (*op. cit.*, n. 2, *supra*) 214 *et seq.*
[92] The approach taken by Bälz (*op. cit.*, n. 17, *supra*) 238 *et seq.*, is too negative.

conflicts can be solved by developing rules based on the concept of fairness of the single transaction. As mentioned elsewhere the policy question is rather under what protective conditions the parent may make use of separate corporate entities within the group in order to pursue an overall group business policy.[93]

C. Law enforcement and/or civil liability

(1) *Criminal law and/or civil liability*

As a general rule, the use of criminal sanctions in the context of groups of companies is problematic. The example of certain countries with a Roman legal system which rely heavily on penal sanctions for directors of the board of the subsidiary who follow the parent's interest instead of the one of their own company is hardly convincing.[94] The reality of the group has remained what it always was. Unless there is a good chance of clearly defining the elements of the offence and of successfully prosecuting infringements, penal offences should be restricted to a necessary minimum of white collar crimes. The imposition of civil liability seems more appropriate, but one must keep in mind that the problem is not primarily one of the behaviour of individual persons, but of attributing chances, risks, rights and duties between business entities. The general tendency in the development of the law of groups goes rightly away from rules of evaluating personal behaviour and towards solving institutional and structural problems.

(2) *Derivative suits and creditors' actions*

As the theme "Groups of Companies—Reality and the Law" indicates, there is a significant gap between both. To cover or at least to narrow down this gap seems one of the most important tasks for modern commercial and company law. Derivative suits of shareholders and creditors' actions[95] may raise many legal problems, but they still appear indispensable. It is interesting to see that several of the more recent German landmark cases on the law of groups (outside the 1965 Act) have been initiated by single shareholders or creditors. One commentator on the *Holzmüller* decision even claimed that this case has established the shareholder's derivative suit in German law generally.[96] It should be borne in mind however that the success of the

---

[93] *cf.* Hopt, "Self-Dealing and Use of Corporate Opportunity and Information: Regulating Directors' Conflicts of Interest," in Hopt, Teubner, eds., *Corporate Governance and Directors' Liabilities*, (Berlin, New York 1985) 285–326.

[94] *Supra* 2 C(2).

[95] Note for example, Brondics, *Die Aktionärsklage*, (Berlin 1988); Eickhoff, *Die Gesellschafterklage im GmbH-Recht*, (Köln 1988); von Gerkan, "Die Gesellschafterklage," (1988) ZGR 441; Raiser, "Das Recht der Gesellschafterklage," (1989) 153 ZHR 1; Zöllner, "Die sogenannten Gesellschafterklagen im Kapitalgesellschaftsrecht," (1988) ZGR 392.

[96] Grossfeld, Brondics, "Die Aktionärsklage—nun auch im deutschen Recht", (1982) JZ 589.

derivative suit is not so much dependent on how extensively it is admitted, but on who pays the costs of the action. Article 10 of the projected Ninth EC Directive is unfortunately silent on this point.

Similarly, the *Autokran* decision has allowed the creditor's action (even though there the liability pattern was rather one of the assumption of losses by the parent towards the subsidiary), provided that the subsidiary is bankrupt.

(3) *The role of the courts*

The role of the courts is of course central to all law enforcement. It is not intended to review the many ways in which a court can get involved in group matters. Instead, two specific points shall be made. The first concerns the question of whether proceedings to establish that a group relationship has come into existence should be instituted. In a legal system which relies so heavily on the formation of contractual groups such as the German one there is less need for such a proceeding since, if the system works, the issue is taken care of by the parties to the enterprise contract. On the other hand, if the protection of the creditors and outside shareholders is linked directly to the existence of a *de facto* group, then such proceedings could make sense, particularly if a way is found to make an affirmative court decision relevant to persons other than the parties to the case. The second point is illustrated by Article 11 of the projected Ninth EC Directive. This draft Article provides for a full range of discretionary sanctions by the court if necessary for the protection of the company, its shareholders or workers, namely for example the suspension of directors, the prevention of further performance of harmful contracts, or the obligation of the parent to make an offer for the shares of the outside shareholders. The latter measure has been characterised as very far-reaching and capable of imposing a heavy financial burden which could have a preventive effect.[97]

(4) *The role of self-regulatory bodies and administrative agencies*

Article 11 of the projected Ninth EC Directive provides that the broad discretion mentioned above is given not only to the court necessarily, but to the administrative bodies which are competent under the national law as well. This takes into consideration the specific role which for example the Belgian *Commission bancaire* and to a lesser degree the French *Commission des Opérations de Bourse* have played in developing, respectively, the Belgian and the French law of groups of companies.[98] However, the achievements of other bodies such as the United Kingdom Panel on Take-overs and Mergers[99] or of

---

[97] Immenga (*op. cit.*, n. 48, *supra*) 854; *cf.* also as to Art. 4 of the draft Directive on takeover bids *supra* 3 A(4).
[98] Ommeslaghe, "Les groupes de sociétés et l'expérience du droit belge," in Hopt, ed., *Groups of Companies*, (*op. cit.* n. 4, *supra*), 59, 66 *et seq.*
[99] *cf.* Lee, "Takeover Regulation in the United Kingdom," (1990) EWS 241.

self-regulatory bodies such as national stock exchanges should also be taken note of in this context. It would seem that the better arguments are for not overburdening the courts, but for also using the experience of capital market agencies in the development of the law governing groups.

D. The international setting

(1) *Problems of conflict of laws*

The general rules of private international law applicable to groups are to be derived from the purpose of the law of groups to protect the creditors and the outside shareholders of the subsidiary in the group. Thus in principle the law of groups follows the system of law applicable to the subsidiary. However, as far as the protection of the shareholders of the parent is concerned, the law applicable to the parent governs. This is true for example as to whether the board of directors of the parent company can decide group questions by itself or whether it has to get the consent of the parent company's general meeting.

The problem can be considered also from the viewpoint of the applicability of a national law of groups. This is as controversial as in other sectors of the law such as antitrust law, securities regulation, and bank supervision law. In general one can say that the national law of groups fails to protect foreign creditors and shareholders. A foreign subsidiary of a German parent does not fall under the protective provisions of the German law of groups: as already indicated, the law applicable to the subsidiary governs. Nevertheless, the question arises as to what happens if the foreign subsidiary enters the German market or has German outside shareholders to a substantial extent? Another question is whether enterprise contracts can also be concluded between national and foreign enterprises. This is usually answered in the affirmative, at least if the subsidiary is German. However, the same should be true if only the parent company is German. In any event a 100 per cent. integration as provided under a German law of groups is not possible between a German subsidiary and a foreign parent. The further details of the conflict of laws and rules governing groups are highly controversial.[1]

(2) *Legal harmonisation and group of companies*

The work of the EC towards harmonisation in this field has been mentioned in various contexts above. As for consolidated group accounts the real breakthrough in many of the Member States including Germany is due to the seventh EC Directive of 1983. On the other hand the projected Ninth Directive on the law of groups has failed,

---

[1] Kronke, "Grenzüberschreitende Personengesellschaftskonzerne—Sachnormen und Internationales Privatrecht," (1989) ZGR 473; Ebenroth, "Neuere Entwicklungen im deutschen internationalen Gesellschaftsrecht, Teil 2," (1988) JZ 75–79.

and one can doubt whether the national legislators are interested in the discussion. In the meantime a group of experts from different Member States has been established by the EC Commission with the difficult task of searching for new approaches. It remains to be seen whether the general impetus towards attaining the single internal market in 1992 will result in significant developments in this area as well. Whilst the difficulties of harmonisation of the law governing business enterprise in general and of the law of groups of companies in particular are very considerable indeed,[2] there is no doubt that the reality of the business enterprise today is not the independent corporation, but the group of companies. The question remains to be discussed whether the lacunae between this reality and the national and European laws should remain unfilled for a significant period of time.

[2] See Buxbaum and Hopt. *Legal Harmonization and the Business Enterprise (op. cit.*, n. 24, *supra)*.

VI

The State and Corporate Groups in the United Kingdom

Professor Alan Page*

INTRODUCTION

The United Kingdom is normally regarded as one of those countries which lacks any law of group enterprises. So far as company law is concerned this is undoubtedly so.[1] And yet looked at from the perspective of the state it is not the case that the problems posed by the emergence of the corporate group as the dominant form of business organisation have not been recognised or indeed tackled. It is therefore with the relationship between the state and corporate groups in the United Kingdom that this chapter is concerned. For the purpose of exposition it is proposed to treat the state's involvement with the group phenomenon under three heads: (a) state assistance; (b) state participation; and (c) state regulation or supervision. While the first two are largely of historical interest, the last is at the forefront of contemporary state-group relations. Nevertheless, as will become apparent, the same issues of responsibility and control arise in relation to all three.

STATE ASSISTANCE

The state's interest in economy of expenditure, in its regularity and in ensuring that the purposes for which it is incurred are in fact achieved may all be advanced as reasons why the state ought not to ignore the group character of companies to which it extends assistance. Such evidence as it has been possible to gather of the practice of state assistance in the United Kingdom suggests that the group character of assisted companies is not in fact ignored. A case in point is that of the assistance granted to Chrysler United Kingdom in 1976. This assistance was provided as part of an agreement between the Secre-

---

* Head of Department of Law, The University of Dundee. This is a slightly revised version of a paper presented at a conference on corporate governance at the European University Institute in 1987. It is published here with the kind permission of the organisers.

[1] See D. D. Prentice, "Groups of Companies: The English Experience" in K. Hopt (ed), *Groups of Companies in European Laws*, W. de Gruyter, Berlin and New York, 1982, p. 99. Note also T. Hadden, *The Control of Corporate Groups*, IALS London 1983 in the same sense.

tary of State for Industry, the Chrysler Corporation, and its subsidiary, Chrysler United Kingdom.[2] In this agreement the Chrysler Corporation undertook to exercise the rights that it was entitled to exercise in relation to its subsidiary so as to enable the provisions of the agreement and the documents accompanying it to be implemented in full. It also undertook not to allow its subsidiary to make any substantial alteration to the general nature of the assisted business without the consent of the Secretary of State, and not to reduce its shareholding in Chrysler United Kingdom below 80 per cent. This last obligation was designed to reinforce the moral, as opposed to legal, obligations assumed by the Chrysler Corporation in a declaration of intent accompanying the agreement.[3] In this declaration the Chrysler Corporation stated that among its intentions in relation to the long-term future of Chrysler United Kingdom were that it should be treated no differently from any other Chrysler subsidiary and that its efforts should be supported to the full extent of its parent's managerial, product planning, engineering, design and world-wide distribution facilities. What this example suggests, therefore, is that the state has sought in a variety of ways, some legally-binding, others not, to control the behaviour not only of subsidiaries, but also of parents *vis-á-viz* their subsidiaries.

A second, but no less important, point which emerges from this and other cases of state assistance is that the state has at the same time been concerned to limit its own responsibility. In the case of Chrysler it sought "the maximum degree of control consistent with our policy of placing overall responsibility firmly upon Chrysler Corporation."[4] This insistence on the retention of overall responsibility by the parent cannot of course relieve the state of responsibility for its own actions. Of particular importance in this regard is section 630 of the Companies Act 1985 (formerly section 332 of the Companies Act 1948) which imposes liability for the debts of a company on those who are knowingly party to the carrying on of any business of the company with intent to defraud its creditors. Although this section is thought not to bind the Crown, the government treats itself as under an obligation to observe its terms. Consequently, it is accepted that the financial position of companies should first be ascertained before assistance is extended to them, and that the progress of assisted companies should be monitored to ensure that liability is not incurred subsequently, as well as to ensure that the purposes for which assistance was granted are in fact being achieved.

More difficult to determine is the extent of the state's responsibility for the actions of third parties which, it is argued, have been materially influenced by the fact of the state's involvement. The difficulties, political as much as legal, which may arise are amply illustrated by the cases of Court Line, where the Parliamentary

---

[2] See Eighth Report from the Expenditure Committee on Public Expenditure on Chrysler UK Ltd., H.C. 596 (1975–6), Vol. 2, p. 9.

[3] *Ibid.*, note 2, Vol. 2, p. 8.

[4] *Ibid.*, note 2, Vol. 2, p. 6.

Commissioner for Administration took the view that the government could not be absolved of all responsibility for losses arising from its collapse, and Upper Clyde Shipbuilders where it was unsuccessfully argued on behalf of its creditors that government was bound, morally if not legally, to meet its liabilities. To prevent a recurrence of these difficulties, it is accepted, partly as a result of the work of the Public Accounts Committee of the House of Commons, that where the government decides to intervene it should make plain the basis upon which assistance is being extended.[5] The basis upon which assistance will normally be extended can be dealt with as part of our examination of state participation.

STATE PARTICIPATION

Turning to participation, it was the Hungarian lawyer, Madl, who observed that: "It is by no means accidental ... that for its economic activities the State, too, migrates into the institutions of private law."[6] Such has certainly been the case in the United Kingdom where the registered company has become the preferred vehicle of state participation in economic activity. This raises in turn the question of the extent of the state's liability for such companies. Is it the normal rules of limited liability, or different rules, that apply?

The starting point in answer to this question is provided by the case of Beagle Aircraft, a wholly government-owned company which government put into liquidation in 1970 while at the same time meeting its liabilities in full. Among the considerations which influenced the decision to meet its liabilities in full was the fact that government had never stated its position in relation to its debts. In the absence of such a statement, the government might have been regarded as occupying a position analogous to that of a holding company. As such, while it would have no legal liability for the debts of its subsidiaries, it might be prudent for it to meet them on the grounds that not to do so would be bad for its commercial reputation. Also relevant was the fact that the possible application of section 332 might have had to be considered in relation to some period at least of Beagle Aircraft's existence.[7]

Following its investigation of what had happened, the Public Accounts Committee expressed the view that if the government intended to accept no liability beyond that of a shareholder in a limited liability company, this should be made clear publicly so that creditors were not misled. If no such declaration was made, the Committee argued, the government might find itself face to face with a moral commitment to creditors and, in consequence, with an open-

[5] Third Report from the Committee of Public Accounts, H.C. 447 (1971–72), para. 97.
[6] F. Madl, *The Law of the European Economic Community*, Akademniai Kiado, Budapest, 1978, p. 280.
[7] Third Report from the Committee of Public Accounts, H.C. 447 (1971–72), p. 420.

ended liability.[8] (This is of course the same problem as we encountered in the context of state assistance.) This recommendation was subsequently acted upon. In a written answer to a parliamentary question on March 7, 1972 the Chief Secretary to the Treasury said:

"I am concerned that there should be no misunderstanding as to the position of creditors in relation to limited liability companies in which the Government has a financial interest—for example as creditor, minority or sole shareholder. I should make it absolutely plain that those doing business with such a company must work on the assumption that liability for the company's debts will be determined solely in accordance with the normal rules applicable to a limited liability company under the Companies Acts except where the Government undertake or have undertaken a specific commitment in relation to its debts.[9]

In the absence of such a commitment, the state's responsibility would be no greater, but by the same token no less, than that of any other shareholder.

The same position would appear to have obtained in relation to state holding companies such as the British Technology Group (formerly the National Enterprise Board), despite earlier attempts to argue that the state's liability should be unlimited.[10] The National Enterprise Board Guidelines 1980 enjoined the Board, in deciding on its practice in relation to the debts of its subsidiaries, to have regard to the position of companies in the private sector. To this obligation there was added the rider that there would be no government guarantee to the creditors of a subsidiary of the Board unless government had undertaken a specific commitment in relation to the company's debts; as happened in the case of British Leyland where the Under-Secretary for Industry stated that the National Enterprise Board would not allow its subsidiaries to be abandoned if British Leyland was to get into difficulties.[11]

This of course raises the question of what is the practice of the private sector. In the case of Beagle Aircraft, above, it was assumed that parents would stand behind their subsidiaries for fear of damaging their commercial reputations were they not to do so. Like several assumptions about corporate behaviour, recession proved this one to be unwarranted: in the case of Chrysler it was accepted as axiomatic that a parent would not stand behind its subsidiary if to do so would threaten its own solvency. The trend, of which the government has been a part, has thus been towards not accepting liability. And this indeed was the practice of the National Enterprise Board which, like

---

[8] Third Report from the Committee of Public Accounts, H.C. 300 (1970–71), para. 58.

[9] House of Commons Debates, Fifth Series, Vol. 832, cols. 282–3.

[10] For an account of these attempts, see G. Ganz, *Government and Industry*, Professional Books, Abingdon 1977, pp. 99–101.

[11] House of Commons Debates, Standing Committee A, Dec. 11, 1979, col. 719.

the government, refused to accept liability for the debts of its subsidiaries in the absence of a guarantee. Thus, in one of the more notorious cases, British Tanners was allowed to go into liquidation with debts of some £6m.

STATE SUPERVISION

Finally, in the area of state supervision of economic activity, the particular sector of interest here is the financial sector, a sector which has seen recently the emergence of a number of financial services groups in anticipation of the ending of single capacity trading on The Stock Exchange. Of The Stock Exchange's 200 or so member firms more than half have become part of larger groupings, and these ownership changes "have had repercussions across the whole of the United Kingdom financial sector, creating groupings which include associated or subsidiary firms active in securities dealing in the United Kingdom and abroad, in commercial and investment banking, in portfolio management, and in the marketing of investment products and property.[12]

Surveying the problems that might be posed by outside ownership of member firms, The Stock Exchange observed in 1984 that it might be argued that it:

> "could only be confident of the standing of a controlled Member Firm if it could also fully regulate the non-member parent. It might be claimed that, if the Member Firm were a subsidiary of a large group, The Stock Exchange would have no assurance that the liquidity margins reported in the regular financial returns were genuine and had not been created by group accounting. As The Stock Exchange would not be able to regulate the parent of such a Member Firm it would have to be in a position to exercise some control over the parent's relationship with the Member Firm, to ensure that the Firm remained a free standing entity; that the activities of the group did not disguise the position of the Firm; and that group management did not lead the Member Firm to breach Stock Exchange Rules."[13]

Given these imperatives how, if at all, has the state responded? What strategies has it developed, and what have been their legal consequences? Five responses can be identified.

(i) Adjustment of supervisory regimes

Supervisory regimes, both statutory and non-statutory, have been framed or adjusted to take account of the organisation of financial actors into groups. Under the Financial Services Act 1986, for example, an investment business that forms part of a group seeking

---

[12] See D. Ingram, "Change in the Stock Exchange and Regulations of the City," 27 *Bank of England Quarterly Bulletin* 54.
[13] See Discussion Paper published by The Stock Exchange in 1984, para. 110.

authorisation directly from the Securities and Investments Board is required to submit as part of its application a "family tree" setting out the relationship between the applicant and other members of the group, and the Board is entitled to take into account matters relating to other members of the group in deciding whether to grant the applicant authorisation. Similarly, the exercise of the Board's powers of intervention and its power to withdraw or suspend authorisation may be triggered by the conduct of other members of the group as well as by the conduct of the authorised member.

(ii) Consolidated supervision

Supervision of banking groups is carried out on a consolidated basis, that is to say an assessment is made of the overall strength of the group, and of the potential impact on a bank of the operations of the other parts of the group to which it belongs.[14]

(iii) Co-ordination between supervisors

Co-ordination between supervisors of different parts of groups has been instituted both to ensure their effective supervision and to ensure that the different supervisory requirements neither leave gaps nor are unreasonably burdensome in total. This has been done through the nomination of one of the supervisors as the lead regulator to co-ordinate action and the exchange of information among individual supervisors. These are extra-statutory arrangements, but their implementation has required the provision of statutory gateways to the flow of information between supervisors, both in the United Kingdom and overseas.[15]

(iv) Regulation of group organisation

Related to these developments, the state has become interested in the functional, managerial and legal organisation of groups. In its most recent annual report the Bank states that:

> "Although there are no formal banking supervisory requirements on group structures and organisation, they are nevertheless important to the Bank's supervision as inappropriate or weak arrangements can lead to poor performance and, in particular, to poor risk controls and internal systems, reducing the ability of group management to direct the business efficiently."[16]

The Bank therefore addresses these issues, often as part of its consolidated supervision of banking groups. In its Notice on Consolidated Supervision it states that it "will wish to discuss with group manage-

---

[14] Bank of England, Annual Report and Accounts (1985), 48–49; Bank of England Annual Report and Accounts (1986), 48–49.

[15] Bank of England, Annual Report and Accounts (1986) 48; Bank of England Annual Report and Accounts (1987), 54.

[16] Bank of England, Annual Report and Accounts (1987), 42.

ment, inter alia, the organisational structure as a whole," and that should group management structures not match the Bank's approach it "will wish to discuss with the relevant group management whether the existing group control arrangements represent an acceptable basis on which to build the Bank's consolidated supervision or what mutually acceptable modifications can be devised."[17]

As well as addressing these issues in relation to particular groups, the Bank has insisted that certain functions should be separated off from the rest of the group. Thus gilt-edged market-makers, Stock Exchange money brokers and inter-broker dealers are required to be separately established companies or partnerships. This, it should be emphasised, is not the same as the "separation theme" which Robert Clark has identified in the regulation of financial holding companies in the United States.[18] One of the purposes of separation in the United States is to prevent, through the control of permitted links, the creation of financial conglomerates. In the United Kingdom, by contrast, the creation of conglomerates has not been impeded (indeed it has been encouraged); instead what has happened is that conglomerates having been created certain parts of them have been separated off. Why has this happened?

Four reasons may be suggested. First, to ensure capital adequacy: "The only sensible framework for assessing capital adequacy in multi-faceted groups is for some part of the overall capital in the business to be identified as backing particular parts of the business."[19] This is the concept of dedicated capital. Second, to reduce the risk of contagion:

> "Allowing cross links between different institutions gives rise to the ... problem that a loss of confidence in a member of one market can more easily contaminate participants in others: losses suffered by a market member could affect confidence in its banking parent—or indeed its banking child, cousin or uncle— with the possibility of further contagion to the rest of the banking system."[20]

This is why the Bank has insisted that gilt-edged market-making entities be insulated as far as possible from any adverse developments in other parts of any groups to which they may belong, though the possibility cannot be excluded that trouble will spread simply through loss of confidence in other parts of the business.[21] For the same reason gilt-edged market-makers, as well as having to be

---

[17] Bank of England, Consolidated Supervision (1986) (BSD/1986/3), paras. 6 and 14.
[18] R. Clark, "The Regulation of Financial Holding Companies," 92 *Harvard Law Review* 787.
[19] P. Cooke, "Some concerns of a banking supervisor" 22 *Bank of England Quarterly Bulletin* (1982), p. 220.
[20] C. McMahon, "Changes in the Structure of Financial Markets: a view from London," 25 *Bank of England Quarterly Bulletin* (1985) 25, 28.
[21] C. McMahon, "Managing Change in International Banking: A Central Banker's View," 25 *Bank of England Quarterly Bulletin*, (1985) 551, 558.

separately incorporated, are not permitted to have operating subsidiaries, as this would involve them in activities outside those being monitored. This highlights a third reason, also stressed by Clark, namely that separation facilitates supervision. Finally, separation plays a part in the equalisation of regulatory burdens: the concept of level playing fields.

Before examining the last strategy, it may be noted that there are other rules, dealing mainly with conflicts of interest, which push in the same direction, albeit this is not their primary purpose. Thus Stock Exchange Dealing Rule 314.1 prohibits member firms from executing transactions in which they have a material interest without full disclosure to clients. The obligation to disclose, however, does not apply where there is a Chinese wall (of silence) in place, that is to say an arrangement for ensuring that information known to a part of the group is not available to other parts. Similarly, an exempt market-maker, that is to say a market-maker which has demonstrated to the Panel on Takeovers and Mergers that the organisation of which it is part has in place arrangements satisfactory to the Panel relating to the separation of the market-making side from other relevant parts of its business, is not presumed to be acting in concert with an offeror when the organisation is advising that offeror. The point about both of these examples is that the rules do not stipulate that functions be separated off; doing so, however, provided one method of compliance.

(v) Letters of comfort

The final strategy, which goes in the opposite direction, involves seeking assurances from substantial shareholders that, should it become necessary, they will support companies (parent and subsidiaries) *beyond* the limited liability attaching to their shareholding. This strategy has both a moral and a functional underpinning. Morally, the Bank of England believes that "owners of banks have an additional responsibility not present in the ownership of most other commercial and industrial undertakings, because of the special fiduciary responsibilities on those who run businesses which take deposits from the public."[22] Functionally, a failure to stand behind a subsidiary which got into difficulties "would quickly cause a loss of confidence in the parent bank itself."[23]

This principle is said to be acknowledged and accepted by British banks. The practice of seeking assurances or letters of comfort in support of it began in the mid-1970s when they were sought from overseas banks with shareholdings in United Kingdom banks. Since then the practice has been extended to non-bank shareholders from within the United Kingdom and overseas and, following the collapse of Johnson Matthey, they are now sought from all shareholder controllers, that is to say institutions or other persons controlling 15 per

---

[22] Report of the Committee set up to consider the system of Banking Supervision, Cmnd. 9550 (1985), para. 8.2.

[23] *Ibid.*, note 22, para. 8.1.

cent. or more of the voting power of a bank. They may also be sought from shareholders with holdings of as little as 10 per cent.[24] And this policy has been extended to gilt-edged market-members and participants in the wholesale money markets.

Like Chrysler's declaration of intent, with which this chapter began, these letters of comfort are not legally binding. For this reason their value has been questioned. However, the fact that they are not legally enforceable does not mean that they are not *administratively* enforceable and, assurances having been obtained, the Banking Supervision Division has begun to *monitor* the ability of givers of letters to honour their responsibilities should the need arise.[25] What we appear to be seeing, therefore, is the *de facto* removal of limited liability: financial holding companies and those with financial interests are in effect being denied limited liability. (Confirmation of this is provided by the Building Societies Act 1986, s.22 of which obliges building societies to discharge the liabilities of associated bodies should these bodies be unable to discharge their liabilities out of their own assets.)

Before pursuing the implications of this development, it may also be noted that just as the state has sought to insist that its assistance of a company or participation in it does not diminish the responsibility of third parties for their own actions, so too it has insisted that its supervision or regulation of economic activity does not diminish their responsibility either:

"However rigorous the standards he lays down and however strictly he demands that they be met, the supervisor must never get into the position of being directly accountable for the running and thus the actual health of any private sector institution that he is supervising. He cannot second guess all the decisions and all the risk-taking of management. There must and should remain the possibility that errors or bad luck can lead to a clearly perceived failure of a particular management. In such circumstances the management and shareholders must be subject to the normal consequences of business failure-dismissal from office, loss of capital and income etc."[26]

The particular problem being addressed here is what supervisors call the problem of "moral hazard," that is the belief that because institutions are supervised, "either the authorities will not allow the institutions to fail, or that if they fail the depositors or policyholders will be 'bailed out.' "[27] It is of course identical to the problem we saw in relation to state assistance and state participation.

Given this problem, is it possible to conclude of the abandonment

[24] Bank of England, Annual Report and Accounts (1985), 53.

[25] Report of the Committee set up to consider the system of Banking Supervision, Cmnd. 9550 (1985), para. 8.4.

[26] C. McMahon, "The Business of Financial Supervision," 24 *Bank of England Quarterly Bulletin* (1984), 46, 48-9.

[27] *Ibid.*, note 26, 48.

of limited liability that its primary significance is as a means of shifting responsibility that has fallen or threatens to fall to the state back where it properly belongs? Theory provides some support for this conclusion in that one of the functions of limited liability is to facilitate the raising of capital by *inter alia* allowing risks to be shifted from shareholders to creditors. While this is perhaps part of it, it is not, in the present author's view, its primary purpose. What we are witnessing is not so much the shifting of risk, as the provision of a further safeguard against the risk of collapse, an additional buttress to the state's liability as lender of last resort designed to ensure the solidity of major actors in the financial system. "Although a comfort letter is not legally binding, being rather a statement of intent, the fact that it has been given can have an important effect in maintaining market confidence in a bank during periods of uncertainty."[28]

This being recognised, and given that it is questionable whether financial groups with banking components could ever be allowed to go into liquidation, the removal of limited liability has the additional merit of forcing managers and shareholders to think about control:

> "we believe that they will be taken very seriously by the controlling board, which will as a result be encouraged to recognises its responsibility towards the gilt-edged market-maker both at the outset and as its business develops. It can be said that the comfort letter is simply an acknowledgement of an underlying commercial reality, which would exist in any case. While this may be true, we believe that such an explicit acknowledgement of that reality also serves a useful purpose for the reasons ... given."[29]

In this respect the removal of limited liability provides a useful antidote to the problem of moral hazard.

CONCLUSION

Looking to the future, the likelihood of the United Kingdom developing a full-blown law of group enterprise must be adjudged remote. Notwithstanding this, the state has responded in a variety of ways to the emergence of the corporate group as the dominant form of business organisation. As has been seen, it has sought to control the behaviour of parents of companies to which it has extended assistance. At the same time it has been forced to address the issue of its liability for the debts of such companies, an issue which has increased in importance as the registered company has become the preferred vehicle of state participation in economic activity. The adoption of the group form in the context of state participation in economic activity also raises the question, not discussed here, of the degree of control which the state should seek to exercise over holding com-

[28] Bank of England, Annual Report and Accounts (1985), 53.
[29] F. George, The City Revolution, 25 *Bank of England Quarterly Bulletin* (1985) 422.

panies and, through them, over their constituent members. It is in the area of financial regulation, however, that groups present perhaps the greatest challenge to the realisation of state objectives and have accordingly provoked the greatest variety of responses, including the *de facto* removal of limited liability. How effective these responses will prove to be remains to be seen.

Appendix I

Consolidated text of an Agreement dated the 28th day of June, 1946 between UNILEVER N.V. (hereinafter called "the Dutch Company") and UNILEVER PLC (hereinafter called "the English Company") as amended by Supplemental Agreement dated the 20th day of July, 1951 and Second Supplemental Agreement dated the 21st day of December, 1981.

NOW THIS AGREEMENT WITNESSETH as follows:

1. In this Agreement unless the context shall otherwise require the following expressions shall have the following meanings:

    "THE PREFERENCE SHARES OF THE DUTCH COMPANY" shall mean the issued shares of the Dutch Company outstanding at any time and ranking in priority to the Ordinary Shares of the Dutch Company.

    "THE PREFERENCE SHARES OF THE ENGLISH COMPANY" shall mean the issued shares of the English Company outstanding at any time and ranking in priority both to the Ordinary Shares and to the Deferred Shares of the English Company.

    "SHARES" shall include Stock.

    "SHAREHOLDERS" shall include Stockholders.

    "FINANCIAL PERIOD" shall mean a financial year of either of the parties hereto or any other period for which the accounts of either party hereto may by mutual agreement be made up for the purpose of ascertaining and paying dividends.

    "DIVIDENDS" shall mean in the case of each Company the full dividends receivable by a Shareholder together with any tax payable by the Company in respect of such dividends but before deducting any tax deductible by the Company from such dividends.

    "OPEN RESERVES" shall mean in the case of each Company all reserves other than:

    (i) reserves not legally available for distribution,

    (ii) reserves properly made and still required to meet any specified loss, liability or contingency and

    (iii) any deferred dividend reserve or equalisation reserve.

    "FREE RESERVES" shall mean in the case of each Company the amount of any open reserves increased or reduced by the balance of profit and loss account existing at the beginning of any financial period.

    "CURRENT PROFITS" shall mean in the case of each

122

Company the profits which may lawfully be distributed at the expiration of each financial period before making any provision for open reserves but excluding any open reserves or balance of profit and loss account (whether credit or debit but in the case of a debit subject to the proviso next hereinafter contained) existing at the beginning of the financial period.

Provided that in the event of there being a deficiency on the Profit and Loss Account at the commencement of the period which is in excess of the open reserves at that date then for the purposes of this definition the profits available for distribution shall be reduced by and to the extent of such excess.

"SURPLUS ASSETS" shall mean in the case of each Company any assets remaining after repayment of all amounts due in liquidation to the holders of the Preference Shares of the Dutch Company or of the English Company as the case may be.

"RELEVANT RATE OF EXCHANGE" shall mean the rate of exchange between the Dutch Florin and the Pound sterling on the last day of the quarterly period ended last before the declaration of a dividend (in the case of an interim dividend) or of the financial period in respect of which a dividend is being resolved to be recommended (in the case of a final dividend) provided that if the parties hereto shall by mutual agreement adopt another rate of exchange for their reporting to shareholders of the combined profit of the two Companies attributable to their Ordinary Share Capitals in respect of the relevant quarterly period or financial period (as the case may be) then such other rate shall be the relevant rate of exchange.

2. So long as this Agreement remains in force the Dutch and English Companies' shall adopt the same financial periods and for the purposes of this Agreement the Dutch and English Companies shall adopt the same principles of accountancy and the same methods of determining current profits and free reserves so as to include the Companies proportion of current profits and free reserves attributable respectively to their interests direct or indirect in subsidiary allied and associated companies less the Companies' proportion of losses so attributable and applying in the case of subsidiary allied and associated companies the same meanings to the expressions "current profits" and "free reserves" as are applied in Clause 1 hereof in the case of the Dutch and English Companies.

3. If the current profits of one Company shall be insufficient to provide in full the dividends (and arrears if any) on its Preference Shares in respect of any financial period or if there be no current profits the other Company shall to the extent of its own current profits for the same financial period after providing for the dividends (and arrears if any) on its own Preference Shares be under obligation to make good any loss incurred by the former Company during the period together

with any amount by which the deficiency (if any) on profit and loss account at the commencement of the period exceeds the open reserves at that date and to make up the current profits of that Company to the amount of the dividends (and arrears if any) on that Company's Preference Shares to the close of such financial period. If after such contribution has been received by the former Company the current profits (including the amount so received) of the former Company are still insufficient for the purpose the deficiency shall in so far as the free reserves of that Company have been utilised but are not sufficient for the purpose be met by a further contribution from the other Company to the extent of its free reserves. Any contribution so made shall in so far as not utilised for making good any such loss and/or deficiency on Profit and Loss Account as aforesaid be distributed by the Company to whom such payment is made but if not so distributed shall be repaid forthwith to the Company by whom the contribution was made.

4. (a) All dividends on the Ordinary Share Capitals of the Dutch and English Companies shall in the case of interim dividends be declared and in the case of final dividends be resolved to be recommended by the Boards of the Dutch and English Companies on the same day.

(b) The Boards of the two Companies shall decide from time to time what portion of the aggregate of the current profits of the two Companies for each financial period and free reserves should be distributed by way of dividend on the Ordinary Share Capitals of the Dutch and English Companies for that period for which purpose the Boards may take into account the existence of the following provisions of this Clause.

(c) The amount so decided shall (subject as provided in this Clause) be utilised in providing for dividends on the Ordinary Share Capitals of the Dutch and English Companies respectively upon the footing that the dividend paid on every Fl. 12 nominal of capital in the Dutch Company at the relevant rate of exchange shall be equal in value to the dividend paid on every £1 nominal of capital in the English Company.

(d) Notwithstanding the foregoing if the application of sub-clause (c) of this Clause to the decision mentioned in sub-clause (b) of this Clause:

(i) would result in the declaration or recommendation of a dividend by one of the Companies which it would be prevented by law from declaring; or

(ii) would because of movements in the relative parties between the Dutch Florin and the Pound sterling result in a level of dividend of one of the Companies which (in the opinion of the Boards of the two Companies) its Board (on the assumption for this purpose that the Company concerned was the parent company of the two Companies) would regard as unreasonable to declare or recommend having regard in particular to (1) the level of the corresponding dividend in respect of the last preceding financial period (2) the development of the aggregate of the current profits of the Dutch and English Companies expressed in the currency of the Company concerned and (3) any special circumstances in the country of incorporation of that Company relevant to the decision as to the level of dividend which would be reasonable;

the Board of that Company may declare or recommend a dividend differing from that resulting from sub-clauses (b) and (c) of this Clause provided that in each case;

    (x) such dividend is of such a level as is reasonable in the opinion of the Boards of both Companies having regard in particular to the factors described in this sub-clause;

    (y) the difference is dealt with in accordance with the following provisions of this Clause; and

    (z) the Boards of the two Companies make available to their shareholders together with and in the same manner as the announcement of the dividend a statement giving the reason why the provisions of this sub-clause have been applied.

(e) For the purpose of the following provisions of this Clause:

    (i) "the Company declaring the lower dividend" shall mean the Company declaring a dividend which upon the footing referred to in sub-clause (c) of this Clause shall be lower in value than the dividend declared by the other Companies; and

    (ii) "the difference" shall mean the difference calculated at the relevant rate of exchange between the total amount of dividend declared on its Ordinary Share Capital by the Company declaring the lower dividend and the total amount of dividend it would have to declare on its Ordinary Share Capital in order to provide for a dividend which upon the footing referred to in sub-clause (c) of this Clause would be equal in value to that declared by the other Company.

(f) Whenever it shall be decided in accordance with the provisions of paragraph (i) of sub-clause (d) of this Clause that a dividend shall be declared or recommended differing from that which would result from sub-clauses (b) and (c) of this Clause an amount equal to the difference shall be credited to a "deferred dividend reserve" to be established or adjusted as the case may be in the books of the

Company declaring the lower dividend and that Company shall apply the whole of such deferred dividend reserve towards declaration and payment of a dividend or dividends on its Ordinary Share Capital as soon as practicable after this becomes permitted by law. If at the date of declaration of any such last-mentioned dividend that Company holds any of its own Ordinary Shares the amount of the dividend which would be payable in respect of them if they were not so held shall be transferred from the deferred dividend reserve to that Company's free reserves.

(g) Whenever it shall be decided in accordance with the provisions of paragraph (ii) of sub-clause (d) of this Clause that a dividend shall be declared or recommended differing from that which would result from sub-clauses (b) and (c) of this Clause an amount equal to the difference shall be credited to an "equalisation reserve" to be established or adjusted as the case may be in the books of the Company declaring the lower dividend provided that if such an equalisation reserve is at that time in existence in the books of the other Company there shall first be deducted from the amount of the difference the amount of that equalisation reserve or such part thereof as is equal to the amount of the difference and provided further that in such case the amount so deducted shall be debited to that existing equalisation reserve. Any amounts so to be deducted and debited shall be calculated at the relevant rate of exchange.

(h) If at any time when a deferred dividend reserve or an equalisation reserve is in existence in the books of either of the two Companies:

  (i) the amount paid up on its Ordinary Share Capital shall be increased (otherwise than as a result of an allotment or issue of shares to the holders of its existing Ordinary Share Capital free of payment or an allotment or issue of shares to the holders of its existing Ordinary Share Capital pursuant to an offer of such shares to such holders whether in any such case the right to such shares or the right to accept such an offer is or is not renounceable) and the amount paid up on its Ordinary Share Capital comprised in such increase ranks or will rank for any dividend to be paid out of the existing deferred dividend reserve or equalisation reserve under the provisions of this Clause the amount of such reserve shall thereupon be increased proportionately to the increase in the paid up amount of its Ordinary Share Capital by the transfer to such reserve of an appropriate part of that Company's free reserves; or

(ii) the amount paid up on its Ordinary Share Capital shall be reduced (otherwise than by a reduction of the amount paid up on each Ordinary Share) the amount of such reserve shall thereupon be reduced proportionately to the reduction in the paid up amount of its Ordinary Share Capital by the transfer of an appropriate part of such reserve to that Company's free reserves. This paragraph shall apply to a reduction of the amount paid up on the Ordinary Shares of either of the two Companies arising on a purchase by that Company of its own shares as well as on a reduction of that Company's capital.

(j) Notwithstanding the foregoing the power under paragraph (ii) of sub-clause (d) of this Clause to declare or recommend a dividend differing from that which would result from sub-clauses (b) and (c) of this Clause shall not be used if and to the extent that as a result thereof the amount to be credited to any equalisation reserve by one of the Companies when added to the amount (if any) already standing to the credit of the equalisation reserve in the books of that Company would exceed an amount equal to the annual average of the aggregate dividends declared or recommended on the Ordinary Share Capital of that Company in respect of the three financial periods immediately preceding the financial period in respect of which the relevant dividend is being declared or recommended. If any Ordinary Share Capital of that Company has at any time been issued (otherwise than as bonus shares as defined in Clause 9(b) hereof) on terms that it ranks or will rank for dividend in respect of a part only of the said three financial periods or for only some and not the whole of the dividends declared or recommended in respect of those periods then for the purposes of the foregoing the said average shall be calculated as if all the Ordinary Share Capital so issued had been issued at the beginning of the first of the said three financial periods and in respect of those periods the same rate or rates of dividend had been declared or recommended on the Ordinary Share Capital so issued as were declared or recommended on that Company's issued Ordinary Share Capital provided that if the increase in the issued Ordinary Share Capital shall be effected by way of a Rights issue as defined in Clause 9(b) hereof the amount of such additional Ordinary Share Capital to be treated as if issued at the beginning of the first of the said financial periods shall be reduced by an amount (to be announced at the time when the issue is made) which the Boards of the two Companies consider to be reasonable having regard to any discount on current market price at which the Rights issue shall be made.

(k) If at any time one of the Companies shall have standing to the credit of its equalisation reserve a sum equal to or exceeding 70 per cent. of the maximum amount permitted in accordance with sub-clause (j) of this Clause that Company shall be entitled to apply the whole or part of its equalisation reserve towards the declaration and payment of a dividend or dividends on its Ordinary Share Capital. If at the date of declaration of any such last-mentioned dividend that Company holds any of its Ordinary Shares the amount of the dividend which would be payable in respect of them if they were not so held shall be transferred from the equalisation reserve to that Company's free reserves.

(l) If the current profits of one Company shall be insufficient to enable it to pay any ordinary dividend declared or recommended under sub-clause (c) or sub-clause (d) of this Clause and if the Boards of the two Companies consider it appropriate that Company shall require the other Company to the extent of its own current profits remaining after providing for the amount required to enable it to pay the ordinary dividend so declared or recommended on its own Ordinary Share Capital to pay forthwith to the first-mentioned Company an amount sufficient to make up the first-mentioned Company's current profits to the sum required to pay such dividend. If the current profits (including the amount of any contribution received pursuant to the provisions of this sub-clause) and the free reserves of one Company are insufficient to enable it to pay such dividend or to credit to deferred dividend reserve or to equalisation reserve the amount required under sub-clauses (f), (g) and (h) of this Clause the deficiency shall be met by a contribution from the other Company to the extent of its free reserves. For the purposes of this Clause the expression "ordinary dividend" shall in the case of the English Company include (where necessary and appropriate) the dividends on the preferential certificates outstanding under the Co-Partnership Trust and on its Deferred Shares.

(m) Neither Company shall pay any dividend on its Ordinary Share Capital larger than the one declared or recommended to be declared by the Board of the Company concerned in accordance with the preceding provisions of this Clause and if notwithstanding this restriction either of the Companies shall pay a larger dividend on its Ordinary Share Capital such Company shall forthwith pay to the other Company a sum equal to the extra amount which the other Company would have to distribute to raise the dividend on its Ordinary Shares for that period accordingly and if necessary in the case of the English Company to pay the dividends on the said preferential certificates and on its Deferred Shares. In such circumstances such other Company may at such times as it may in its discretion decide utilise the amount so received by it in paying an extra dividend or such dividends as the case may be and so long as and to the extent that such extra dividend or such dividends are not so paid the said amount together with interest thereon at the rate of four per cent. per annum shall be excluded in computing the current profits and free reserves of that Company for each subsequent financial period.

5. Any sums due from one Company to the other in accordance with the provisions of Clauses 3 or 4 hereof shall be deemed to have become due on the last day of the financial period in respect of which the obligation has arisen and shall bear interest from that date at the rate of four per cent. per annum until payment.

6. Neither Company shall (except as provided in Clause 7 hereof) distribute a dividend in specie.

7. If one of the parties hereto shall go into liquidation whether compulsory or voluntary

(a) Accounts shall from time to time as and when necessary be prepared and certified by the Auditors for the time being (or the last Auditors) of both Companies showing at the date of any account what amounts are in the case of the liquidating Company available for distribution amongst the shareholders of the liquidating Company and in the case of the non-liquidating Company what amounts would be available for distribution amongst the shareholders of the non-liquidating Company on the footing that such Company was then in liquidation and its assets realised and the liabilities discharged.

(b) The amounts certified from time to time to be available in cash for distribution amongst the shareholders of the liquidating Company shall be applied to the payment to the holders of the Preference Shares of the liquidating Company of the amounts due to such shareholders in their due priorities. In the event of the amounts finally available for distribution amongst the shareholders of the liquidating Company being insufficient to pay in full all sums due to the holders of the Preference Shares of the liquidating Company but the account of the non-liquidating Company showing a surplus after provision has been made for the full discharge of all amounts payable to the holders of the Preference Shares of the non-liquidating Company in a liquidation such surplus shall be applied to making good the deficiency aforesaid. Conversely if the accounts of the non-liquidating Company shall show that the non-

129

liquidating Company is not in a position to provide in full all amounts due in a liquidation of such Company to its Preference Shareholders any deficiency shall be made good by the liquidating Company out of any surplus after payment in full of all amounts due in the liquidation to the Preference Shareholders of the liquidating Company.

(c) The surplus assets of both Companies after payment in full to or provision made for the holders of the Preference Shares of both Companies shall be available for making distributions to the holders of the Ordinary Shares of the liquidating Company on the basis that the surplus assets of both Companies are deemed to be pooled and distributed or allocated amongst the holders of the Ordinary Shares of both Companies upon the footing that the sum paid or allocated on every Fl. 12 nominal of capital in the Dutch Company at the rate of exchange on the day of certification of the Accounts so to be prepared as aforesaid on which the distribution and allocation are made shall be equal in value to the sum allocated or paid on every £1 nominal of capital in the English Company on the basis that each Company has borne or has to bear any tax payable by the Company in respect of such distributions but before deducting any tax deductible by the Company from the sums so distributed provided always that before making such distribution and allocation there shall be allocated to the holders of Ordinary Shares of the relevant Company or Companies sums equal to the amounts (if any) standing for the time being to the credit of any deferred dividend reserve and of any equalisation reserve. Any amounts allocated under the provisions of this sub-clause to the holders of the Ordinary Shares in the non-liquidating Company shall be paid to or retained by the non-liquidating Company.

(d) On the occasion of each account (except the final account) no greater amount shall be distributed than is available in cash for distribution in the liquidating Company and if there shall be shown to be due by the liquidating Company to the non-liquidating Company any sum necessary to enable the non-liquidating Company to make provision for a distribution on the above basis such sum shall be paid for forthwith to the non-liquidating Company by the liquidating Company. No contribution shall be made by the non-liquidating Company to the liquidating Company until the final account has been taken.

(e) Any distribution which may be made in specie shall be made in a manner certified by the Auditors for the time being (or the last Auditors) of both Companies as complying with the above basis.

(f) In calculating any amounts available for distribution

amongst the holders of the Ordinary Shares of both Companies there shall be deducted an amount equal to any contributions made by one Company to the other pursuant to the provisions of Clause 4 hereof and not distributed by way of dividend on the Ordinary Shares of such other Company together with interest thereon as provided in Clause 4 hereof which amount and interest shall be exclusively applied for the benefit of the holders of the Ordinary Shares of such other Company.

(g) In making any distribution or allocation under sub-Clause (c) hereof there shall be taken into account the amounts due in a liquidation of the English Company to the holders of its Deferred Shares.

8. If both the Dutch and English Companies shall be in liquidation at the same time the provisions of Clause 7 hereof shall be applied *mutatis mutandis*.

9. (a) Neither Company shall at any time issue any capital without the consent in writing of the other nor reduce its capital without the like consent.

(b) With regard to any future issue of Ordinary Capital the following provisions shall apply:

(i) Issue of bonus shares, that is to say the issue free of payment to shareholders of shares credited as fully paid up, shall in principle only be made by the Dutch and English Companies simultaneously and then only upon the terms that the shares by way of bonus shall be Ordinary Shares.

The Boards of the two Companies shall decide from time to time what amounts should be distributed by way of bonus shares. The amount decided shall be utilised in issuing bonus shares to the Ordinary Shareholders of the Dutch and English Companies respectively upon the footing that the nominal amount of bonus capital to be received by the holder of Fl. 12 nominal of capital in the Dutch Company shall bear the same proportion to such Fl. 12 nominal of capital held by him as the nominal amount of bonus capital to be received by the holder of £1 nominal of capital in the English Company bears to such £1 nominal of capital held by him. If the undistributed profits (including free reserves but excluding any contributions made by one Company to the other in pursuance of Clause 4 hereof and not utilised for the purpose therein mentioned) of one of the Companies shall be insufficient to provide for the issue by that Company of bonus shares as so decided the other Company shall be under obligation to pay to it forthwith out of its undistributed profits (including as aforesaid) any

131

amount required to enable it to make an issue as so decided.

Any sums due from one Company to the other in accordance with the provisions of this Clause shall be deemed to have become due on the day of authorisation of the issue of the bonus shares and shall bear interest from that date at the rate of four per cent. per annum until payment.

(ii) "Rights" issues, that is to say the issue to shareholders of shares on terms that each holder of a specified number of shares is entitled to apply for and have allotted a specified number of new shares at a price less than the best obtainable on a public issue, shall in principle be made by the Dutch and English Companies simultaneously and then only upon the terms that the shares issued as "rights" shall be Ordinary Shares and upon the footing that the nominal amount of capital offered for subscription to every holder of Fl. 12 nominal of capital in the Dutch Company shall bear the same proportion to such Fl. 12 nominal of capital held by him as the nominal amount of capital offered for subscription to every holder of £1 nominal of capital in the English Company shall bear to such £1 nominal of capital held by him and so that the amounts to be paid by the subscriber of each Fl. 12 nominal of capital in the Dutch Company shall at the rate of exchange on the day of decision by the Boards to make the issues be equal in value to the amount to be paid by the subscriber of each £1 nominal of capital in the English Company.

(iii) Neither Company shall in principle issue Ordinary Shares at any time at a price which when converted into sterling or florins as the case may be at the rate of exchange on the day of such issue would for a share of a nominal amount of Fl. 12 or £1 as the case may be represent a subscription price lower than £1 or Fl. 12 as the case may be.

(iv) If at any time the Boards of the two Companies decide that it is in the interests of the two Companies that the principles set out in Sections (i), (ii) and (iii) of this sub-Clause should not be applied then and in every such case such measures shall be taken as will be equitable to the Shareholders of both Companies having regard to the recitals and the provisions in these presents.

10. This agreement shall be construed and have effect in all respects as a contract made in England in accordance with the laws of England and any dispute shall be settled by arbitration

in England under the Arbitration Acts 1950 to 1979 or any statutory modification or re-enactment thereof from time to time in force.

The original agreement dated June 28, 1946 was signed on behalf of Lever Brothers & Unilever N.V. by Mr. A. Hartog and Mr. R. G. Jurgens, Directors and on behalf of Lever Brothers & Unilever Limited by Mr. R. E. Huffam and Mr. A. G. Short, Directors.

[This Equalisation Agreement is reproduced by kind permission of Unilever plc.]

Appendix II

Definitions of a "subsidiary" etc. under the Companies Act 1989

1. FOR GENERAL PURPOSES

"Subsidiary," "holding company" and "wholly-owned subsidiary"

144.—(1) In Part XXVI of the Companies Act 1985 (general interpretation provisions), for section 736 substitute—

> **" "Subsidiary," holding company" and "wholly-owned subsidiary"**
>
> 736.—(1) A company is a "subsidiary" of another company, its "holding company," if that other company—
>
> (a) holds a majority of the voting rights in it, or
> (b) is a member of it and had the right to appoint or remove a majority of its board of directors, or
> (c) is a member of it and controls alone, pursuant to an agreement with other shareholders or members, a majority of the voting rights in it.
>
> or if it is a subsidiary of a company which is itself a subsidiary of that other company.
>
> (2) A company is a "wholly-owned subsidiary" of another company if it has no members except that other and that other's wholly-owned subsidiaries or persons acting on behalf of that other or its wholly-owned subsidiaries.
>
> (3) In this section "company" includes any body corporate.

Provisions supplementing s.736

736A.—(1) The provisions of this section explain expressions used in section 736 and otherwise supplement that section.

(2) In section 736(1)(a) and (c) the references to the voting rights in a company are to the rights conferred on shareholders in respect of their shares or, in the case of a company not having a share capital, on members, to vote at general meetings of the company on all, or substantially all, matters.

(3) In section 736(1)(b) the reference to the right to appoint or remove a majority of the board of directors is to the right to appoint or remove directors holding a majority of the voting

134

rights at meetings of the board on all, or substantially all, matters; and for the purposes of that provision—

(a) a company shall be treated as having the right to appoint a directorship if—

    (i) a person's appointment to it follows necessarily from his appointment as director of the company, or

    (ii) the directorship is held by the company itself; and

(b) a right to appoint or remove which is exercisable only with the consent or concurrence of another person shall be left out of account unless no other person has a right to appoint or, as the case may be, remove in relation to that directorship.

(4) Rights which are exercisable only in certain circumstances shall be taken into account only—

(a) when the circumstances have arisen, and for so long as they continue to obtain, or

(b) when the circumstances are within the control of the person having the rights;

and rights which are normally exercisable but are temporarily incapable of exercise shall continue to be taken into account.

(5) Rights held by a person in fiduciary capacity shall be treated as not held by him.

(6) Rights held by a person as nominee for another shall be treated as held by the other; and rights shall be regarded as held as nominee for another if they are exercisable only on his instructions or with his consent or concurrence.

(7) Rights attached to shares held by way of security shall be treated as held by the person providing the security—

(a) where apart from the right to exercise them for the purpose of preserving the value of the security, or of realising it, the rights are exercisable only in accordance with his instructions;

(b) where the shares are held in connection with the granting of loans as part of normal business activities and apart from the right to exercise them for the purpose of preserving the value of the security, or of realising it, the rights are exercisable only in his interests.

(8) Rights shall be treated as held by a company if they are held by any of its subsidiaries; and nothing in subsection (6) or (7) shall be construed as requiring rights held by a company to be treated as held by any of its subsidiaries.

(9) For the purposes of subsection (7) rights shall be treated as being exercisable in accordance with the instructions or in the interests of a company if they are exercisable in accordance with the instructions of or, as the case may be, in the interest of—

(a) any subsidiary or holding company of that company, or

(b) any subsidiary of a holding company of that company.

(10) The voting rights in a company shall be reduced by any rights held by the company itself.

(11) References in any provision of subsections (5) to (10) to rights held by a person include rights falling to be treated as held by him by virtue of any other provision of those subsections but not rights which by virtue of any such provision are to be treated as not held by him.

(12) In this section "company" includes any body corporate.".

(2) Any reference in any enactment (including any enactment contained in subordinate legislation within the meaning of the Interpretation Act 1978) to a "subsidiary" or "holding company" within the meaning of section 736 of the Companies Act 1985 shall, subject to any express amendment or saving made by or under this Act, be read as referring to a subsidiary or holding company as defined in section 736 as substituted by subsection (1) above.

This applies whether the reference is specific or general, or express or implied.

(3) In Part XXVI of the Companies Act 1985 (general interpretation provisions), after section 736A insert—

"Power to amend ss.736 and 736A

736B.—(1) The Secretary of State may by regulations amend sections 736 and 736A so as to alter the meaning of the expressions "holding company," "subsidiary" or "wholly-owned subsidiary."

(2) The regulations may make different provision for different cases or classes of case and may contain such incidental and supplementary provisions as the Secretary of State thinks fit.

(3) Regulations under this section shall be made by statutory instrument which shall be subject to annulment in pursuance of a resolution of either House of Parliament.

(4) Any amendment made by regulations under this section does not apply for the purposes of enactments outside the Companies Acts unless the regulations so provide.

(5) So much of section 23(3) of the Interpretation Act 1978 as applies section 17(2)(a) of that Act (effect of repeal and re-enactment) to deeds, instruments and documents other than enactments shall not apply in relation to any repeal and re-enactment effected by regulations made under this section."

(4) Schedule 18 contains amendments and savings consequential on the amendments made by this section; and the Secretary of State may by regulations make such further amendments or savings as appear to him to be necessary or expedient.

(5) Regulations under this section shall be made by statutory

instrument which shall be subject to annulment in pursuance of a resolution of either House of Parliament.

(6) So much of section 23(3) of the Interpretation Act 1978 as applies section 17(2)(a) of that Act (presumption as to meaning of references to enactments repealed and re-enacted) to deeds or other instruments or documents does not apply in relation to the repeal and re-enactment by this section of section 736 of the Companies Act 1985.

FOR ACCOUNTING PURPOSE

Parent and subsidiary undertakings

21.—(1) The following section is inserted in Part VII of the Companies Act 1985—

"Parent and subsidiary undertakings

Parent and subsidiary undertakings

258.—(1) The expressions "parent undertaking" and "subsidiary undertaking" in this Part shall be construed as follows; and a "parent company" means a parent undertaking which is a company.

(2) An undertaking is a parent undertaking in relation to another undertaking, a subsidiary undertaking, if—

(a) it holds a majority of the voting rights in the undertaking, or

(b) it is a member of the undertaking and has the right to appoint or remove a majority of its board of directors, or

(c) it has the right to exercise a dominant influence over the undertaking—
  (i) by virtue of provisions contained in the undertaking's memorandum or articles, or
  (ii) by virtue of a control contract, or

(d) it is a member of the undertaking and controls alone, pursuant to an agreement with other shareholders or members, a majority of the voting rights in the undertaking.

(3) For the purposes of subsection (2) an undertaking shall be treated as a member of another undertaking—

(a) if any of its subsidiary undertakings is a member of that undertaking, or

(b) if any shares in that other undertaking are held by a person acting on behalf of the undertaking or any of its subsidiary undertakings.

(4) An undertaking is also a parent undertaking in relation to another undertaking, a subsidiary undertaking, if it has a participating interest in the undertaking and—

(a) it actually exercises a dominant influence over it, or

(b) it and the subsidiary undertaking are managed on a unified basis.

(5) A parent undertaking shall be treated as the parent undertaking of undertakings in relation to which any of its subsidiary undertakings are, or are to be treated as, parent undertakings, and references to its subsidiary undertakings shall be construed accordingly.

(6) Schedule 10A contains provisions explaining expressions used in this section and otherwise supplementing this section."

(2) Schedule 9 to this Act (parent and subsidiary undertakings: supplementary provisions) is inserted after Schedule 10 to the Companies Act 1985, as Schedule 10A.

Section 21(2)   SCHEDULE 9

[SCHEDULE 10A TO THE COMPANIES ACT 1985]

PARENT AND SUBSIDIARY UNDERTAKINGS: SUPPLEMENTARY
PROVISIONS

Introduction

1. The provisions of this Schedule explain expressions used in section 258 (parent and subsidiary undertakings) and otherwise supplement that section.

Voting rights in an undertaking

2.—(2) In section 258(2)(a) and (d) the references to the voting rights in an undertaking are to the rights conferred on shareholders in respect of their shares or, in the case of an undertaking not having a share capital, on members, to vote at general meetings of the undertaking on all, or substantially all, matters.

(2) In relation to an undertaking which does not have general meetings at which matters are decided by the exercise of voting rights, the references to holding a majority of the voting rights in the undertaking shall be construed as reference to having the right under the constitution of the undertaking to direct the overall policy of the undertaking or to alter the terms of its constitution.

Right to appoint or remove a majority of the directors

3.—(1) In section 258(2)(b) the reference to the right to appoint or remove a majority of the board of directors is to the right to appoint or remove directors holding a majority of the voting rights at meetings of the board on all, or substantially all, matters.

(2) An undertaking shall be treated as having the right to appoint a directorship if—

(a) a person's appointment to it follows necessarily from his appointment as director of the undertaking, or
(b) the directorship is held by the undertaking itself.

(3) A right to appoint or remove which is exercisable only with the consent or concurrence of another person shall be left out of account unless no other person has a right to appoint or, as the case may be, remove in relation to that directorship.

Right to exercise dominant influence

4.—(1) For the purposes of section 258(2)(c) an undertaking shall not be regarded as having the right to exercise a dominant influence over another undertaking unless it has a right to give directions with respect to the operating and financial policies of that other undertaking which its directors are obliged to comply with whether or not they are for the benefit of that other undertaking.

(2) A "control contract" means a contract in writing conferring such a right which—

(a) is a kind authorised by the memorandum or articles of the undertaking in relation to which the right is exercisable, and
(b) is permitted by the law under which that undertaking is established.

(3) This paragraph shall not be read as affecting the construction of the expression "actually exercises a dominant influence" in section 258(4)(a).

Rights exercisable only in certain circumstances or temporarily incapable of exercise

5.—(1) Rights which are exercisable only in certain circumstances shall be taken into account only—

(a) when the circumstances have arisen, and for so long as they continue to obtain, or
(b) when the circumstances are within the control of the person having the rights.

(2) Rights which are normally exercisable but are temporarily incapable of exercise shall continue to be taken into account.

Rights held by one person on behalf of another

6. Rights held by a person in a fiduciary capacity shall be treated as not held by him.

7.—(1) Rights held by a person as nominee for another shall be treated as held by the other.

(2) Rights shall be regarded as held as nominee for another if they

are exercisable only on his instructions or with his consent or concurrence.

Rights attached to shares held by way of security

8. Rights attached to shares held by way of security shall be treated as held by the person providing the security—

(a) where apart from the right to exercise them for the purpose of preserving the value of the security, or of realising it, the rights are exercisable only in accordance with his instructions, and

(b) where the shares are held in connection with the granting of loans as part of normal business activities and apart from the right to exercise them for the purpose of preserving the value of the security, or of realising it, the rights are exercisable only in his interests.

Rights attributed to parent undertaking

9.—(1) Rights shall be treated as held by a parent undertaking if they are held by any of its subsidiary undertakings.

(2) Nothing in paragraph 7 or 8 shall be construed as requiring rights held by a parent undertaking to be treated as held by any of its subsidiary undertakings.

(3) For the purposes of paragraph 8 rights shall be treated as being exercisable in accordance with the instructions or in the interests of an undertaking if they are exercisable in accordance with the instructions of or, as the case may be, in the interests of any group undertaking.

Disregard of certain rights

10. The voting rights in an undertaking shall be reduced by any rights held by the undertaking itself.

Supplementary

11. References in any provision of paragraphs 6 to 10 to rights held by a person include rights falling to be treated as held by him by virtue of any other provision of those paragraphs but not rights which by virtue of any such provision are to be treated as not held by him.

Appendix III

Book III of the German *Aktiengesetz* of 1965 (as amended) on Connected Enterprises[1]

First Part

Enterprise Contracts

First Division

Kinds of Enterprise Contracts

§ 291

Contract of domination. Contract to transfer profits

(1) Enterprise contracts are contracts by which a stock corporation or an association limited by shares subjects the direction of its association to another enterprise (contract of domination) or by which it obligates itself to transfer all its profits to another enterprise (contract to transfer profits). A contract by which a stock corporation or an association limited by shares undertakes to conduct its enterprise for the account of another enterprise is also considered as a contract to transfer all of the profit.

(2) If enterprises which are not dependent on each other submit themselves by contract to a uniform direction, without having one of them become therewith dependent on another of the contracting enterprises, then this contract does not constitute a contract of domination.

---

[1] The present text consists principally of the relevant paragraphs of the 1976 translation by R. Mueller and E. G. Galbraith of the German *Aktiengesetz* into English, entitled "The German Stock Corporation Law" (2nd edition). Permission to use this text was kindly granted by Fritz Knapp Verlag, Frankfurt am Main. Account has been taken of the amendments made to these provisions by the *Bilanzrichtliniengesetz* of 1985, BG. Bl 1.2355, which implemented the Fourth, Seventh and Eighth Company Law Directives in the Federal Republic of Germany, and made a number of amendments to the Commercial Code, the Stock Corporation Law, and the law governing private companies of that country.

(3) Consideration from the association on the basis of a contract of domination or to transfer profits is not considered as a violation of §§ 57, 58 and 60.

§ 292

Other enterprise contracts

(1) In addition enterprise contracts are contracts by which a stock corporation or an association limited by shares
1. obligates itself to pool its profit or the profit of one or more of its establishments wholly or partly with the profit of other enterprises or of one or more establishments of other enterprises for the purpose of dividing a joint profit (profit pool),
2. obligates itself to transfer a part of its profit or the profit of one or more of its establishments wholly or partly to another (contract to transfer profits in part),
3. leases or otherwise leaves the business of its enterprise to another (shop leasing contract, business transfer contract).

(2) A contract for profit sharing with members of the board of management and of the supervisory board or with individual employees of the association as well as a stipulation of profit sharing in current business contracts or in license contracts does not constitute a contract to transfer profits in part.

(3) A shop leasing contract or a business transfer contract and the resolution by which the shareholders' meetings has consented to the contract are not void for the reason that the contract violates §§ 57, 58 and 60. Sentence 1 does not exclude the contesting of the resolution for this violation.

Second Division

Conclusion, Amendments and Termination of Enterprise Contracts

§ 293

Consent of the shareholders' meeting

(1) An enterprise contract only becomes effective with the consent of the shareholders' meeting. The resolution requires a majority which comprises at least three fourths of the share capital represented at the passing of the resolution. The articles of association may determine a greater capital majority and additional requirements. The provisions of the law and of

the articles of association regarding amendments of the articles of association are not to be applied to the resolution.

(2) A contract of domination or to transfer profits to which the other party is a stock corporation or an association limited by shares, only becomes effective if the shareholders' meeting of this association consents as well. Para. 1 sentences 2 to 4 apply accordingly to the resolution.

(3) It is required that the contract be in writing. It is to be made available for inspection by the shareholders in the premises of the association as of the call of the shareholders' meeting which is to decide the consent. At his request a copy shall be given to every shareholder without undue delay. The contract shall be made available for inspection in the shareholders' meeting. It shall be explained by the board of management at the beginning of the proceedings. It shall be attached to the record as an exhibit.

(4) In the shareholders' meeting which decides the consent to a contract of domination or to transfer profits, information shall also be given to every shareholder on his request on all matters of the enterprise with which the contract shall be concluded which are material for the conclusion of the contract.

§ 294

Registration. Effectiveness

(1) The board of management of the association shall apply for entry into the trade register of the existence and the kind of the enterprise contract as well as of the name of the other party to the contract, in the case of contracts to transfer profits in part, also the agreement on the amount of the profit to be transferred. To the application there shall be attached the contract and in case it is only effective with the consent of the shareholders' meeting of the other party to the contract, the record of this resolution and its exhibits, in the original, an authorized record or an officially certified copy.

(2) The contract only becomes effective after its existence has been entered into the trade register of the domicile of the association.

§ 295

Amendments

(1) An enterprise contract may only be amended with the consent of the shareholders' meeting. §§ 293, 294 apply accordingly.

(2) The consent of the shareholders' meeting to an amendment in the provisions of the contract which provide for the obligation to compensate the outside shareholders' of the association or to acquire their shares requires a special resolution of the outside

143

shareholders to become effective. § 293 para. 1 sentences 2 and 3 apply to the special resolution. Information shall also be given to every outside shareholder on his request in the meeting which decides the consent on all matters of the other party to the contract which are material to the amendment.

§ 296

Cancellation

(1) An enterprise contract may only be cancelled as of the end of the fiscal year or the otherwise contractually stipulated accounting period. A retroactive cancellation is not permitted. It is required that the cancellation be in writing.

(2) A contract which gives rise to an obligation to compensate outside shareholders or to acquire their shares can only be cancelled if the outside shareholders consent by special resolution. § 293 para. 1 sentences 2 and 3, § 295 para. 2 sentence 3 apply accordingly to the special resolution.

§ 297

Termination

(1) An enterprise contract may be terminated for cause without observing a notice period. Cause exists in particular if it can be foreseen that the other party to the contract will not be able to perform its obligations existing on the basis of the contract.

(2) The board of management of the association may only terminate without cause a contract which gives rise to an obligation to compensate the outside shareholders of the association or to acquire their shares if the outside shareholders consent by special resolution. § 293 para. 1 sentences 2 and 3, § 295 para. 2 sentence 3 apply accordingly to the special resolution.

(3) It is required that the termination notice be in writing.

§ 298

Application and registration

The board of management of the association shall apply without undue delay for the entry into the trade register of the termination of an enterprise contract, the reason and the date of the termination.

§ 299

Exclusion of directives

The association may not, on the basis of an enterprise contract, be directed to amend, maintain or terminate the contract.

Securing the Association and the Creditors

§ 300

Legal reserve

The legal reserve shall be credited in place of the credit determined in § 150 para. 2,

1. if a contract to transfer profits exists, with a credit out of the profit for the year as results without the profit transfer and after deducting a loss carried forward from the previous year, which is necessary to replenish the legal reserve [the capital reserve being added thereto] evenly in the first five fiscal years which begin during the existence of the contract or after the execution of a capital increase, up to a tenth or a higher part of the share capital determined by the articles of association, at least however with the credit stated in no. 2;

2. if a contract to transfer profits in part exists, with a credit which would have to be credited to the legal reserve pursuant to § 150 para. 2 no. 1 out of the profit for the year, as results without the profit transfer and after deducting a loss carried forward from the previous year;

3. if a contract of domination exists without the association being also obligated to transfer all its profit, with the credit required to replenish the legal reserve pursuant to no. 1, at least however with the credit stated in § 150 para. 2 or, if the association is obligated to transfer its profit in part, the credit stated in no. 2.

§ 301

Maximum amount of the profit transfer

Irrespective of agreements which have been made for the calculation of the profit to be transferred, an association may transfer as its maximum profit the profit for the year as results without the profit transfer and after deducting a loss carried forward from the previous year and the credit which is to be credited to the legal reserve pursuant to § 300. If credits were credited to [other unappropriated earned surplus] during the term of the contract, then these credits may be taken from the [other unappropriated earned surplus] and be transferred as profit.

Assuming losses

(1) If a contract of domination or to transfer profits exists, then the other party to the contract must, to the extent it is not compensated by amounts withdrawn from the [other unappropriated earned surplus] which were credited thereto during the term of the contract, compensate for every loss for the year which otherwise results during the term of the contract.

(2) If a dependent association has leased or has otherwise left the business of its enterprise to the dominating enterprise, then the dominating enterprise must compensate every loss for the year which otherwise results during the term of the contract, to the extent the stipulated consideration is not equal to an adequate compensation.

(3) The association may only waive or compromise a claim to compensate three years after the date at which the entry of the termination of the contract into the trade register is considered to be published pursuant to § 10 of the Commercial Code. This does not apply if the party obliged to compensate is insolvent and enters into a composition with its creditors to avert or remove bankruptcy proceedings. The waiver or composition is only effective if the outside shareholders consent by special resolution and a minority, the aggregate shares of which equal one tenth of the share capital represented at the passing of the resolution, does not object in the record of the meeting.

§ 303

Protection of creditors

(1) If a contract of domination or to transfer profits terminates, then the other party to the contract must render security to the creditors of the association for claims which were founded before the entry of the termination of the contract into the trade register is considered to be published pursuant to § 10 of the Commercial Code, provided they report to it for this purpose within six months after the publication of the registration. The creditors shall be advised of this right in the publication of the registration.

(2) The right to request security does not pertain to creditors who have a right in the case of bankruptcy proceedings to obtain preferred satisfaction from a fund which is established and supervised by the government for their protection pursuant to statutory provisions.

(3) The other party to the contract may guarantee the claim instead of rendering security. § 49 of the Commercial Code regarding the exclusion of the objection of first suing the debtor is not to be applied.

Securing the Outside Shareholders in Contracts of Domination and to Transfer Profits

§ 304

Adequate compensation

(1) A contract to transfer profits must provide an adequate compensation for the outside shareholders by a recurring consideration in money related to the nominal amounts of the shares (compensation payment). Provided the association is not also obligated to transfer all its profit a contract of domination must guarantee to the outside shareholders, as adequate compensation, a specific annual dividend following the amount as determined for the compensation payment. The determination of an adequate compensation may only be dispensed with if the association has no outside shareholder at the date of the passing of the resolution on the contract by its shareholders' meeting.

(2) A compensation payment msut be promised in the amount of at least the annual payment which foreseeably could be distributed as an average dividend to the individual share pursuant to the theretofore operating results of the association and its future income expectations, considering adequate depreciations and diminutions in value, however without the formation of [other unappropriated earned surplus]. If the other party to the contract is a stock corporation or an association limited by shares, then a payment that may also be promised as a compensation payment is the amount which is distributed as a dividend each time on the shares of the other association, having at least the respective nominal amount. The respective nominal amount is determined in accordance with the ratio by which, in case of a merger, shares of the other association would have to be granted in exchange for one share of the association.

(3) A contract which contrary to para. 1 does not provide for compensation at all is void. The resolution by which the shareholders' meeting of the association has consented to the contract or to an amendment of the contract pursuant to § 295 para. 2 cannot be contested on the basis of § 243 para. 2 by the fact that the compensation stipulated in the contract is inadequate. If the compensation stipulated in the context is inadequate, then the court determined in § 306 shall upon motion determine the compensation contractually owed, it must thereby determine the compensation pursuant to para. 2 sentence 2 if the contract provides for a compensation so calculated.

(4) Every outside shareholder is entitled to make the motion. The motion may only be made within two months from the date at which the entry of the existence or of an amendment of the contract pursuant to § 295 para. 2 into the trade register is considered to be published pursuant to § 10 of the Commercial Code.

(5) If the court determines the compensation, then the other party to the contract may terminate the contract within two months after the decision is final, without observing a period of notice.

§ 305

Indemnity

(1) Apart from the obligation to compensate pursuant to § 304, a contract of domination or to transfer profits must contain the obligation of the party to the contract to acquire the shares of an outside shareholder, at his request, for an adequate indemnity stipulated in the contract.

(2) As an indemnity the contract must provide
1. if the other party to the contract is a not dependent and not majority held stock corporation or association limited by shares with a domestic domicile, for the granting of its own shares of this association,
2. if the other party to the contract is a dependant or majority held stock corporation or association limited by shares and if the dominating enterprise is a stock corporation or association limited by shares with a domestic domicile, either for the granting of shares of the dominating or of the majority holding association or for an indemnity in cash,
3. in all other cases for an indemnity in cash.

(3) If shares of another association are granted as an indemnity, then the indemnity is to be considered as adequate if the shares are granted in accordance with the ratio by which shares of the other association would have to be granted in exchange for one share of the association in case of a merger, whereby residual amounts may be compensated by additional cash payments. The adequate compensation in cash must consider the association's financial position and its operating results at the date of the passing of the resolution on the contract by it shareholders' meeting.

(4) The obligation to acquire the shares may be subject to a time limit. The period terminates at the earliest two month after the date at which the entry of the existence of the contract into the trade register is considered to be published pursuant to § 10 of the Commercial Code. If a motion has been made to let the court referred to in § 306 determine the compensation or the indemnity, then the period terminates, at the earliest two

months after the date at which the decision on the last decided motion was published in the Federal Gazette.

(5) The resolution by which the shareholders' meeting of the association has consented to the contract or to an amendment of the contract pursuant to § 295 para. 2 cannot be contested on the basis of the fact that the contract does not provide for an adequate indemnity. If the contract does not provide for an indemnity at all or for one which does not conform to paras. 1 to 3, then the court referred to in § 306 shall upon motion determine the indemnity to be granted by the contract. It shall thereby in the cases of para. 2 no. 2, if the contract provides for the granting of shares of the dominating or majority holding association, determine the ratio by which these shares are to be granted, and if the contract does not provide for the granting of shares of the dominating or majority holding association, an adequate indemnity in cash. § 304 paras. 4 and 5 apply accordingly.

§ 306

Procedure

(1) The Landgericht in the district of the domicile of the association whose outside shareholders are entitled to the motion is competent. § 132 para. 1 sentences 2 to 4 are to be applied.

(2) § 99 para. 1, para. 3 sentences 1, 2, 4 to 9, para. 5 apply accordingly.

(3) The Landgericht shall publish the motion in the journal of the association whose outside shareholders are entitled to the motion. Outside shareholders may still make motions of their own within a period of two months after this publication. This right shall be indicated in the publication.

(4) The Landgericht shall hear the parties to the enterprise contract. It shall appoint a joint representative who enjoys the position of a legal representative to guard the rights of the outside shareholders who are not applicants pursuant to § 304 para. 4 or § 305 para. 5 or have made motions of their own pursuant to para. 3 sentence 2. If a determination of an adequate compensation and the determination of an adequate indemnity has been applied for, then it shall appoint a joint representative for each motion. The appointment may be dispensed with if the rights of these outside shareholders are secured in another way. The Landgericht shall publish the appointment of the joint representative in the association's journal. The representative may claim from the association a refund for reasonable cash disbursements and for compensation for his services. The disbursements and the compensation are assessed by the Landgericht. At the request of the representative it may charge the association with the payment of

149

advances. The judicial execution of the assessment follows the Code of Civil Procedure.

(5) The Landgericht shall serve its decision on the parties to the enterprise contract as well as on the applicants pursuant to § 304 para. 4, § 305 para. 5, on the outside shareholders who have made motions of their own pursuant to para. 3 sentence 2 and if a joint representative is appointed, on him.

(6) The board of management of the association shall publish the final decision, without the reasons, in the association's journal.

(7) The Regulation of Court Costs applies to the costs of the proceeedings. For proceedings of the first instance the double of the full fee is assessed. For proceedings of the second instance the same fee is assessed; this applies even if the appeal is successful. If the motion or the appeal is withdrawn before a decision has been rendered, then the fee is reduced by one half. The litigation value shall be determined ex officio. It is determined pursuant to § 30 para. 1 of the Regulation of the Court Costs. Advances on costs are not collected. The debtors for the costs are the parties to the enterprise contract. The costs may however be charged wholly or partly to another of the parties if this corresponds to equity.

§ 307

Termination of the contract to secure outside shareholders

If the association has no outside shareholder at the date of the passing of the resolution by its shareholders' meeting for a contract of domination or to transfer profits, then the contract terminates at the latest by the end of the fiscal year in which an outside shareholder participates.

Part Two

Power to Direct and Liability in Case of Dependence of Enterprises

First Division

Power to Direct and Liability if a Contract of Domination Exists

§ 308

Power to direct

(1) If a contract of domination exists, then the dominating enterprise has the right to give directives to the board of

management of the association with regard to the direction of the association. Unless otherwise provided in the contract, directives which are disadvantageous for the association may also be given, if they serve the interests of the dominating enterprise or of the enterprises connected with it and the association in a combine.

(2) The board of management is obligated to follow the directives of the dominating enterprise. It has no right to refuse to follow a directive because it does not, in its opinion, serve the interests of the dominant enterprise or of the enterprises connected with it and the association in a combine, except when it obviously does not serve these interests.

(3) If the board of management is directed to enter into a transaction which may only be entered into with the consent of the supervisory board of the association and if this consent is not given within a reasonable period, then the board of management must communicate this fact to the dominating enterprise. If the dominating enterprise repeats the directive after this communication, then the consent of the supervisory board is no longer required; if the dominating enterprise has a supervisory board, the directive may only be repeated with its consent.

§ 309

Liability of the legal representatives of the dominating enterprise

(1) If a contract of domination exists, then the legal representatives (the owner in the case of a single trader) of the dominating enterprise shall employ the diligence of an orderly and conscientious manager towards the association in giving directives to it.

(2) If they violate their duties, then they are jointly and severally liable to the association for the damage resulting therefrom. If it is contested whether or not they have employed the diligence of an orderly and conscientious manager, then the burden of proof is on them.

(3) The association may only waive or compromise the damage claims three years after the accrual of the claim and only if the outside shareholders consent by special resolution and unless a minority, the aggregate shares of which equal at least one tenth of the share capital represented at the passing of the resolution, objects in the record. The time limit does not apply if the person liable for the damage is insolvent and enters into composition with his creditors to avert or remove the bankruptcy proceedings.

(4) The damage claim of the association may also be asserted by every shareholder. The shareholder may however demand the

151

compensation only for the association. In addition the damage claim may be asserted by the creditors of the association, to the extent they are unable to obtain satisfaction from it. The liability for damages towards the creditors is not excluded by a waiver or composition by the association. If bankruptcy proceedings have been instituted against the assets of the association, then as long as they continue, the receiver in bankruptcy exercises the right of the shareholders and the creditors to assert the damage claim of the association.

(5) The claims from these provisions are barred after five years.

§ 310

Liability of the members of the boards of the association

(1) The members of the board of management and of the supervisory board of the association are jointly and severally liable, apart from the persons liable for damage pursuant to § 309, if they have acted in violation of their duties. If it is contested whether or not they have employed the diligence of an orderly and conscientious manager, then the burden of proof is on them.

(2) The liability for damages is not excluded by the fact that the supervisory board has approved the action.

(3) No liability for damages by the members of the boards of the association exists if the damaging action rests upon a directive which was to be followed pursuant to § 308 para. 2.

(4) § 309 paras. 3 to 5 are to be applied.

Second Division

Liability in the Absence of a Contract of Domination

§ 311

Limits of the influence

(1) If no contract of domination exists, then a dominating enterprise may not use its influence to cause a dependent stock corporation or association limited by shares to take legal transactions disadvantageous to it or to take or omit measures to its disadvantage except when the disadvantages are compensated for.

(2) If the compensation does not in fact take place during the fiscal year, then it must be determined when and by which advantages the disadvantage shall be compensated for, at the latest

at the end of the fiscal year in which the disadvantage was caused to the dependent association. The dependent association shall be granted a legal claim to the advantages determined as compensation.

§ 312

Report of the board of management on the relations with connected enterprises

(1) If no contract of domination exists, then the board of management of a dependent association shall within the first three months of the fiscal year prepare a report on the relations of the association with connected enterprises. The report shall list all legal transactions which the association has taken in the past fiscal year with the dominating enterprise or with an enterprise connected with it or caused by or in the interest of these enterprises, and all other measures which it has taken or omitted in the past fiscal year, caused by or in the interest of these enterprises. There shall be stated as to the legal transactions, the performance and the consideration, as to the measures, the reasons for the measure and its advantages and disadvantages for the association. As to a compensation for disadvantages, there shall be stated in detail how the compensation did in fact take place during the fiscal year or for which advantages the association has been granted a legal claim.

(2) The report shall accord with the principles of conscientious and faithful accounting.

(3) At the end of the report the board of management shall state whether or not pursuant to the circumstances which were known to it at the date on which the legal transaction was concluded or the measure taken or omitted, the association has received in each legal transaction an adequate compensation and was not put at a disadvantage by the fact that the measure was taken or omitted. If the association was put to a disadvantage, it shall also state whether or not the disadvantages were compensated for. The statement shall also be included in the report [on the business and position of the combine].

§ 313

Examination by the [auditor] of the financial statements

(1) [If the annual financial statements have to be audited by an auditor, the report on the relations with connected enterprises shall be submitted to him simultaneously with the annual financial statements and the report on the business and position of the combine. He shall examine whether or not]

1. the factual statements of the report are correct,

153

2. the consideration of the association for the legal transactions stated in the report was not inadequately high pursuant to the circumstances which were known at the date of their taking; to the extent this was the case, whether or not the disadvantages were compensated for,

3. the measures stated in the report must be judged, pursuant to the circumstances to be essentially different from the opinion of the board of management.

[Para. 320(1) sentence 2 and 320(2) sentences 1 and 2 of the Commercial Code apply accordingly. The rights granted to the auditor under the latter provisions are also available to him against the company's fellow subsidiary, parent company, or subsidiary company.]

(2) [The auditor shall report on the results of the examination in writing. If he finds when examining the annual financial statements, the report on the business and position of the combine, and the report on the relations with connected enterprises that the latter report is incomplete, he must also report on this circumstance. The auditor must sign his report and submit it to the board of management.]

(3) If no objections are raised pursuant to the final result of the examination, then the auditor shall confirm this by the following attestation of the report on the relations with connected enterprises:

On the basis of my/our dutiful examination and judgment I/we confirm that

1. the factual statements of the report are correct,

2. the consideration of the association for the legal transactions stated in the report was not unreasonably high or that disadvantages were compensated for,

3. the measures stated in the report must not be judged, pursuant to the circumstances to be essentially different from the opinion expressed by the board of management.

If the report does not list a legal transaction, then no. 2 of the attestation, if it does not list a measure, then no. 3 shall be omitted. If the auditor [. . .] [has] found that in no legal transaction listed in the report was the consideration of the association unreasonably high, then no. 2 of the attestation is to be limited to this confirmation.

(4) If objections are raised or if the auditor [. . .] [has] found that the report on the relations with connected enterprises is incomplete, then he shall qualify or refuse the attestation. If the board of management itself has stated that the association was put to a disadvantage by certain legal transactions or measures without the disadvantages having been compensated for, then this shall be stated in the attestation and the attesta-

154

tion shall be limited to the remaining legal transactions or measures.

(5) The auditor [...] shall sign the attestation by indicating the location and the date. The attestation shall also be included in the examination report.

§ 314

Examination by the supervisory board

(1) The board of management shall submit the report on the relations with connected enterprises and [when the financial statements have to be audited by an auditor, the report of the auditor, together with the documents referred to in § 170 to the supervisory board.]

Every member of the supervisory board is entitled to take notice of the reports. The reports shall also on request be handed to every member of the supervisory board, to the extent the supervisory board has not decided otherwise.

(2) The supervisory board shall examine the report on the relations with connected enterprises and report on the results of its examination in its report to the shareholders' meeting (§ 171 para. 2). [If the annual financial statements have to be audited by an auditor, it shall give an opinion on the result of the examination of the report on relations with connected enterprises by the auditor.] An attestation given by the auditor [...] shall be included in the report, a refusal of the attestation must be expressly indicated.

(3) At the end of the report the supervisory board shall state whether or not as a final result of its examination, objections must be raised against the statement of the board of management at the end of the report on the relations with connected enterprises.

(4) [If the annual financial statement has to be audited by an auditor, the auditor shall on request of the supervisory board take part in this board's deliberations regarding the report on the relations with connected enterprises.]

§ 315

Special examination

Upon motion of a shareholder the court must appoint special auditors to examine the business relations of the association with the dominating enterprise or an enterprise connected with it, if

1. the auditor [...] [has] qualified or refused the attestation of the report on the relations with connected enterprises,

2. the supervisory board has stated that objections are to be raised against the statement of the board of management in the

end of the report on the relations with connected enterprises,

3. the board of management itself has stated that the association has been put to a disadvantage by certain legal transactions or measures without the disadvantages having been compensated for.

Against the decision an immediate appeal is permissible. If the shareholders' meeting has appointed special auditors to examine the identical facts, then every shareholder may make the motion pursuant to § 142 para. 4.

§ 316

No report on relations with connected enterprises for the contract to transfer profits

§§ 312 to 315 do not apply if a contract to transfer profits exists between the dependent association and the dominating enterprise.

§ 317

Liability of the dominating enterprise and its legal representatives

(1) If a dominating enterprise causes a dependent association with which no contract of domination exists to take a legal transaction disadvantageous to it or to take or omit a measure to its disadvantage without in fact compensating for the disadvantage until the end of the fiscal year nor granting a legal claim to the dependent association for an advantage determined as compensation, then it is liable to the association for the damage resulting therefrom. In addition it is liable for the damage resulting therefrom to the shareholders, to the extent they have suffered damage apart from the damage they have suffered by the association being damaged.

(2) The liability for damage does not arise if an orderly and conscientious manager of an independent association would also have taken the legal transaction or would have taken or omitted the measure.

(3) Apart from the dominating enterprise, the legal representatives of the enterprise who have caused the association to take the legal transaction or the measure are jointly and severally liable.

(4) § 309 paras. 3 to 5 apply accordingly.

§ 318

Liability of the members of the boards of the association

(1) The members of the board of management of the association are jointly and severally liable, apart from the persons liable

for damages pursuant to § 317, if they have omitted in violation of their duties to list in the report on the relations of the association with connected enterprises the disadvantageous legal transaction or the disadvantageous measure or to state that the association was put to a disadvantage by the legal transaction or the measure and that the disadvantage was not compensated for. If it is contested whether or not they have employed the diligence of an orderly and conscientious manager, then the burden of proof is on them.

(2) The members of the supervisory board of the association are jointly and severally liable, apart from the persons liable for damages pursuant to § 317, if they have violated their duty, with regard to the disadvantageous legal transaction or the disadvantageous measure, to examine the report on the relations with connected enterprises and to report to the shareholders' meeting the result of the examination (§ 314); para. 1 sentence 2 applies accordingly.

(3) Liability for damages to the association and also to the shareholders does not arise if the action rests upon a legally valid resolution of the shareholders' meeting.

(4) § 309 paras. 3 to 5 apply accordingly.

Part Three

Integrated Associations

§ 319

Integration

(1) The shareholders' meeting of a stock corporation may decide the integration of the association into another stock corporation with domestic domicile (main association), provided all shares of the association are held by the future main association. The provisions of the law and of the articles of association regarding amendments of the articles of association are not to be applied to the resolution.

(2) The resolution for the integration only becomes effective if the shareholders' meeting of the future main association consents. The resolution for the consent requires a majority which comprises at least three fourths of the share capital represented at the passing of the resolution. The articles of association may determine a greater capital majority and additional requirements. Para. 1 sentence 2 is to be applied. On request every shareholder is also to be given information in the shareholders' meeting which decides the consent, on all matters of the

association to be integrated which are material in connection with the integration.

(3) The board of management of the association to be integrated shall apply for the entry of the integration and of the name of the main association into the trade register. The board of management shall state in the application that the resolutions of the shareholders' meetings were not contested within the period allowed or that the contesting action was refused by final judgment. There shall be attached to the application the records of the shareholders' meetings and their exhibits, in an authorized record or an officially certified copy.

(4) The association is integrated into the main association with the entry of the integration into the trade register of the domicile of the association.

§ 320

Integration by majority resolution

(1) The shareholders' meeting of a stock corporation may also decide the integration of the association into another stock corporation with domestic domicile provided shares of the association in the aggregate nominal amount of 95 per cent. of the share capital are held by the future main association. Its own shares and shares which belong to another for the account of the association are to be deducted from the share capital. Paras. 2 to 7 apply to the integration, apart from § 319 para. 1 sentence 2, paras. 2 to 4.

(2) The publication of the integration as a subject on the agenda is correct only, if

1. it contains the name and the domicile of the future main association,
2. a statement of the future main association is attached by which it offers its own shares to the retiring shareholders in exchange for their shares as an indemnity and in the case of para. 5 sentence 3 an additional indemnity in cash.

Sentence 1 no. 2 also applies to the publication of the future main association.

(3) On request every shareholder is also to be given information, in the shareholders' meeting which decides the integration, on all matters on the future main association which are material in connection with the integration.

(4) All shares which are not held by the main association pass over to it with the entry of the integration into the trade register. If share certificates for these shares were issued, then until rendered to the main association they only certify to the claim to an indemnity.

(5) The retired shareholders have a claim to an adequate indem-

nity. As an indemnity they shall be granted the main association's own shares. If the main association is a dependent association, then the retired shareholders shall be granted, at their choice, the main association's own shares, or an adequate indemnity in cash. If shares of the main association are granted as an indemnity, then the indemnity is to be considered as adequate if the shares are granted in accordance with the ratio by which shares of the main association would have to be granted in exchange for one share of the association in case of a merger, whereby residual amounts may be compensated by additional cash payments. The adequate indemnity in cash must consider the association's financial position and its operating results at the date of the passing of the resolution for the integration by the shareholders' meeting. For the indemnity in cash as well as for additional cash payments, five per cent. interest per annum shall be paid as of the publication of the registration of the integration; asserting an additional damage is not excluded.

(6) The resolution by which the shareholders' meeting of the integrated association has decided the integration of the association cannot be contested on the basis of § 243 para. 2 or by the fact that the indemnity offered by the main association pursuant to para. 2 no. 2 is inadequate. If the offered indemnity is inadequate, then upon motion the court determined in § 306 shall determine the adequate indemnity. The same applies if the main association has not or not properly offered an indemnity and a contesting action based thereupon has not been brought within the period allowed or has been withdrawn or refused by a final judgment.

(7) Every retired shareholder is entitled to the motion. The motion may only be made within two months after the date on which the entry of the integration into the trade register is considered to be published pursuant to § 10 of the Commercial Code. § 306 applies accordingly to the procedure.

§ 321

Protection of creditors

(1) To the extent they cannot demand satisfaction the creditors of the integrated association whose claims were founded before the entry of the integration into the trade register was published shall be rendered security provided they report for this purpose within six months after the publication. The creditors shall be advised of this right in the publication of the registration.

(2) The right to request security does not pertain to creditors who have a right in the case of bankruptcy proceedings to obtain preferred satisfaction from a fund which is established and

159

supervised by the government for their protection pursuant to statutory provisions.

§ 322

Liability of the main association

(1) As of the integration, the main association is accountable to the creditors of the integrated association jointly and severally for this association's liabilities which were founded before this date. It is in the same way accountable for all liabilities of the integrated association which are founded after the integration. An agreement to the contrary is ineffective towards third persons.

(2) If a claim for a liability of the integrated association is asserted against the main association, then it may raise objections, which are not based on its own position, only to the extent they may be raised by the integrated association.

(3) The main association may refuse to satisfy the creditor as long as the integrated association has the right to contest the legal transaction on which the liability is based. The same right pertains to the main association as long as the creditor may satisfy himself by a set-off against a due claim of the integrated association.

(4) A judicial execution based on an executable document of debt directed against the integrated association cannot take place against the main association.

§ 323

Power of the main association to direct and liability of the members of the board of management

(1) The main association has the right to give directives to the board of management of the integrated association with regard to the direction of the association. § 308 para. 2 sentence 1, para. 3, §§ 309, 310 apply accordingly. §§ 311 to 318 are not to be applied.

(2) Consideration the integrated association pays to the main association is not considered as a violation of §§ 57, 58 and 60.

§ 324

Legal reserve. Transfer of profit. Assuming losses

(1) The legal provisions for the formation of a legal reserve, for its application and for credits of amounts to the legal reserve are not to be applied to integrated associations.

(2) §§ 293 to 296, 298 to 303 are not to be applied to a contract, between the integrated association and the main association,

to transfer profits, a profit pool or a contract to transfer profits in part. It is required that the contract, its amendment and its cancellation be in writing. The maximum profit which may be transferred is accumulated earnings as they result without the transfer of the profit. The contract ends, at the latest, with the end of the fiscal year in which the integration ends.

(3) The main association is liable to compensate for any accumulated losses otherwise resulting to the integrated association, to the extent they exceed the amount of the [capital reserves and the unappropriated earned surplus].

[§ 325 was repealed by *Bilanzrichtliniengesetz* of 1985, BG. Bl 1. 2355.]

§ 326

Right of information of the shareholders of the main association

Every shareholder of the main association is to be given information on matters of the integrated association in the same measure as on matters of the main association.

§ 327

Termination of the integration

(1) The integration terminates

1. by resolution of the shareholders' meeting of the integrated association,
2. if the main association ceases to be a stock corporation with domestic domicile,
3. if all shares of the integrated association are no longer held by the main association,
4. by dissolution of the main association.

(2) If all shares of the integrated association are no longer held by the main association, then the main association shall communicate this to the integrated association in writing without undue delay.

(3) The board of management of the previously integrated association shall report the termination of the integration, its reason and its date, for entry into the trade register of the domicile of the association without undue delay.

(4) The claims against the former main association for liabilities of the previously integrated association are barred after five years from the date on which the entry of the termination of the integration into the trade register is considered to be published pursuant to § 10 of the Commercial Code, unless the claim against the previously integrated association is subject to a

shorter statute of limitation. If the claim of the creditor becomes due only after the date on which the entry of the termination of the integration into the trade register is considered to be published, then the period of the limitation begins with the due date.

Part Four

Mutually Participating Enterprises

§ 328

Limitation of rights

(1) If a stock corporation or an association limited by shares and another enterprise constitute mutually participating enterprises, then as soon as the existence of the mutual participation has become known to one enterprise or the other enterprise has made a communication to it pursuant to § 20 para. 3 or § 21 para. 1, rights from the participations of the other enterprise which belong to it may only be exercised in the maximum of one fourth of the aggregate participations of the other enterprise. This does not apply to the right to new shares from a capital increase from reserves. § 16 para. 4 is to be applied.

(2) The limitation of para. 1 does not apply if before it had received such a communication from the other enterprise and before the existence of the mutual participation has become known to it, the enterprise has made a communication on its own to the other enterprise pursuant to § 20 para. 3 or § 21 para. 1.

(3) If a stock corporation or an association limited by shares and another enterprise constitute mutually participating enterprises, then the enterprises shall communicate to each other the amount of their participation and every change in writing without undue delay.

Accounting of the Combine

[Paras. 329–336 were repealed by the *Bilanzrichtliniengesetz* of 1985 Bt. Bl 1.2355.]

§ 337

Submission of the consolidated financial statements and of the report [on the business and position of the combine]

(1) Without undue delay after receipt of the examination report of the [auditor] of the consolidated financial statements, the board of management of the [parent] association shall submit the con,olidated financial statements, the report [on the business and position of the combine] and the examination report to the supervisory board of the [parent] association for information. Every member of the supervisory board is entitled to take notice of the submitted documents. The submitted documents shall also be handed on request to every member of the supervisory board to the extent the supervisory board has not decided otherwise.

(2) If the consolidated financial statements are prepared as of the closing date of the annual financial statements of the [parent] association, then the consolidated financial statements and the report [on the business and position of the combine] shall be submitted to the shareholders' meeting which has to receive or to determine these annual financial statements. If the closing date of the consolidated financial statements deviates from the closing date of the annual financial statements of the [parent] association, then the consolidated financial statements and the report [on the business and position of the combine] shall be submitted to the shareholders' meeting which shall receive or determine the next following annual financial statements after the closing date of the consolidated financial statements.

(3) § 175 para. 2 applies [accordingly] to making available for inspection the consolidated financial statements and the report [on the business and position of the combine] and to giving copies § 176 para. 1 applies [accordingly] to the submission to the shareholders' meeting and to reporting by the board of management.

(4) The duty of the board of management of the [parent] association to give information in the shareholders' meeting in which the consolidated financial statements and the report [on the business and position of the combine] are submitted extends also to the situation of the combine and of the enterprises included in the consolidated financial statements.

[§ 338 was repealed by *Bilanzrichtliniengesetz* of 1985, BG Bl 1.2355.]

Appendix IV

Seventh Council Directive of June 13, 1983 (83/349/EEC) based on Article 54(3)(g) EEC on consolidated accounts, (O.J. 1983 193/1)

SECTION 1.

Conditions for the preparation of consolidated accounts

Article 1

1. A Member State shall require any undertaking governed by its national law to draw up consolidated accounts and a consolidated annual report if that undertaking (a parent undertaking):

   (a) has a majority of the shareholders' or members' voting rights in another undertaking (a subsidiary undertaking); or

   (b) has the right to appoint or remove a majority of the members of the administrative, management or supervisory body of another undertaking (a subsidiary undertaking) and is at the same time a shareholder in or member of that undertaking; or

   (c) has the right to exercise a dominant influence over an undertaking (a subsidiary undertaking) of which it is a shareholder or member, pursuant to a contract entered into with that undertaking or to a provision in its memorandum or articles of association, where the law governing that subsidiary undertaking permits its being subject to such contracts or provisions. A Member State need not prescribe that a parent undertaking must be a shareholder in or member of its subsidiary undertaking. Those Member States the laws of which do not provide for such contracts or clauses shall not be required to apply this provision; or

   (d) is a shareholder in or member of an undertaking, and:

      (aa) a majority of the members of the administrative, management or supervisory bodies of that undertaking (a subsidiary undertaking) who have held office during the financial year, during the preceding financial year and up to the time when the consolidated accounts are drawn up, have been appointed solely as a result of the exercise of its voting rights; or

(bb) controls alone, pursuant to an agreement with other shareholders in or members of that undertaking (a subsidiary undertaking), a majority of shareholders' or members' voting rights in that undertaking. The Member States may introduce more detailed provisions concerning the form and contents of such agreements.

The Member States shall prescribe at least the arrangements referred to in (bb) above.

They may make the application of (aa) above dependent upon the holding's representing 20 per cent. or more of the shareholders' or members' voting rights.

However, (aa) above shall not apply where another undertaking has the rights referred to in subparagraphs (a), (b) or (c) above with regard to that subsidiary undertaking.

2. Apart from the cases mentioned in paragraph 1 above and pending subsequent coordination, the Member States may require any undertaking governed by their national law to draw up consolidated accounts and a consolidated annual report if that undertaking (a parent undertaking) holds a participating interest as defined in Article 17 of Directive 78/660/EEC in another undertaking (a subsidiary undertaking), and:

(a) it actually exercises a dominant influence over it; or

(b) it and the subsidiary undertaking are managed on a unified basis by the parent undertaking.

Article 2

1. For the purposes of Article 1(1)(a), (b) and (d), the voting rights and the rights of appointment and removal of any other subsidiary undertaking as well as those of any person acting in his own name but on behalf of the parent undertaking or of another subsidiary undertaking must be added to those of the parent undertaking.

2. For the purposes of Articles 1(1)(a), (b) and (d), the rights mentioned in paragraph 1 above must be reduced by the rights:

(a) attaching to shares held on behalf of a person who is neither the parent undertaking nor a subsidiary thereof; or

(b) attaching to shares held by way of security, provided that the rights in question are exercised in accordance with the instructions received, or held in connection with the granting of loans as part of normal business activities, provided

165

that the voting rights are exercised in the interests of the person providing the security.

3. For the purposes of Article 1(1)(a) and (d), the total of the shareholders' or members' voting rights in the subsidiary undertaking must be reduced by the voting rights attaching to the shares held by that undertaking itself by a subsidiary undertaking of that undertaking or by a person acting in his own name but on behalf of those undertakings.

Article 3

1. Without prejudice to Articles 13, 14 and 15, a parent *undertaking and all of its subsidiary undertakings* shall be undertakings to be consolidated regardless of where the *registered offices of such subsidiary undertakings are situated.*

2. For the purposes of paragraph 1 above, any subsidiary undertaking of a subsidiary undertaking shall be considered a subsidiary undertaking of the parent undertaking which is the parent of the undertakings to be consolidated.

Article 4

1. For the purposes of this Directive, a parent undertaking and all of its subsidiary undertakings shall be undertakings to be consolidated where either the parent undertaking or one or more subsidiary undertakings is established as one of the following types of company:

   (a) *in Germany:*

   die Aktiengesellschaft, die Kommanditgesellschaft auf Aktien, die Gesellschaft mit beschränkter Haftung;

   (b) *in Belgium:*

   la société anonyme/de naamloze vennootschap—la société en commandite par actions/de commanditaire vennootschap op aandelen—la société de personnes à responsabilité limitée/de personenvennootschap met beperkte aansprakelijkheid;

   (c) *in Denmark:*

   aktieselskaber,   kommanditaktieselskaber, anpartsselskaber;

   (d) *in France:*

   la société anonyme, la société en commandite par actions, la société à responsabilité limitée;

(e) *in Greece:*

η ανώνυμη εταιρία, η ταιρία κεριορισμένης ευθύνης, η ετερόρρυθμῆ κατά μετοχές εταιρία;

(f) *in Ireland:*

public companies limited by shares or by guarantee, private companies limited by shares or by guarantee;

(g) *in Italy:*

la società per azioni, la società in accomandita per azioni, la società a responsabilità limitata;

(h) *in Luxembourg:*

la société anonyme, la société en commandite par actions, la société à responsabilité limitée;

(i) *in the Netherlands:*

de naamloze vennootschap, de besloten vennootschap met beperkte aansprakelijkheid;

(j) *in the United Kingdom:*

public companies limited by shares or by guarantee, private companies limited by shares or by guarantee.

(k) *in Spain:*

la sociedad anónima, la sociedad comanditara por acciones, la sociedad de responsabilidad limitada;

(l) *in Portugal:*

a sociedade anonima de responsabilidade limitada, a sociedade em coimanditara por acções, a sociedade por quotas de responsabilidade limitada.[1]

2. A Member State may, however, grant exemption from the obligation imposed in Article 1(1) where the parent undertaking is not established as one of the types of company listed in paragraph 1 above.

---

[1] The table takes account of the Act of Accession with Spain and Portugal (1985) art. 26, Annex I, Part II(d), point 5, which made amendments to the original text of Article 4(1).

Draft Ninth Company Law Directive on the Conduct of Groups containing a Public Limited Company as a subsidiary (unpublished).

Definitions

Article 2

1. For the purposes of this Directive, a subsidiary undertaking is one in which another undertaking (the parent undertaking):
   (a) has a majority of the shareholders' or members' voting rights; or
   (b) has the right to appoint or remove a majority of the members of the administrative, management or supervisory body, and is at the same time a shareholder or member, or
   (c) is a shareholder or member and a majority of the members of the administrative, management or supervisory body who have held office during the financial year have been appointed solely as a result of the exercise of its rights, or
   (d) is a shareholder or member and controls alone, pursuant to an agreement with other shareholders or members of the undertaking (subsidiary undertaking), a majority of shareholders' or members' voting rights in that undertaking.

2. For the purposes of applying paragraph 1, the voting rights and rights of appointment or removal of any other subsidiary undertaking as well as those of any person acting in his own name but on behalf of the parent undertaking or another subsidiary undertaking, must be added to those of the parent undertaking.

3. For the purposes of applying paragraph 1, the rights mentioned in paragraph 2 must be reduced by the rights:
   (a) attaching to shares held on behalf of a person who is neither the parent undertaking nor a subsidiary undertaking or held in connection with the granting of loans as part of normal business activities, provided that the voting rights are exercised in the interests of the person providing the security.
   (b) attaching to shares held by way of security, provided that such rights are exercised in accordance with the instructions received, or held in connection with the granting of Loans as part of normal business activities, provided that the voting rights are exercised in the interests of the person providing the security.

4. For the purposes of applying paragraph 1(a), (c) and (d), the total of the shareholders' or members' voting rights in the subsidiary undertaking must be reduced by the voting rights attaching to shares held by that undertaking itself, by another undertaking which is its subsidiary or by a person acting in his own name but on behalf of those undertakings.

Council Directive of December 12, 1988 (88/627/EEC) on the information to be published when a major holding in a listed Company is acquired or deposed of, OJL 348/62, 17.12.88.

Article 8

1. For the purposes of this Directive, "controlled undertaking" shall mean any undertaking in which a natural person or legal entity:
    (a) has a majority of the shareholders or members' voting rights; or
    (b) has the right to appoint or remove a majority of the members of the administrative, management or supervisory body and is at the same time a shareholder in, or member of, the undertaking in question; or
    (c) is a shareholder or member and alone controls a majority of the shareholders' or members' voting rights pursuant to an agreement entered into with other shareholders or members of the undertaking.
2. For the purposes of paragraph 1, a parent undertaking's rights as regards voting, appointment and removal shall include the rights of any other controlled undertaking and those of any person or entity acting in his own name but on behalf of the parent undertaking or of any other controlled undertaking.

Appendix V

1

Council Regulation (EEC) No. 2137/85 of July 25, 1985 on the European Economic Interest Grouping (EEIG) (O.J. 1985 199/1)

The Council of the European Communities

Having regard to the Treaty establishing the European Economic Community, and in particular Article 235 thereof.

Having regard to the proposal from the Commission.[1]

Having regard to the opinion of the European Parliament.[2]

Having regard to the opinion of the Economic and Social Committee.[3]

Whereas a harmonious development of economic activities and a continuous and balanced expansion throughout the Community depend on the establishment and smooth functioning of a common market offering conditions analogous to those of a national market: whereas to bring about this single market and to increase its unity a legal framework which facilitates the adaption of their activities to the economic conditions of the Community should be created for natural persons, companies, firms and other legal bodies in particular: whereas to that end it is necessary that those natural persons, companies, firms and other legal bodies should be able to cooperate effectively across frontiers;

Whereas co-operation of this nature can encounter legal, fiscal or psychological difficulties: whereas the creation of an appropriate Community legal instrument in the form of a European Economic Interest Grouping would contribute to the achievement of the above mentioned objectives and therefore proves necessary;

Whereas the Treaty does not provide the necessary powers for the creation of such a legal instrument;

---

[1] OJ No C 14, 15, 2, 1974, p. 30 and OJ No C 103, 28, 4, 1978, p. 4.
[2] OJ No C 163, 11, 7, 1977, p. 17.
[3] OJ No C 108, 15, 5, 1975, p. 46.

Whereas a grouping's ability to adapt to economic conditions must be guaranteed by the considerable freedom for its members in their contractual relations and the internal organization of the grouping;

Whereas a grouping differs from a firm or company principally in its purpose, which is only to facilitate or develop the economic activities of its members to enable them to improve their own results: whereas, by reason of that ancillary nature, a grouping's activities must be related to the economic activities of its members but not replace them so that, to that extent, for example, a grouping may not itself with regard to third parties, practise a profession, the concept of economic activities being interpreted in the widest sense;

Whereas access to grouping form must be made as widely available as possible to natural persons, companies, firms and other legal bodies, in keeping with the aims of this Regulation: whereas this Regulation shall not, however, prejudice the application at national level of legal rules and/or ethical codes concerning the conditions for the pursuit of business and professional activities;

Whereas this Regulation does not itself confer on any person the right to participate in a grouping even where the conditions it lays down are fulfilled;

Whereas the power provided by this Regulation to prohibit or restrict participation in grouping on grounds of public interest is without prejudice to the laws of Member States which govern the pursuit of activities and which may provide further prohibitions or restrictions or otherwise control or supervise participation in a grouping by any natural person, company, firm or other legal body or any class of them;

Whereas to enable a grouping to achieve its purpose it should be endowed with legal capacity and provision should be made for it to be represented *vis-à-vis* third parties by an organ legally separate from its membership.

Whereas the protection of third parties requires wide-spread publicity: whereas the members of a grouping have unlimited joint and several liability for the grouping's debts and other liabilities, including those relating to tax or social security without however, that principle's affecting the freedom to exclude or restrict the liability of one or more of its members in respect of a particular debt or other liability by means of a specific contract between the grouping and a third party;

Whereas matters relating to the status or capacity of natural persons and to the capacity of legal persons are governed by national law;

Whereas the grounds for winding up which are peculiar to the grouping should be specific while referring to national law for its liquidation and the conclusion thereof.

171

Whereas groupings are subject to national laws relating to insolvency and cessation of payments; whereas such laws may provide other grounds for the winding up of groupings;

Whereas this Regulation provides that the profits or losses resulting from the activities of a grouping shall be taxable only in the hands of its members; whereas it is understood that otherwise national tax laws apply, particularly as regards the apportionment of profits, tax procedures and any obligations imposed by national tax law;

Whereas in matters not covered by this Regulation the laws of the Member States and Community law are applicable, for example with regard to:

— social and labour laws,
— competition laws,
— intellectual property laws;

Whereas the activities of groupings are subject to the provisions of Member States' laws on the pursuit and supervision of activities: whereas in the event of abuse or circumvention of the laws of a Member State by a grouping or its members that Member State may impose appropriate sanctions;

Whereas the Member States are free to apply or to adopt any laws, regulations or administrative measures which do not conflict with the scope or objectives of this Regulation;

Whereas this Regulation must enter into force immediately in its entirety: whereas the implementation of some provisions must nevertheless be deferred in order to allow the Member States first to set up the necessary machinery for the registration of groupings in their territories and the disclosure of certain matters relating to groupings: whereas with effect from the date of implementation of this Regulation, groupings set up may operate without territorial restrictions.

HAS ADOPTED THIS REGULATION:

Article 1

1. European Economic Interest Groupings shall be formed upon the terms, in the manner and with the effects laid down in this Regulation.

    Accordingly, parties intending to form a grouping must conclude a contract and have the registration provided for in Article 6 carried out.

2. A grouping so formed shall, from the date of its registration as provided for in Article 6, have the capacity, in its own name, to have rights and obligations of all kinds, to make contracts or accomplish other legal acts, and to sue and be sued.

3. The Members States shall determine whether or not groupings registered at their registries, pursuant to Article 6, have legal personality.

Article 2

1. Subject to the provisions of this Regulation, the law applicable, on the one hand, to the contract for the formation of a grouping, except as regards matters relating to the status or capacity of natural persons and to the capacity of legal persons and, on the other hand, to the internal organization of a grouping shall be the internal law of the State in which the official address is situated, as laid down in the contract for the formation of the grouping.

2. Where a State comprises several territorial units each of which has its own rules of law applicable to the matters referred to in paragraph 1, each territorial unit shall be considered as a State for the purposes of identifying the law applicable under this Article.

Article 3

1. The purpose of a grouping shall be to facilitate or develop the economic activities of its members and to improve or increase the results of those activities: its purpose is not to make profits for itself.

   Its activity shall be related to the economic activities of its members and must not be more than ancillary to those activities,

2. Consequently, a grouping may not

   (a) exercise, directly or indirectly, a power of management or supervision over its members own activities or over the activities of another undertaking in particular in the fields of personnel, finance and investment;

   (b) directly or indirectly, on any basis whatsoever, hold shares of any kind in a member undertaking: the holding of shares in another undertaking shall be possible only in so far as it is necessary for the achievement of the grouping's objects and if it is done on its members' behalf;

   (c) employ more than 500 persons;

   (d) be used by a company to make a loan to a director of a company, or any person connected with him, when the making of such loans is restricted or controlled under the Member States' laws governing companies. Nor must a grouping be used for the transfer of any property between a company and a director, or any person connected with him, except to the extent allowed by the Member States' laws governing companies. For the purposes of this provision the making of a loan includes entering into any transaction or arrangement of similar effect and property includes moveable and immoveable property;

   (e) be a member of another European Economic Interest Grouping.

Article 4

1. Only the following may be members of a grouping:

   (a) companies or firms within the meaning of the second paragraph of Article 58 of the Treaty and other legal bodies governed by public or private law, which have been formed in accordance with the law of a Member State and which have their registered or statutory office and central administration in the Community; where, under the law of a Member State, a company, firm or other legal body is not obliged to have a registered or statutory office, it shall be sufficient for such a company, firm or other legal body to have its central administration in the Community;

   (b) natural persons who carry on any industrial, commercial, craft or agricultural activity or who provide professional or other services in the Community.

2. A grouping must comprise at least:

   (a) two companies, firms or other legal bodies, within the meaning of paragraph 1, which have their central administrations in different Member States, or

   (b) two natural persons, within the meaning of paragraph 1, who carry on their principal activities in different Member States, or

   (c) a company, firm or other legal body within the meaning of paragraph 1 and a natural person, of which the first has its central administration in one Member State and the second carries on his principal activity in another Member State.

3. A Member State may provide that groupings registered at its registries in accordance with Article 6 may have no more than 20 members. For this purpose, that Member State may provide that, in accordance with its laws, each member of a legal body formed under its laws, other than a registered company, shall be treated as a separate member of a grouping.

4. Any Member State may, on grounds of that State's public interest, prohibit or restrict participation in groupings by certain classes of natural persons, companies, firms, or other legal bodies.

Article 5

A contract for the formation of a grouping shall include at least:

(a) the name of the grouping preceded or followed either by the words 'European Economic Interest Grouping' or by the initials 'EEIG,' unless those words or initials already form part of the name;

(b) the official address of the grouping;

174

grouping has been concluded stating the number, date and place of registration and the date, place and title of publication, shall be given in the *Official Journal of the European Communities* after it has been published in the gazette referred to in Article 39(1).

Article 12

The official address referred to in the contract for the formation of a grouping must be situated in the Community.

The official address must be fixed either:

    (a) where the grouping has its central administration, or

    (b) where one of the members of the grouping has its central administration or, in the case of a natural person, his principal activity, provided that the grouping carries on an activity there.

Article 13

The official address of a grouping may be transferred within the Community.

When such a transfer does not result in a change in the law applicable pursuant to Article 2, the decision to transfer shall be taken in accordance with the conditions laid down in the contract for the formation of the grouping.

Article 14

1. When the transfer of the official address results in a change in the law applicable pursuant to Article 2, a transfer proposal must be drawn up, filed and published in accordance with the conditions laid down in Articles 7 and 8.

    No decision to transfer may be taken for two months after publication of the proposal. Any such decision must be taken by the members of the grouping unanimously. The transfer shall take effect on the date on which the grouping is registered, in accordance with Article 6, at the registry for the new official address. That registration may not be effected until evidence has been produced that the proposal to transfer the official address has been published.

2. The termination of a grouping's registration at the registry for its old official address may not be effected until evidence has been produced that the grouping has been registered at the registry for its new official address.

3. Upon publication of a grouping's new registration the new official address may be relied on as against third parties in accordance with the conditions referred to in Article 9(1); however, as long as the termination of the grouping's registration at the registry for the old official address has not been published, third parties may continue to rely on the old official

address unless the grouping proves that such third parties were aware of the new official address.

4. The laws of a Member State may provide that, as regards groupings registered under Article 6 in that Member State, the transfer of an official address which would result in a change of the law applicable shall not take effect if, within the two-month period referred to in paragraph 1, a competent authority in that Member State opposes it. Such opposition may be based only on grounds of public interest. Review by a judicial authority must be possible.

Article 15

1. Where the law applicable to a grouping by virtue of Article 2 provides for the nullity of that grouping, such nullity must be established or declared by judicial decision. However, the court to which the matter is referred must, where it is possible for the affairs of the grouping to be put in order, allow time to permit that to be done.

2. The nullity of a grouping shall entail its liquidation in accordance with the conditions laid down in Article 35.

3. A decision establishing or declaring the nullity of a grouping may be relied on as against third parties in accordance with the conditions laid down in Article 9(1).

   Such a decision shall not of itself affect the validity of liability owed by or to a grouping, which originated before it could be relied on as against third parties in accordance with the conditions laid down in the previous subparagraph.

Article 16

1. The organs of a grouping shall be the members acting collectively and the manager or managers.

   A contract for the formation of a grouping may provide for other organs; if it does it shall determine their powers.

2. The members of a grouping, acting as a body, may take any decision for the purposes of achieving the objects of the grouping.

Article 17

1. Each member shall have one vote. The contract for the formation of a grouping may, however, give more than one vote to certain members, provided that no one member holds a majority of the votes.

2. A unanimous decision by the members shall be required to:

   (a) alter the objects of a grouping;
   (b) alter the number of votes allotted to each member;
   (c) alter the conditions for the taking of decisions;

(d) extend the duration of a grouping beyond any period fixed in the contract for the formation of the grouping;

(e) alter the contribution by every member or by some members to the grouping's financing;

(f) alter any other obligation of a member, unless otherwise provided by the contract for the formation of the grouping;

(g) make any alteration to the contract for the formation of the grouping not covered by this paragraph, unless otherwise provided by that contract.

3. Except where this Regulation provides that decisions must be taken unanimously, the contract for the formation of a grouping may prescribe the conditions for a quorum and for a majority, in accordance with which the decisions, or some of them shall be taken. Unless otherwise provided for by the contract, decisions shall be taken unanimously.

4. On the initiative of a manager or at the request of a member, the manager or managers must arrange for the members to be consulted so that the latter can take a decision.

Article 18

Each member shall be entitled to obtain information from the manager or managers concerning the grouping's business and to inspect the grouping's books and business records.

Article 19

1. A grouping shall be managed by one or more natural persons appointed in the contract for the formation of the grouping or by decision of the members.

No person may be a manager of a grouping if:

— by virtue of the law applicable to him, or
— by virtue of the internal law of the State in which the grouping has its official address, or
— following a judicial or administrative decision made or recognised in a Member State

he may not belong to the administrative or management body of a company, may not manage an undertaking or may not act as manager of a European Economic Interest Grouping.

2. A Member State may, in the case of groupings registered at their registries pursuant to Article 6, provide that legal persons may be managers on condition that such legal persons designate one or more natural persons, whose particulars shall be the subject of the filing provisions of Article 7(d) to represent them.

If a Member State exercises this option, it must provide that the representative or representatives shall be liable as if they were themselves managers of the grouping concerned.

The restrictions imposed in paragraph 1 shall also apply to those representatives.

3. The contract for the formation of a grouping or, failing that, a unanimous decision by the members shall determine the conditions for the appointment and removal of the manager or managers and shall lay down their powers.

Article 20

1. Only the manager or, where there are two or more, each of the managers shall represent a grouping in respect of dealings with third parties.

   Each of the managers shall bind the grouping as regards third parties when he acts on behalf of the grouping, even where his acts do not fall within the objects of the grouping, unless the grouping proves that the third party knew or could not, under the circumstances, have been unaware that the act fell outside the objects of the grouping; publication of the particulars referred to in Article 5(c) shall not of itself be proof thereof.

   No limitation on the powers of the manager or managers, whether deriving from the contract for the formation of the grouping or from a decision by the members, may be relied on as against third parties even if it is published.

2. The contract for the formation of the grouping may provide that the grouping shall be validly bound only by two or more managers acting jointly. Such a clause may be relied on as against third parties in accordance with the conditions referred to in Article 9(1) only if it is published in accordance with Article 8.

Article 21

1. The profits resulting from a grouping's activities shall be deemed to be the profits of the members and shall be apportioned among them in the proportions laid down in the contract for the formation of grouping or, in the absence of any such provision, in equal shares.

2. The members of a grouping shall contribute to the payment of the amount by which expenditure exceeds income in the proportions laid down in the contract for the formation of the grouping or, in the absence of any such provision, in equal shares.

Article 22

1. Any member of a grouping may assign his participation in the grouping, or a proportion thereof, either to another member or

to a third party; the assignment shall not take effect without the unanimous authorisation of the other members.

2. A member of a grouping may use his participation in the grouping as security only after the other members have given their unanimous authorisation, unless otherwise laid down in the contact for the formation of the grouping. The holder of the security may not at any time become a member of the grouping by virtue of that security.

Article 23

No grouping may invite investment by the public.

Article 24

1. The members of a grouping shall have unlimited joint and several liability for its debts and other liabilities of whatever nature. National law shall determine the consequences of such liability.

2. Creditors may not proceed against a member for payment in respect of debts and other liabilities, in accordance with the conditions laid down in paragraph 1, before the liquidation of a grouping is concluded, unless they have first requested the grouping to pay and payment has not been made within an appropriate period.

Article 25

Letters, order forms and similar documents must indicate legibly:

(a) the name of the grouping preceded or followed either by the words 'European Economic Interest Grouping' or by the initials 'EEIG,' unless those words or initials already occur in the name;

(b) the location of the registry referred to in Article 6, in which the grouping is registered, together with the number of the grouping's entry at the registry;

(c) the grouping's official address;

(d) where applicable, that the managers must act jointly;

(e) where applicable, that the grouping is in liquidation, pursuant to Articles 15, 31, 32 or 36.

Every establishment of a grouping, when registered in accordance with Article 10, must give the above particulars, together with those relating to its own registration, on the documents referred to in the first paragraph of this Article uttered by it.

Article 26

1. A decision to admit new members shall be taken unanimously by the members of the grouping.

2. Every new member shall be liable, in accordance with the

conditions laid down in Article 24, for the grouping's debts and other liabilities, including those arising out of the grouping's activities before his admission.

He may, however, be exempted by a clause in the contract for the formation of the grouping or in the instrument of admission from the payment of debts and other liabilities which originated before his admission. Such a clause may be relied on as against third parties, under the conditions referred to in Article 9(1), only if it is published in accordance with Article 8.

Article 27

1. A member of a grouping may withdraw in accordance with the conditions laid down in the contract for the formation of a grouping or, in the absence of such conditions, with the unanimous agreement of the other members.

   Any member of a grouping may, in addition withdraw on just and proper grounds.

2. Any member of a grouping may be expelled for the reasons listed in the contract for the formation of the grouping and, in any case, if he seriously fails in his obligations or if he causes or threatens to cause serious disruption in the operation of the grouping.

   Such expulsion may occur only by the decision of a court to which joint application has been made by a majority of the other members, unless otherwise provided by the contract for the formation of a grouping.

Article 28

1. A member of a grouping shall cease to belong to it on death or when he no longer complies with the conditions laid down in Article 4(1).

   In addition, a Member State may provide, for the purposes of its liquidation, winding up, insolvency or cessation of payments laws, that a member shall cease to be a member of any grouping at the moment determined by those laws.

2. In the event of the death of a natural person who is a member of a grouping, no person may become a member in his place except under the conditions laid down in the contract for the formation of the grouping or, failing that, with the unanimous agreement of the remaining members.

Article 29

As soon as a member ceases to belong to a grouping, the manager or managers must inform the other members of that fact; they must also take the steps required as listed in Articles 7 and 8. In addition, any person concerned may take those steps.

Article 30

Except where the contract for the formation of grouping provides otherwise and without prejudice to the rights acquired by a person under Articles 22(1) or 28(2), a grouping shall continue to exist for the remaining members after a member has ceased to belong to it, in accordance with the conditions làid down in the contract for the formation of the grouping or determined by unanimous decision of the members in question.

Article 31

1. A grouping may be wound up by a decision of its members ordering its winding up. Such a decision shall b•· taken unanimously, unless otherwise laid down in the contract for the formation of the grouping.
2. A grouping must be wound up by a decision of its members.
    (a) noting the expiry of the period fixed in the contract for the formation of the grouping or the existence of any other cause for winding up provided for in the contract, or
    (b) noting the accomplishment of the grouping's purpose or the impossibility of pursuing it further.

    Where, three months after one of the situation referred to in the first subparagraph has occurred, a members' decision establishing the winding up of the grouping has not been taken, any member may petition the court to order winding up.

3. A grouping must also be wound up by a decision of its members or of the remaining member when the conditions laid down in Article 4(2) are no longer fulfilled,
4. After a grouping has been wound up by decision of its members, the manager or managers must take the steps required as listed in Article 7 and 8. In addition, any person concerned may take those steps.

Article 32

1. On application by any person concerned or by a competent authority, in the event of the infringement of Article 3, 12 or 31(3), the court must order a grouping to be wound up, unless its affairs can be and are put in order before the court has delivered a substantive ruling.
2. On application by a member, the court may order a grouping to be wound up on just and proper grounds.
3. A Member State may provide that the court may, on application by a competent authority, order the winding up of a grouping which has its official address in the State to which that authority belongs, wherever the grouping acts in contravention of that State's public interests, if the law of that State provides for such a possibility in respect of registered companies or other legal bodies subject to it.

Article 33

When a member ceases to belong to a grouping for any reason other than the assignment of his rights in accordance with the conditions laid down in Article 22(1), the value of his rights and obligations shall be determined taking into account the assets and liabilities of the grouping as they stand when he ceases to belong to it.

The value of the rights, and obligations of a departing member may not be fixed in advance.

Article 34

Without prejudice to Article 37(1), any member who ceases to belong to a grouping shall remain answerable, in accordance with the conditions laid down in Article 24, for the debts and other liabilities arising out of the grouping's activities before he ceased to be a member.

Article 35

1. The winding up of a grouping shall entail its liquidation.
2. The liquidation of a grouping and the conclusion of its liquidation shall be governed by national law.
3. A grouping shall retain its capacity, within the meaning of Article 1(2), until its liquidation is concluded.
4. The liquidator or liquidators shall take the steps required as listed in Articles 7 and 8.

Article 36

Groupings shall be subject to national laws governing insolvency and cessation of payments. The commencement of proceedings against a grouping on grounds of its insolvency or cessation of payments shall not by itself cause the commencement of such proceedings against its members.

Article 37

1. A period of limitation of five years after the publication, pursuant to Article 8, of notice of a member's ceasing to belong to a grouping shall be substituted for any longer period which may be laid down by the relevant national law for actions against that member in connection with debts and other liabilities arising out of the grouping's activities before he ceased to be a member.
2. A period of limitation of five years after the publication, pursuant to Article 8, of notice of the conclusion of the liquidation of a grouping shall be substituted for any longer period which may be laid down by the relevant national law for actions against a member of the grouping in connection with debts and other liabilities arising out of the grouping's activities.

Article 38

Where a grouping carries on any activity in a Member State in contravention of that State's public interest, a competent authority of that State may prohibit that activity. Review of that competent authority's decision by a judicial authority shall be possible.

Article 39

1. The Member States shall designate the registry or registries responsible for effecting the registration referred to in Articles 6 and 10 and shall lay down the rules governing registration. They shall prescribe the conditions under which the documents referred to in Articles 7 and 10 shall be filed. They shall ensure that the documents and particulars referred to in Article 8 are published in the appropriate official gazette of the Member State in which the grouping has its official address, and may prescribe the manner of publication of the documents and particulars referred to in Article 8(c).

    The Member States shall also ensure that anyone may, at the appropriate registry pursuant to Article 6 or, where appropriate. Article 10, inspect the documents referred to in Article 7 and obtain, even by post, full or partial copies thereof.

    The Member States may provide for the payment of fees in connection with the operations referred to in the preceding subparagraphs; those fees may not, however, exceed the administrative cost thereof.

2. The Member States shall ensure that the information to be published in the *Official Journal of the European Communities* pursuant to Article 11 is forwarded to the Office for Official Publications of the European Communities within one month of its publication in the official gazette referred to in paragraph 1.

3. The Member State shall provide for appropriate penalties in the event of failure to comply with the provisions of Articles 7, 8 and 10 on disclosure and in the event of failure to comply with Article 25.

Article 40

The profits or losses resulting from the activities of a grouping shall be taxable only in the hands of its members.

Article 41

1. The Member States shall take the measures required by virtue of Article 39 before July 1, 1989. They shall immediately communicate them to the Commission.

2. For information purposes, the Member States shall inform the Commission of the classes of natural persons, companies, firms and other legal bodies which they prohibit from participating

in groupings pursuant to Article 4(4). The Commission shall inform the other Member States.

Article 42

1. Upon the adoption of this Regulation, a Contact Committee shall be set up under the auspices of the Commission. Its function shall be:
   (a) to facilitate, without prejudice to Articles 169 and 170 of the Treaty, application of this Regulation through regular consultation dealing in particular with practical problems arising in connection with its application;
   (b) to advise the Commission, if necessary, on additions or amendments to this Regulation.
2. The Contact Committee shall be composed of representatives of the Member States and representatives of the Commission. The chairman shall be a representative of the Commission. The Commission shall provide the secretariat.
3. The Contact Committee shall be convened by its chairman either on his own initiative or at the request of one of its members.

Article 43

This Regulation shall enter into force on the third day following its publication in the *Official Journal of the European Communities*.

It shall apply from July 1, 1989, with the exception of Articles 39, 41 and 42 which shall apply as from the entry into force of the Regulation.

This Regulation shall be binding in its entirety and directly applicable in all Member States.

Done at Brussels, 25 July 1985.

For the Council
The President
J. POOS

Index